"The legal profession has always been conservative and rightly so. However, the transformation of industry after industry by the digital revolution means that in order to stay relevant to it's clients, the legal profession must also embrace the technology enablers that exist in both the business and practice of law. *The LegalTech Book*, crowdsourced from leading industry experts and thought leaders, provides important insights into the use of technology in the law, as well as the debates surrounding its use. It is an invaluable resource to help understand the LegalTech ecosystem."

Steve Schiff, Independent Disruptive Technology Consultant and Former CEO of ReMATCH LTD

"AI is already changing both the practice of law, the courts and the legal system through which we govern ourselves as a society. Automation is changing the nature of legal jobs, while AI increasingly allows us to identify patterns in human conduct – from financial decisions to risky behaviours governed by criminal or private law – in ways that both hold great promise, but also pose grave risks to the legitimacy and transparency of our legal institutions. Whether you are a legal practitioner, entrepreneur, executive, investor or academic, *The LegalTech Book* is an essential resource for anyone seeking to better understand how AI is changing legal practice, adjudication and the rule of law itself. Highly recommended reading for experts and non-experts alike."

Professor Alexander Sarch, Head of School, University of Surrey School of Law

"Truly excellent legal technology depends on deep understanding and collaboration between many different disciplines. However, the mother tongue of lawyers, developers, data scientists, knowledge managers and ontologists, to name a few, differ from each other. *The LegalTech Book* brings together a vast array of contributors, each on the cutting edge of their respective LegalTech projects. It will undoubtedly foster the necessary understanding, as well as keys to being understood, to the end of excellent multi-disciplinary LegalTech collaboration. It is a must read no matter what your discipline."

Garth Watson, Co-Founder and CLO, Libryo

"The largest and most impac[...] know it – I am free to say will [...] regulations are brought to lig[...] change the legal industry an[...] brilliant book and amazing m[...] this book bring the full light to us in a very powerful way."

Milos Kresojevic, Founder, AI.Legal Labs

"While automation has played a role in the legal profession for some time, the legal industry is reaching a tipping point – not only are intelligent systems on the verge of taking over, but clients also ask for them.

This book provides an excellent insight into the new role that LegalTech plays in the workplace. Intelligent applications based on artificial intelligence, smart contracts, and advanced document management, are the next wave of technology transforming how lawyers, law firms and legal technology consulting firms work and learn."

Djuro Stojanovic, Founder and CEO, Uhura Solutions

"Bringing together insights in an easily understood framework, this well-written and lucid book looks at LegalTech from a wide range of perspectives. The use of AI, smart contracts, RegTech, contract management, and digital due diligence are some of the areas of LegalTech which promise to reshape the legal profession for good. This excellent and timely book will be useful to experts in the field and of interest to general readers and policy-makers thinking ahead of time."

Ana Odorović, Lecturer at the University of Belgrade, Faculty of Law, Research Affiliate at the Cambridge Centre for Alternative Finance, Judge Business School

"Technology is redefining whole industries and the legal sector is not immune. Technological innovation and adoption will be the major defining drivers as to which firms prosper and those which struggle to survive over the next decade. Clients are looking for technological solutions and technology enabled efficiencies and expecting firms to spend in order to deliver this. Those that do not will find themselves priced out of the market. *The LegalTech Book* will enable law firms to consider some of the innovations that are underway and develop a strategy to best position themselves for the changes that are about to come."

Martin Bartlam, Partner, Head of Finance, Projects & Restructuring, DLA PIPER

"Legal tech is a growing movement globally. We are fortunate to have a world leading legal tech hub in the UK which complements the strengths of its internationally renowned legal sector. As an active supporter, the Corporation sees the potential for legal tech to be a game changer right across the economy. The role of technology in supporting and transforming the delivery of legal services has been accelerated as a result of the global lockdown in response to the COVID-19 outbreak. This includes a significant increase across all parts of the legal sector in the use of existing and emerging technology. The need is greater than ever for lawyers and clients to develop their understanding of the potential benefits of legal tech and increasing awareness and understanding."

Catherine McGuiness, Chair of the Policy & Resources Committee, City of London Corporation

The LegalTech Book

Library of Congress Cataloging-in-Publication Data

Names: Chishti, Susanne, editor.
Title: The legaltech book : the legal technology handbook for investors, entrepreneurs and FinTech visionaries / edited by Susanne Chishti,
    Sophia Adams Bhatti, Akber Datoo, Dr. Drago Indjic.
Description: Chichester, West Sussex, United Kingdom : John Wiley & Sons, 2020. | Includes bibliographical references and index.
Identifiers: LCCN 2020008305 (print) | LCCN 2020008306 (ebook) | ISBN 9781119574279 (paperback) | ISBN 9781119574286 (adobe pdf) | ISBN 9781119574354 (epub)
Subjects: LCSH: Practice of law—Automation. | Law—Data processing. | Information technology. | Technology and law.
Classification: LCC K87 .L459 2020 (print) | LCC K87 (ebook) | DDC 340.0285—dc2 3
LC record available at https://lccn.loc.gov/2020008305
LC ebook record available at https://lccn.loc.gov/2020008306

A catalogue record for this book is available from the British Library.

ISBN 978-1-119-57427-9 (paperback)   ISBN 978-1-119-57428-6 (ePDF)
ISBN 978-1-119-57435-4 (ePub)   ISBN 978-1-119-70806-3 (obook)

10 9 8 7 6 5 4 3 2 1

Cover design: Wiley
Cover image: pkproject/Shutterstock

Set in 10/13pt Helvetica Lt Std by Aptara, New Delhi, India
Printed in Great Britain by TJ International Ltd, Padstow, Cornwall, UK

The LegalTech Book

The Legal Technology Handbook for Investors, Entrepreneurs and FinTech Visionaries

Edited by

Sophia Adams Bhatti

Susanne Chishti

Akber Datoo

Dr Drago Indjic

Contents

1. An Introduction to LegalTech: The Law Boosted by AI and Technology

2. Law and Data

3. Technology vs Law

4. Cryptocurrencies, Distributed Ledger Technology and the Law

5. Smart Contracts and Applications

6. Legal Technology: Increasing or Impeding Access to Justice?

7. LegalTech Around the World

8. The Future of LegalTech

Preface

Global investment in legal technology (also referred to as "LegalTech" or "LawTech") is about $1 billion and likely to increase. The industry is backed by angel and seed-stage investors and venture capital funds globally. LegalTech benefits established law and financial services firms who seek to leverage legal technology innovations to provide better services to their clients, reduce costs and increase efficiency. In fact, LegalTech will benefit any corporation which employs in-house lawyers. In addition, legal technology has the opportunity to positively impact our wider society at large.

This book covers a wide range of applications of LegalTech, including collaboration tools, document management, intellectual property management, e-Billing, e-Discovery, legal research and analytics, legal project management, governance and compliance and contract management, including contract review and due diligence. In terms of technologies and their use cases we will cover LegalTech adoption using artificial intelligence, machine learning, blockchain and distributed ledger technologies, robotic process automation and chatbots, among many more.

The LegalTech Book is the first crowdsourced book globally showing how much technology can achieve in the legal and financial services sector – a book that provides food for thought to newbies, pioneers and well-seasoned experts alike. The reason we decided to reach out to the global LegalTech and financial technology (FinTech) community in sourcing the book's contributors lies in the inherently fragmented nature of the field of

LegalTech. There was no single author, group of authors or indeed region in the world that could cover all the facets and nuances of legal technology and its potential in an exhaustive manner. What is more, by being able to reach out to a truly global contributors' base, we not only stayed true to the spirit of technology startups and the LegalTech community, making use of technological channels of communication in reaching out to, selecting and reviewing our would-be contributors, we also made sure that every corner of the globe had the chance to have its say. Thus, we aimed to fulfil one of the most important purposes of The LegalTech Book, namely – to give a voice to those who would remain unheard, those who did not belong to a true legal and technology community in their local areas, and spread that voice to an international audience. We have immensely enjoyed the journey of editing The LegalTech Book and sincerely hope that you will enjoy reading it.

More than 110 contributors submitted 140 abstracts to be part of the book. We asked our global FinTech and LegalTech communities for their views regarding which abstracts they would like to have fully expanded for The LegalTech Book. Out of all contributors, we selected sixty-four who were asked to write their full articles, which have now been included in this book. We conducted a questionnaire among all our selected authors to further understand their background and expertise. In summary, our selected authors come from twenty countries. More than 70% of our authors have postgraduate university degrees (78%) and have strong domain expertise across many fields (see Tables 1 and 2), and 81% of our finalist authors had their articles published before.

Tables 3 and 4 show that more than 36% of our finalist authors are entrepreneurs working for startups and scaleups (many of them part of the founding team), 31% work in law firms, 6% come from established financial and technology companies and more than a quarter come from service providers such as consulting firms servicing the financial services sectors.

Almost 42% of our authors work for startups with up to ten people and another 25% for startups/small medium-sized enterprises

Table 1: What is the highest educational qualification of our finalist authors?

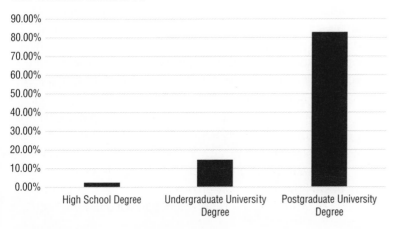

Table 2: A list of all areas our authors have domain expertise in, multiple choices were possible

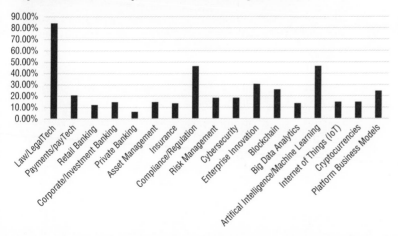

Table 3: Authors selected by the type of company they are working in

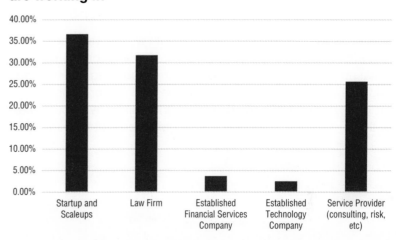

Table 4: Size of companies our authors work for

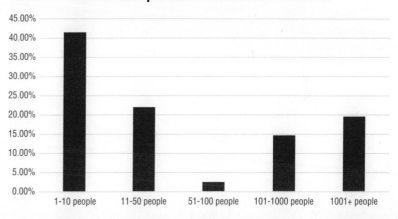

with up to 100 people. Thirty-three per cent of our authors are employed by a large organization of more than 100 employees.

We are very proud of our highly qualified authors, their strong expertise and passion for legal technology. They are either entrepreneurs or often "intrapreneurs" in law firms and large established organizations who all are committed to play a significant role in the global LegalTech revolution. These remarkable people are willing to share their insights with all of us over the next pages.

This book would not have been possible without the dedication and efforts of all contributors (both those who submitted their initial abstracts for consideration by the global legal technology and FinTech community, as well as the final authors whose insights you will be reading shortly). In addition, we would like to thank our editors at Wiley whose guidance and help made

sure that what started off as an idea, you are now holding in your hands.

Finally, I would like to thank my fantastic co-editors Sophia Adams Bhatti, public policy and regulation expert, former director at the UK's Law Society and Head of Strategy and Policy at Simmons Wavelength Limited; Akber Datoo, founding partner of D2 Legal Technology LLP with a background as both a technologist and derivatives lawyer; and Dr Drago Indjic, co-founder of several startups and director of an alternative investment fund and the Oxquant consulting firm in Oxford. Editing a crowdsourced book naturally takes several months and Sophia, Akber and Drago were always a pleasure to work with inspired by their strong domain expertise and vision for the future!

Susanne Chishti
Bestselling Co-Editor, The FinTech Book Series
CEO FINTECH Circle and FINTECH Circle Institute

About the Editors

Sophia Adams Bhatti

Sophia is a Public Policy Expert with 20 years' experience across a range of sectors. Currently, she is the Head of Strategy and Policy at Simmons Wavelength where she is leading work at the intersection of technology, law and policy. She is driven by a passion of what law reimagined can deliver for clients and wider societal outcomes.

Previously, she was the Director of Policy at the Law Society of England and Wales where she was credited with supercharging its role in legal technology and most notably was the creator of the groundbreaking Commission on the Use of AI in Criminal Justice. Prior to that she has held senior roles at the FCA, CMA, OFT and GMC, and has worked in both domestic government agencies and international organizations, including the UN.

Susanne Chishti (Editor in Chief)

Susanne Chishti is the CEO of FINTECH Circle, Europe's first angel network focused on FinTech investments and founder of the FINTECH Circle Institute, the leading FinTech learning and innovation platform offering corporate innovation workshops to C-level executives and FinTech courses. She is also the bestselling co-editor of *The FinTech Book*, *The WealthTech Book*, *The InsurTech Book* and *The PayTech Book* (all published by Wiley).

Awards:

1. Fintech Champion of the Year 2019 (Women in Finance Awards)
2. Social Media Influencer of the Year 2018 (*Investment Week*)
3. Top 7 Crypto Experts globally 2018 (*Inc. Magazine*)
4. City Innovator – Inspirational Woman in 2016
5. European Digital Financial Services "Power 50", an independent ranking of the most influential people in digital financial services in Europe (2015)

When completing her MBA she started her career working for a FinTech company (before the term was being invented) in Silicon Valley 25 years ago. She then worked more than 15 years across Deutsche Bank, Lloyds Banking Group, Morgan Stanley and Accenture in London and Hong Kong. Susanne is an award-winning entrepreneur and investor with strong FinTech expertise. She is a judge and coach at global FinTech events and competitions and a conference keynote speaker. Susanne leads a global community of more than 130,000 FinTech entrepreneurs, investors and financial services professionals (www.fintechcircle.com).

Akber Datoo

Akber Datoo is the Founder and CEO of D2 Legal Technology (D2LT), an award-winning global legal consulting firm advising clients on the use of technology and data to unlock business value through legal change. D2LT operates at the exciting intersection of FinTech and LegalTech.

After graduating with a first-class honours in computer science from Cambridge University, Akber began his career as a technologist at the investment bank UBS. Through this, he saw an opportunity for digital transformation across the legal profession and decided to retrain and qualify as a lawyer, working at magic circle law firm Allen & Overy. Akber founded D2LT in 2011 where he has overseen its growth across Europe, the US and Asia. He was appointed to the Law Society's Technology and Law Committee in 2016 and is the author of the Wiley textbook *Legal Data – Banking & Finance*, published in May 2019. Akber was highlighted as a "Market Shaper" in the Financial Times Intelligent Awards 2019, with D2LT winning an award for its legal agreement data strategy work with ISDA, the OTC derivatives trade association.

Dr Drago Indjic

Drago is Managing Director at Oxquant, a firm involved in consulting, research and training in AI and machine learning for many knowledge-based and data science industries. He is also a co-founder and an advisor to several technology (Soft-Finance, Technology Partnership) and financial (Richfox Capital, ETFmatic) businesses across Europe, and lectures part-time on FinTech and investment management at Queen Mary University of London, Regent's University, London, and London Business School.

Drago has been a EU expert since 1997. He has also worked as an investment portfolio manager and in research at several hedge funds, including his own hedge fund venture, a family office and at a sovereign wealth fund. Drago holds two engineering degrees, a Dipl Ing from the University of Belgrade and a PhD from Imperial College, London. He is also known as @dindjic on Twitter and other professional and academic networks ranging from ResearchGate to F6S. He is a member of the IEEE, the IET and a holder of various FCA CF authorizations over 20 years.

Acknowledgements

After the global book launch events of *The FinTech Book*, *The WealthTech Book* and *The InsurTech Book*, we met many legal and financial technology entrepreneurs, investors, law firms and financial services and technology professionals who all loved the books and wanted to learn more about how legal technology will impact the corporate sector and our world overall.

We came up with the idea for *The LegalTech Book* and spoke to our legal and technology friends globally. Entrepreneurs across all continents were eager to share their powerful insights. They wanted to explain the new business models empowered by LegalTech and the technologies they were working on to improve the world of law. Investors, "intrapreneurs", innovation leaders at leading financial and technology institutions and thought leaders were keen to describe their embrace of the data and LegalTech revolution. Legal technologies will become part of our lives and also provide access to justice for millions of people.

The global effort of crowdsourcing such insights was born with *The FinTech Book*, which became a global bestseller across 107 countries in ten languages. We continued this success with *The WealthTech Book*, *The InsurTech Book*, *The PayTech Book* and *The AI Book*, which were published in 2020. We hope we can satisfy the appetite for knowledge and insights about the future of legal innovation with this book.

We are aware that this book would not have been possible without the global FINTECH Circle community and our own personal networks in the legal industry. We are very grateful to more than 130,000 members of FINTECH Circle for joining us daily across our website www.FINTECHCircle.com and our Twitter accounts and LinkedIn groups. Without public support and the engagement of our global LegalTech and FinTech communities, this book would not have been possible.

The authors you will read about have been chosen by our global ecosystem purely on merit, thus no matter how big or small their organization, no matter in which country they work, no matter if they were well known or still undiscovered, everybody had the same chance to apply and be part of *The LegalTech Book*. We are proud of this because we believe that legal technologies will drive the corporate world and will ultimately make our society a fairer place. The global legal, finance and technology community is made up of the smartest, most innovative and nicest people we know. Thank you for being part of our journey. It is difficult to name you all here, but you are all listed in the directory at the end of this book.

Our publisher Wiley has been a great partner for *The FinTech Book* Series and we are delighted that Wiley will again publish *The LegalTech Book* in paperback and e-book formats globally. A special thanks go to our fantastic editor Gemma Valler. Thank you and your team – we could not have done it without your amazing support!

We look forward to hearing from you. Please visit our website https://fintechcircle.com/LegalTech-book/ for additional bonus content from our global community! Please send us your comments on *The LegalTech Book* and let us know how you wish to be engaged by dropping us a line at info@FINTECHCircle.com.

Sophia Adams Bhatti
Twitter: @adams_bhatti
Akber Datoo
Twitter: @akber_datoo

Susanne Chishti
Twitter: @SusanneChishti
Dr Drago Indjic
Twitter: @dindjic

ACKNOWLEDGEMENTS

An Introduction to LegalTech: The Law Boosted by AI and Technology

① What is AI

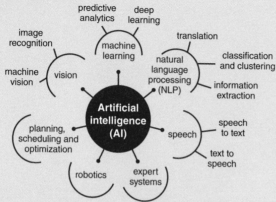

- predictive analytics
- deep learning
- image recognition
- machine vision
- vision
- machine learning
- translation
- classification and clustering
- natural language processing (NLP)
- information extraction
- **Artificial intelligence (AI)**
- planning, scheduling and optimization
- speech
- speech to text
- text to speech
- robotics
- expert systems

② Emerging AI

Computational Law

Data Driven
- prediction models and methods
- natural language processing
- visual law
- network analytic methods

Rules Based
- expert systems
- self executing law
- computable codes

③ The Four V's of Big Data

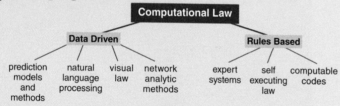

Volume
- 6 million people have cell phones (World population 7 billion)
- An estimated 2.3 trillion gigabytes of data are created each day

Variety
- By 2014 it is expected there will be 420 million wearable wireless health monitors
- 400 million tweets are sent per day by around 200 million monthly active users

Veracity
- 1 in 3 business lenders don't trust the information they use to make decisions
- Poor data quality costs the US economy around $3.1 trillion a year

Velocity
- Modern cars have around 100 sensors monitoring fuel levels, tyre pressure etc
- The NYSE captures 1 TB of trade information during each trading session

④ Ethics

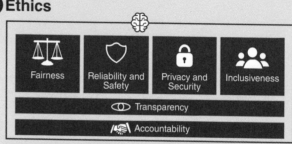

- Fairness
- Reliability and Safety
- Privacy and Security
- Inclusiveness
- Transparency
- Accountability

⑤ What is LegalTech

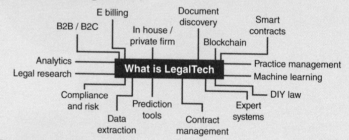

- E billing
- Document discovery
- Smart contracts
- B2B / B2C
- In house / private firm
- Blockchain
- Analytics
- **What is LegalTech**
- Practice management
- Legal research
- Machine learning
- Compliance and risk
- Prediction tools
- DIY law
- Data extraction
- Contract management
- Expert systems

⑥ The hype and Adoption

AI is already at work
Many of the data-intensive tasks that legal professionals do today – from legal research and ediscovery to pricing and billing – can be streamlined with legal AI technologies.

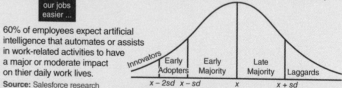

AI makes our jobs easier ...

Higher efficiency = higher profits
More than 75% of law firms that changed their approach to efficiency saw increases in both revenue and profit.

Source: Altman Well, Law Firms in Transition Study, 2015

AI does not replace humans, it assists them
It's not a question of whether machines are more accurate than humans, but whether humans assisted by machines are more accurate than humans alone. And the answer, of course, is yes.

60% of employees expect artificial intelligence that automates or assists in work-related activities to have a major or moderate impact on thier daily work lives.
Source: Salesforce research

Innovators | Early Adopters | Early Majority | Late Majority | Laggards
$x - 2sd$ $x - sd$ x $x + sd$

Relationship between types of adopters classified by innovativeness and their location on the adoption curve.
Source: *Everett M. Rogers, Diffusions of Innovations,* 5th ed. (New York: Free Press, 2003), p. 281.

Executive Summary

LegalTech has seen a huge boom over the last few years, and although still short of revolutionizing the legal services market, there is much to play for. In this part our authors explore the journey of LegalTech, alongside the role that artificial intelligence (AI) is playing now and might play in the future.

The part begins with an overview of how the market came to be where it is, and goes on to explore the classification of technologies, the role of education and skills, the perspective of the in-house counsel and how in one sector, LegalTech, plays a part. The role of AI in the law is explored from both the regulatory and legislative perspective as well as how tools deploying AI and machine learning are beginning to change the delivery of legal services.

In "We Are Voyagers", Liam Brown charts a short history of legal technology, examining the waves of advancements and the speed of change. Alongside this he also sets out some of the key drivers such as digitalization and economic efficiencies as well as a looks over the horizon as to what we might expect next.

Ever felt a sense of confusion when talking about LegalTech – what is the difference between all these tools? In his chapter, "An Introduction to Mapping and Classifying LegalTech", Alessandro Galtieri seeks to help demystify this by providing a helpful no-nonsense explanation of key terms and areas of development. Before this, Daan Vansimpsen provides a useful outline of how to handle the plethora of LegalTech solutions on the market.

Struan Britland and Elly May in their paper "Educating for Disruption, Innovation and Legal Technology" consider the nature of disruption and what sorts of things those involved in training the talent of the future need to be thinking about now.

Paul Massey examines the pivotal role of the in-house legal team, looking at both the role of the in-house team in the ecosystem as a whole alongside how LegalTech is being adopted by the in-house community.

In a case study, Brie Lam looks at the interesting convergence of LegalTech and financial services – necessity may well have been the mother of invention the author argues, and looks at interesting lessons for the wider deployment of LegalTech.

Laura Stoskute in her chapter examines the impact on the legal profession of AI and how legal teams should start to prepare for the future.

Charlotte Gerrish and Lily Morrison examine in their chapter the question of whether the law can keep up with the growth of AI, using copyright as an illustration of the difficulties to be overcome.

In "Fairness, Accountability and Transparency – Trust in AI and Machine Learning", Cemil Cakir examines the impact of AI on fundamental rights. This chapter is followed by Brian Tang and his analysis of the importance of "human in the loop". Turning from societal debates to the role of the individual, Laura van Wyngaarden addresses the debate of the ethical responsibilities of lawyers and the deployment of AI.

Paula Hodges and Charlie Morgan move the debate to the practical realm of the application of big data, focusing on the changing nature of dispute resolution.

Ben Stoneham looks towards the future in his chapter on why all LegalTech roads point to a platform strategy. There are hundreds of point-to-point solutions out there, but how do we move from this to a more consolidated and coordinated set of options?

And finally, Simon George provides a small glimpse into the world of the Internet of Things (IoT), and argues that despite all the drawbacks and concerns, businesses and consumers alike will continue to fuel the demand for IoT devices.

We Are Voyagers

Liam Brown
Chairman and CEO, Elevate

You are headed somewhere. That somewhere is your future. To navigate there successfully, you need to know where you started, decide where you want to go, be realistic about the resources at your disposal and understand the forces acting on you along the way.

I hope you get there. And I believe LegalTech can help you, but it won't if you don't choose wisely – or you don't choose at all.

I care a great deal about LegalTech. I'm the founder and leader of a law company that builds legal software and provides legal services augmented by technology. My company's strategy depends upon LegalTech, and I constantly scan the horizon for trends, insights and ideas that will be useful to our customers.

On the fear of missing out sea of LegalTech, today's shiny new object may end up on tomorrow's scrapheap of "brilliant ideas that were ahead of their time". But sometimes new legal software becomes a business tool that we use every day, and which we come to take for granted.

I recommend we each develop our own framework for evaluating LegalTech so that we can plan our route and course-correct as our journey unfolds. I'd like to share my own perspective, as someone with a vested interest in this topic.

The Journey so Far

As Bill Gates said, "In the next ten years, business will change more than it did in the previous fifty." Technology has brought massive change to almost every industry, and the pace of change is increasing.

Consider the last fifty years of LegalTech history:

50 years ago	All legal documents were paper, all phones had cords, the internet didn't exist, the majority of lawyers couldn't type and books were the only way to search case law.
45 years ago	A very small percentage of lawyers were able to search case law electronically, using the Lexis UBIQ terminal (introduced in 1973).
40 years ago	Law firms began using fax machines, and IBM was about to introduce the first "personal computer" (in 1981).
35 years ago	A few lawyers were just starting to create documents using personal computers, mostly on systems where file sharing required physically moving floppy disks from computer to computer.
30 years ago	Networked databases were enabling law firms to index complex litigation matters that previously would have been nearly impossible to handle manually.
26 years ago	The first law firm website was launched.
24 years ago	The Law Society of England and Wales denounced Richard Susskind's prediction that email would become the primary mode of communication between lawyers and clients.
20 years ago	LegalZoom was launched online (2001), and the first Blackberry device was launched.
15 years ago	The first version of the Electronic Discovery Reference Model was published. The beta version of Google Scholar was released a year later (2004), making hundreds of millions of cases, filings and research articles searchable and free.
13 years ago	The first iPhone was released, followed by the first iPad three years later. Lawyers began using smartphones and tablets for work.

10 years ago	Technology-assisted review (TAR) was first used. US Magistrate Judge Peck issued his first opinion endorsing TAR two years later.
7 years ago	Blockchain-based "smart contracts" began to appear.
6 years ago	Information processing volume in the cloud surpassed the on-premise volume in traditional IT environments in companies and firms.
3 years ago	Investment in legal technology was $233 million; the following year (2018), it catapulted to $1.7 billion.
2 years ago	95% of all lawyers were using smartphones for work.[1]
1 year ago	The Global Legal Blockchain Consortium grew to 250 members, including large companies, law firms, software companies and universities, all collaborating to develop standards that will govern the use of blockchain technology in the business of law.
	and
	The first LegalTech "app store" launched with backing from 18 of the largest law firms in the US and UK.

Reflecting on this, I find myself surprised and inspired by how much the legal world has changed technologically within my own lifetime. Being an entrepreneur, I see this as an incredible opportunity. As evidenced by the recent investment boom in the LegalTech market, I'm clearly not alone.[2]

---

[1] ABA Legal Technology Survey Report, 2018.

[2] Valentin Pivovarav, "713% Growth: Legal Tech Set an Investment Record in 2018", *Forbes*, January 2018. Found online at https://www.forbes.com/sites/valentinpivovarov/2019/01/15/legaltechinvestment2018/#3bea5adc7c2b.

Speed of Travel

Ray Kurzweil, a leading futurist, illustrates the accelerating rate of technology change with a great deal of supporting data in his essay, "The Law of Accelerating Returns."[3]

A simple way to visualize this concept is to picture changes as a series of waves that are increasing in frequency, like Figure 1.

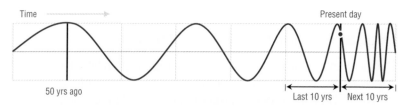

Figure 1: Change increasing in frequency

The more frequently changes occur, the more their effects overlap, amplifying the net impact. Conceptually, this can be visualized as a wave increasing in both frequency and amplitude, as shown in Figure 2.

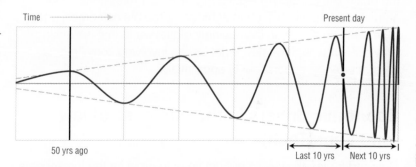

Figure 2: Change increasing in both frequency and amplitude

---

[3] Ray Kurzweil, "The Law of Accelerating Returns", 2001. Found online at https://www.kurzweilai.net/the-law-of-accelerating-returns.

Looking at both of these illustrations, it's easy to see what Bill Gates meant in predicting that business will change more in the next ten years than it did in the previous fifty!

Direction of Travel

If we agree that the speed of change is accelerating, it seems prudent to figure out where it's taking us! Rather than predicting specific destinations, let's think about the general direction of travel.

Digital – if not today, tomorrow

Businesses are becoming increasingly digital, from how they interact with customers and suppliers to how they function internally. Digital is replacing paper and manual processes. A 2018 survey by Gartner of over 450 CEOs and senior business executives found that 62% have a management initiative or transformation plan to make their business more digital.[4]

The law department must keep pace with this tsunami of digitization, which leads to three challenges: (1) selecting, implementing and integrating legal technology to better support the business; (2) getting legal and business professionals to actually use the LegalTech to achieve incredible outcomes; and (3) managing risk in an increasingly digital world that is creating previously unimagined new legal issues involving social media, cryptocurrency, cybersecurity and privacy.

Economic drivers in the business of law (and LegalTech)

Demand for legal services will continue to grow for the foreseeable future, fuelled by many factors. The worldwide regulatory environment is becoming more complex, requiring greater legal awareness, guidance and oversight. Advances in science, from genomics to drones to driverless vehicles, not to mention a more connected, always-on fabric of people and devices, will generate new legal issues that we have yet to imagine.

Despite this growing demand for legal services, legal departments will continue to experience increased pressure to spend less. That dynamic will drive demand for new ways of getting legal work done, including using legal technology as a force multiplier instead of paying more lawyers to work harder.

The most progressive general counsels already run their legal departments with business discipline, increasingly relying on technology. More will follow their lead. They use tech to measure their activity, cost and outcomes in order to predict and manage more effectively. They will continue to do more with less, turning increasingly to legal automation and self-service legal tools to support the rest of the business. Legal operations as a discipline will flourish, driving ongoing improvement in efficiency and quality by reimagining how people, process and technology are used. Legal departments will work more closely with procurement to systematically ensure greater value in exchange for outside legal spend. A few legal departments will shift from being a cost centre to being seen as a strategic asset of the business.

Follow the money

Building technology requires funding and resources, so we must consider access to capital to anticipate where and how LegalTech will develop. As previously mentioned, investment in LegalTech surged in 2018 to over 700% of the prior year and was already at $1.2 billion as of September 2019. Investors have developed keen awareness and become believers in the opportunity for LegalTech.[5]

---

[4] Gartner, Inc., "CEO Views on Digital Business: Takeaways for Finance Leaders", 2018.

[5] Bob Ambrogi, "At $1.2 Billion, 2019 is a Record Year for Legal Tech Investments – and it's only September", 2019. Found online at https://www.lawsitesblog.com/2019/09/at-1-1-billion-2019-is-a-record-year-for-legal-tech-investments-and-its-only-september.html.

These investments took a variety of forms, ranging from substantial late-stage raises by mature LegalTech companies to modest venture investments in startups. In other words, some institutional investors are betting big on established players, while others are betting on the promise of new entrants or "the next big thing". Investment like this will likely continue, fuelling development and innovation at all stages.

While law firms are restricted in their ability to take outside investment, pure-play LegalTech companies and law companies (like Elevate) have many sources of capital available to secure funding for growth.

Scanning the Horizon

As we voyage, we see new blips appear on the LegalTech radar with growing frequency. Do they represent ships under full sail, or shipwrecks beneath the waves?

Historical analogues

Technology has been developed and adopted more slowly in the legal industry than in most other areas of the business world generally. Many factors contributed to this, ranging from the caution of lawyers as market buyers, to the forces acting on investment capital, such as the (relatively) small size of the legal market. Regardless, since many other sectors *have* already undergone more dramatic technological change, we can study and learn from them. Asking ourselves "What worked (or didn't) and why?" gives us insight into what's unfolding in the legal sector.

Generational change is upon us

German physicist Max Planck said that science advances one funeral at a time. So too for LegalTech. Users of technology are human, and humans can be finicky, irrational creatures. As Richard Susskind has famously joked, "It's very difficult to tell a roomful of millionaires that their business model is wrong." The emerging tech-savvy generation of lawyers is emotionally invested in the LegalTech future they believe in, compared to the current generation of lawyers comfortable with the status quo. Even so, if the benefits of a new tool aren't immediately clear to the user or the user interface isn't intuitive, software languishes in disuse.

Natural selection

As legal catches up with the rest of the business world, technology will prove to be a double-edged sword: it is simultaneously a tool to help us *do more with less* and a catalyst that drives even more change, *requiring us to do more*. This will create disruption, uncertainty, winners and losers, but that is hardly new. Humans are, after all, toolmakers and tool users. Technology is at the heart of our species; it's simply unfolding at a rate we've never seen before. As always, those who adapt will succeed, while those who don't will be subject to natural selection.

The tools themselves are subject to the forces of selection. Many tools do one thing quite well, but prove to be of limited use to address the next problem we will need to solve in the future (such as the next General Data Protection Regulation, Brexit, London Inter-bank Offered Rate, California Consumer Privacy Act or A606 challenge). Specialization can be a strength in some contexts, but a liability in others. In the long run, flexible, reconfigurable *tool sets* will be less vulnerable to obsolescence.

Where Are We Headed?

Most of us make decisions about the future based on our experience of the past, which is a flawed method for evaluating disruptive technologies when the pace of change is increasing.

In a TED talk about predicting technology trends, Chris Anderson, then editor of *Wired* magazine, said he found that almost all technology predictions come true – they just don't happen *when* they were predicted to happen.[6]

He explained his methodology for spotting trends, which uses the technology hype cycle, a conceptual model developed by Gartner. He tracks when promising new ideas hit an initially overhyped peak and subsequently bottom out, then he monitors for indicators that they are poised to resurge into widespread adoption.

Anderson says there are four key markers he watches for:

1. Critical price, making the new tech a viable option for buyers

2. Critical mass (market penetration), indicating that buyers are voting with their wallets

3. Displacement, demonstrating that the new technology is taking the place of something else

4. Commoditization (sometimes becoming nearly free), often near the end of a technology's life cycle

Monitoring the progression of these markers, he explained, is a reliable method for identifying the arrival of game-changing trends.

Obviously, some people are better at predicting the future than others, but I believe we can all develop greater confidence and success by developing a mental framework of indicators that any of us can monitor. And, of course, you can gain an advantage by tapping into other people's ideas – including those of the contributors to this very book. Enjoy!

---

[6] Chris Anderson, "Technology's Long Tail" [Video file], February 2004. Retrieved from https://www.ted.com/talks/chris_anderson_of_wired_on_tech_s_long_tail#t-231365.

Mapping and Classifying LegalTechs

Daan Vansimpsen
CIO, Ethel

Why Is Classification Necessary?

Having already done quite extensive research into the existing FinTech, InsurTech and LegalTech applications and their providers, it's far from easy to classify them, but it is helpful to have some sense of order in order for both developers and users to understand the tools available and their uses.

Heaps of national LegalTech initiatives and associations have popped up over the past two years, and the internet has seen a number of LegalTech maps, albeit mostly incomplete and rapidly outdated (yet we should all be thankful to the creators for being catalysts!).

A Mapping Frenzy

There have been a few efforts globally which have mapped the LegalTech landscape. The most known probably being the Stanford CodeX index, partly due to the law school's frontrunner position with regards to LegalTech and legal design. If you want to gain a broader understanding and scope out existing initiatives, you might want to have a look at these directories first. Whether you're looking for details on funding, features or an overview per country, this is a great starting point.

Here is a list of others:

- Stanford Law Tech Index – the biggest and most known database out there
- Dealtech – providing the most elaborate company profiles
- LawSites – a classifying attempt by Robert Ambrogi

- Ethel LegalTech and design directory – the broadest legal innovation directory out there (mapping facilitators, LegalTechs and modern practitioners)
- Legal Geek Startup Map – the quirkiest map you'll find
- AngelList – a startup database overview with a focus on founders
- Crunchbase – a database with a particular focus on founders, funding and related news
- Legalcomplex and Legalpioneer – the most elaborate LegalTech funding research-oriented database by Raymond Blijd
- Comparador Legal Tech – directory of LegalTech solutions for legal practitioners and citizens (mostly Spanish providers)
- Legital LegalTech Library – a database with an extensive focus on features

Approaching the Classification Effort

This section provides a sort of checklist for setting up your own directory. Whether you want to perform research, benchmark versus competitors or want to build your own knowledge centre on LegalTech, you'll want to think about the following topics before diving in.

Defining the general scope

The first thing you want to know is which type of companies will be included in the list. So, let's first set out a company definition: a LegalTech company is one that applies technology to:

1. help facilitate the practice of law for lawyers and other legal practitioners, or
2. help consumers gain access to legal expertise and the judicial system.

And maybe consider excluding incumbent providers and instead focus on startups, in most cases providing a completely different value proposition.

Setting a geographical scope

Next up is defining the global scope. Limiting your scope to arbitrary or natural borders won't do your innovation strategy any good, so let's agree not to do that. Could continents be a good alternative? No, they're not. Technology has no borders. One of the directories mentioned above, however, decided to list solutions available only in Spanish or provided by Spanish companies. Taking this language-based approach probably won't do your innovation strategy any good either. But it makes sense if language is a business requirement you're limited to when selecting the best provider.

The ability to search your database

Probably the most elaborate LegalTech database in the world is the "Stanford CodeX Law Tech Index", containing over 1200 companies at the moment of writing. To make it easy for everyone to search the list, the number of main categories has been limited to only nine. In addition, you are able to select the target audience and a series of tags.

In the database I have published with my own LegalTech and design agency, Ethel, we worked the other way around. We've set it up in such a way that you can start looking for keywords, either the target audience and/or the category (which we didn't limit to nine), in the order you like. So, although we both offer similar search options, it's important to realize that the way in which you can initiate your search is the dealmaker here.

In case you're more into visual representations, be sure to check out the Underground-style overview published by Legal Geek. A great example of legal design! And since everyone has a different angle when looking into LegalTech solutions, a full text search of all details is a true blessing. When setting up your own database, consider using a no-code platform like Notion or Airtable (like some of the prominent databases mentioned earlier do) as they provide this off the shelf. Or you could even try creating your own mobile application like David Bushby from Law Hackers did (be sure to check this one too!).

Gazing Into the FinTech Abyss

The financial industry has been under attack by nifty new fin- and InsurTech players for nearly a decade now. Therefore, it's wise to have a look at the way in which they are dealing with mapping and classifying providers and solutions. One of the most renowned advisory players in this particular field is probably 11FS, a London-based consultancy and startup foundry. They've been working on their own database, 11FS Pulse, for a few years now and it's become a true beauty. You're able to benchmark your progress against peers, and access thousands of user journeys across finance, FinTech and digital technology. A similar platform was set up by Fintechdb to help incumbents find, understand and compare financial technology companies with the ultimate goal of speeding up partnerships and supplier relationships between tech vendors and financial services companies. Obviously, AngelList and Crunchbase provide a wealth of information on lots of companies in this industry too. The same goes for CB Insights and Gartner, which regularly publish on the topic, including startup maps, which is something we'll probably see happening in LegalTech too in the near future. However, all of the examples listed above require you to buy into a paying subscription to get to the information you'll

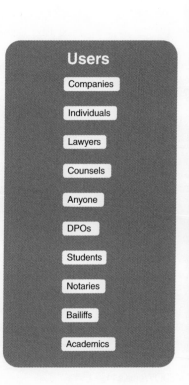

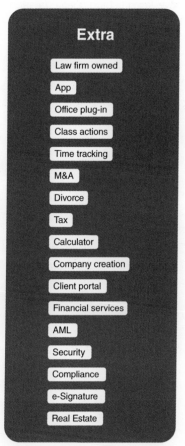

Figure 1: A classification example by Ethel

most probably need. Apart from the Law Hackers app,[1] I haven't seen this in the LegalTech industry yet. Another prediction of what the future will bring for LegalTech?

Links

Stanford Law Tech Index: http://techindex.law.stanford.edu/
Dealtech: https://dealtech.io/
LawSites blog: https://www.lawsitesblog.com/legal-tech-startups
Ethel LegalTech and design directory: https://bit.ly/ethellegal

Legal Geek Startup Map: https://www.legalgeek.co/startup-map/
AngelList: https://angel.co/companies?markets[]=Legal±Tech
Crunchbase: https://www.crunchbase.com/hub/legal-tech-companies
Legalcomplex and Legalpioneer: https://www.legalcomplex.com/
Comparador Legal Tech: https://www.comparador-legaltech.com/
Legital LegalTech Library: https://airtable.com/shrmrR5PGFTCKrWe9/tblZ9HD2a5CfILuvX/viwvoqfdTiylxAxxX?blocks=hide
Law Hackers: https://app.lawhackers.co/
https:// www.getrevue.co/profile/lawhackers/issues/law-hackers-weekly-192familyproperty-juit-atticus-altaclaro-166052

---

[1] https://docs.google.com/presentation/d/1LnKsFW6sF-2 CwlZ9OWesiKs11_Ovx_uSgE7bcwUxVpjA/edit#slide=id.p https://www.getrevue.co/profile/lawhackers/issues/law-hackers-weekly-192-familyproperty-juit-atticus-altaclaro-166052.

Educating for Disruption, Innovation and Legal Technology

Struan Britland
Head of Legal Operations Solutions, Simmons Wavelength

and Elly May
Legal Engineer, Simmons Wavelength

Introduction

The legal services industry has been one of the last bastions of resistance to the kind of disruption that has driven change across many other industries and sectors, but that is fast changing. In this chapter we will consider the nature of disruption and innovation seen in legal services to date, and the role technology is increasingly playing in service delivery. Most importantly, we will also consider what the people involved in, or training to be involved in, providing legal services today need to be thinking about and doing in order to be fit for the future.

The Nature of Disruption and Innovation in Legal Services to Date and the Increasing Role of Technology

Use of automation, artificial intelligence and machine learning technology within legal services has been increasing at a dramatic rate since 2014.[1] Law firms and legal teams, known for being risk averse, increasingly welcome the idea of leveraging their data and using technology to improve their systems and processes. This has been reflected by investments made in the LegalTech market, which was estimated to be worth $3,245 million in 2018.

However, the nature of this disruption is not only in the form of LegalTech but also thought leadership. One of the main challenges faced is breaking the "we've always done it that way" mindset, which, in the finance industry, started to shift with the boom of "FinTech".

Another area of change is in job roles. "Legal engineering" has emerged as a profession which aims to bridge the gap between legal services and technology implementation. Legal engineers provide a methodology and tools to legal teams to help identify problems and opportunities. From there they can reconceive legal processes to deliver better results to end users. Decisions around whether to use LegalTech, which technology to use and the extent to which it is used in the implementation of a re-engineered solution or process will vary depending on the problem and its underlying causes.

There are various capabilities available within a legal engineering toolkit. For example, text extraction, which simplifies the process of document review, machine learning, which aids automation of mundane and repetitive tasks, and expert systems, which use logic to build triaging solutions to complex legal scenarios and decision-making.

"Legal design" is another new role which focuses on applying human-centred creativity to legal systems, services and outputs to make them more accessible and user-friendly in a profession previously largely devoid of design thinking. Take, for example, an individual signing an employment contract. Asking a lawyer to look over the contract might be too expensive to justify, but contracts tend to be difficult to understand. Contract design seeks to address the issue of complexity of contracts. It applies design thinking to include colour, images, graphics or illustrations to a contract, making it easier to understand; and sometimes a reformatting of the layout to make it easier to navigate.

---

[1] https://www.legalgeek.co/read/how-much-is-invested-in-law-tech/.

Why the sudden change of pace?

The legal profession has to an extent been shielded from the need to change due to regulatory protections and has been largely blindsided by growing demand from clients for new and innovative ways to deliver. Scepticism towards technology is a part of the problem, with vendors (and the legal media) unable to make a compelling case to overcome lawyers' natural instincts that technology implementation leads to commoditization or redundancy. Both law firm partners and in-house lawyers see themselves as "trusted advisors", and can struggle to see how technology can coexist as a partner, rather than a competitor, to a trusted human lawyer.

This hasn't deterred legal companies, software vendors and other entrepreneurs who have identified this gap in the market for an acceleration in how law firms and legal teams embrace and utilize technology. Whilst the rest of the world moves forward with digital and mobile transformation – clients are wondering why their legal services cannot be delivered in the same way, with efficiency and cost benefits being passed on. While we may well be nearing the apex of a hype curve, only the most obdurate of lawyers is now able to ignore the growing confluence of demand and capability.

Although it may seem as though all legal technology companies are disrupting the LegalTech space with new technology and products, many are actually "sustaining" along with legacy providers because they are playing in the current legal services market by making it cheaper, more efficient and more effective. However, the disruptive slice of the market is tending to cater to the hitherto completely unserved, such as those who are unable to obtain legal advice due to the high cost, complexity of procedure or lack of approachability. In response, we have seen startups provide solutions such as "the world's first robot lawyer" to help individuals gain access to the expensive and lengthy process by essentially using technology to commoditize the legal service, for example to dispute parking tickets or challenge a landlord in violation of regulations or contractual obligations. Other platforms offer a service to match the right lawyer with an individual using expert systems and an intuitive user interface, but also help with education of the legal process by providing free legal education materials and guidance.

Where Do We Go From Here?

We have seen formal education begin to respond to this need with a rise in LegalTech degrees across universities in the UK, Europe and America where the curriculum spans from exploring and harnessing technology in legal services to using expert systems and software development platforms to build real-world applications. There is still, however, a long way to go, particularly in terms of integrating and embedding new ways of thinking into legal courses, rather than this being an ancillary "bolt-on" to legal education.

However, there is also a need for informal, ongoing learning for personal and professional development. This benefits modern legal solutions, which need to be delivered through collaboration from diverse teams with a wide range of thought, skill and capability. To put it another way, lawyers need to think like legal engineers. In our experience, no two legal engineers are the same. Each one has a different journey, background and skill set, but a common goal in changing legal services for the better by bridging the wide gap between legal services and technology.

Traditionally, lawyers are very narrow specialists. However, this does not mean that all lawyers need to retrain or expand their skill set by learning to code. When it comes to engineering in the legal world, soft skills are just as important as the hard ones. For some, this may start with basic computer training in MS Excel, Word or Outlook, but there are a wide variety of skill sets and competencies required in the LegalTech world. Simple approaches such as attending LegalTech events and workshops provide opportunities for discussion around real-life applications of LegalTech, for example how to harness the value from thousands of data points lawyers work with every day through machine learning and automation tools. By understanding the framework of what could be possible, lawyers can participate in conversations around innovation in their own practices. A key shift that needs to happen, and is being seen in forward-thinking organizations more broadly (and so in some cases taking the in-house legal team along on the journey), but less so in law firms, is a focus on competencies rather than just the skills needed to do a job. Being ready for how this new world continues to develop will also be an ongoing challenge – transformation in any context is never finished, just ready for the next iteration.

Some firms are realizing the importance of LegalTech by introducing training and programmes to support lawyers with an autodidactic approach to embracing LegalTech and hopefully honing an interest towards technology and data to change the archaic functioning of many traditional law firms.

Conclusion

With so much noise, it can be hard for lawyers to get a true understanding of the market today and make future predictions. Though clients may not be dreaming of digital lawyers, they are demanding more efficient and effective legal input. Lifting the lid on the legal services black box puts greater transparency on service delivery and billing, but also leads to more questions. There is still a fear of trusting a robot lawyer to give accurate legal advice. However, this is not the goal.

There is resistance to legal innovation, but one of the aims of artificial intelligence is to cut out banal tasks and improve efficiency. After all, no one went into law to spend hours scrolling through hundreds of thousands of documents hunting for variations of one clause. It is true that legal technology will replace jobs, but this does not mean it will replace people who provide something artificial intelligence cannot – a mixture of intelligence quotient and emotional intelligence, such as empathy, persuasiveness and sympathy, and above all – creativity.

Although we are far away from full automation of legal services, what we have seen is room for lawyers to be more productive and focus on the law itself by taking away the mundane, repetitive or administrative tasks around legal practice in many instances. This in turn has led to a more efficient and effective delivery of legal services and advice from lawyers to their clients. Lawyers need to continue the trend, so as not to be left behind.

An Introduction to Mapping and Classifying LegalTech

Alessandro Galtieri
Deputy General Counsel, Colt Technology Services

It is often difficult to keep track of all the technology that is dramatically changing the landscape of traditional lawyering. The following chapter will provide an introduction on how to approach this field and an overview of some solutions now available.

It may be useful to set the scene and reflect on the evolution of this area so far. The origin of LegalTech can to a certain degree be made to coincide with the emergence of legal research, e-Discovery and e-Billing solutions. The following technological advance in big data processing and in the "intelligence" of these systems was the enabler for the creation and development of other, more complex offerings.

Broadly speaking, the parallel shift of most enterprise systems (somewhat later than consumers) to cloud computing also enabled new providers to offer solutions which could be deployed in – and tied to – an environment in which customers were comfortable.

There is undoubtedly a lot of noise in the current markets, with literally hundreds of solution providers and a certain amount of marketing and "dressing up". However, truly innovative systems do exist, and may entail a sea change in age-old practices.

It is important, however, to appreciate that any new technology – be it a matter management system or a contract drafting tool – introduces changes in the way legal teams work, as it affects the way legal knowledge is accessed, acquired, processed and delivered. A holistic view of the impact of any such technology is therefore paramount.

This is because any team (and arguably, especially a team of highly trained professionals such as lawyers) is naturally resistant to change, and that rolling out a new technology would be pointless unless the team has been primed for its adoption. There is a risk that the introduction of technology will be perceived as devaluing the lawyers' contribution. It is not about the technology itself, but about the underlying change in working practices. Therefore, any new technology will require change management – and that is about people, not tech. Involving all stakeholders is crucial: from internal and external customers, to the whole supply ecosystem, and everyone who may be impacted by the change.

In order to take full advantage of the new solutions, it may help to have a basic taxonomy to understand what needs we are trying to address.

The first area is that of **legal research** – that we probably give for granted given that we are now using online tools on a daily basis (be it free resources such as BAILII, or paid subscriptions such as the ones offered by LexisNexis, Thomson Reuters, etc.), but that were really not so common until a couple of decades ago.

Matter management is a very varied and crowded field, as there are many activities that are covered by matter management software: the automation of reporting, standardization of workflows, collaboration facilitation, faster search, maintenance of precedents, recording approvals, etc. It may therefore be useful to break this section down further into areas:

1. Billing/legal spend management. This is usually the first step in the adoption of technology in legal departments, and the reason is obvious. The ability to track and analyse external legal spend allows for a very quick demonstration of the return on investment to other stakeholders. This is because these tools allow for automatic rejection of invoices that contain items not agreed in the engagement terms (hourly rates,

number of associates, internal travel, administration expenses, etc.). Other solutions are slightly different, being rather a sort of legal analytics tool, in order to analyse the data contained in the processed invoices, a function offered by the more complex systems already mentioned, but that increasingly can be purchased as a stand-alone (typically simpler and cheaper) service.

2. Knowledge management and expertise automation. Knowledge management has for years now covered the issue of centralizing a team's know-how. There are now innovative solutions to tackle what is logically the next problem: the intelligent searching and delivery of such knowledge to legal team members.

Contracts are, of course, another area of intense LegalTech innovation. Solutions include:

1. Drafting aides. Contract drafting software helps automate the creation of new contracts. These tools can be based on existing templates or can be more sophisticated, such as software that creates a contract when the user answers a number of questions.

2. Contract review (including due diligence). This software is used to automate the review of existing contracts and other agreements. At its most basic level, it can compare against a given template. More complex programs can identify a number of clauses that have been tagged as being of interest, even without a specific clause template to compare against. At its most sophisticated, new systems can "learn" and create "standard" clauses from a large number of contracts, and identify which contracts in that sample have provisions that deviate from the "median". This feature is more useful in large extraction exercises, such as the need to identify risky provisions in a large number of contracts during due diligence. Recently, these tools have been used not just for "traditional" due diligence processes (i.e. acquisitions) but to identify potentially problematic clauses in an existing contract database. For instance, they have been used in the case of Brexit to identify all contractual provisions that defined "territory" as the territory of the European Union or that made reference to EU legislation as being applicable.

3. Management. These tools start from the basic contract repository and continue to more advanced solutions offering obligation mapping and tracking, task management, analytics, etc.

4. Analytics. This is a feature of due diligence and management tools, allowing extraction and monitoring of data related to an organization's contractual obligations, contracting trends, efficiency, etc.

Digital signature. The advantages of digital or electronic signature are becoming widely known and include not just speed of execution, but also a third-party certified, time-stamped repository of the executed documents, which helps in case of disputes. Another feature greatly appreciated by signatories is the fact that contracts can be signed using a mobile app while on the move. The existing solutions also offer additional benefits: the implementation is easy as this is a change affecting a single task (execution), but from which may derive a number of positive consequences, in terms of governance (right signatory every time), contract retention (automated), speed (with multiple signatories, there is no need to check availability – documents are sent to all signatories and the first one that signs completes the process) and future-proofing (most systems integrate with matter management and contracts systems).

e-Discovery. This now feels like "old hat" to many lawyers, but there are constant advances in new litigation discovery tools in managing the identification, collection and analysis of electronically stored information.

IPRs. Although there is nothing "different" about the management of intellectual property rights compared to other legal matters, this highly standardized world has seen an explosive growth of tools to automate the tracking of patents, trademarks, and other IPRs.

Process automation is to a certain extent a category overlapping with matter management but there is a growing number of stand-alone solutions.

Specific solutions also exist to support **privacy** obligations and more generally to help with **compliance** matters, some of which increase the effectiveness of traditional tools and training. And, of course, there are a growing number of **online dispute resolution** providers that are helping reduce costs and increase speed of resolving potential and actual litigation.

The really new (and fast-developing) area is that of **litigation prediction** technology. As more and more cases of many courts are accessible online, there are now tools that can quite accurately predict the outcome of a case based on the court's (or even a specific judge's) past track record, to the extent that litigation

strategies and tactics can be adapted in order to maximize the chances of the desired outcome.

It is, of course, impossible to predict how future developments will impact all of these areas. However, it is possible, if counterintuitive, that it is where technology is providing a genuine disruption in the way legal services are conceived and delivered – as supposed to the areas where it simply serves as an enhancement of the work currently performed by lawyers – that we will see the fastest adoption. After all, one can still decide to handle matters in a traditional way with files/folders, etc., and simply forsake the efficiency gain of a modern matter management system. However, it would be difficult to resist clients' demands to use digital signatures, or to provide information in a certain format. Let's not forget that only thirty years ago lawyers certainly did not anticipate how virtually all client communications would be handled by email. Outside pressure – be it from clients or competitors – will determine which one of these innovations will transform into daily business practices.

In-House Counsel Can Drive Industry Change Through Legal Technology

Paul Massey
CEO, Tabled.io

Introduction and My Journey to LegalTech

When I moved from being an in-house lawyer to launching a LegalTech business, I expected life as an entrepreneur to become much harder. It will come as no surprise that building a startup is an enormous challenge! But in many ways, my work now is more streamlined and easier to manage than it ever was as a lawyer. Dashboards manage and display key company data and metrics, intuitive platforms help design our products and customer management and marketing are all catered for by well-designed online applications. Even accounting, the area I dreaded the most, is effortless, with seamless integration with my accountants through Xero.

As a General Counsel, I looked for platforms like this to help run my legal team, from accessible document management to innovative artificial intelligence (AI) solutions to help streamline workflows. I generally found products designed for law firms at unattainable prices or too difficult to adopt. That is why I decided to launch Tabled, to address the everyday problems facing legal teams. It is also why I think in-house counsel should lead on legal technology adoption, to ensure that the tools to improve their legal operations are readily available.

The Law Society's recent report on LegalTech adoption[1] concludes that "Lawtech is not yet fundamentally transforming the provision of law… Looking at the maturity of the LawTech sector as a whole, it is hard to argue that it is anything other than in the 'innovation' or 'early adoption' stage." This demonstrates the huge potential of legal technology and raises the question of why existing technologies have not yet changed the face of legal services.

Adoption of Legal Technology – In-House vs Law Firms

Building a complete picture of the adoption rates of legal technology is difficult, with patchy surveys and no publicly available longitudinal data. Until we have that data, we can piece together a general picture to compare in-house and law firm LegalTech adoption.

In private practice, PwC found that 97% of firms had adopted or were piloting client collaboration tools (e.g. external portals and data rooms), with 78% adopting or piloting automated document production. Over 50% were piloting AI applications and over 50% were researching robotic process automation.[2]

In-house, the level of adoption is generally lower. The Association of Corporate Counsel (ACC) found that only 16% and 41% had implemented collaboration and contract management solutions, respectively, with contract management tools potentially including automated document production. Both categories were dominated by legacy Microsoft SharePoint systems. Higher numbers were adopting e-signatures, demonstrating a first win for in-house LegalTech solutions.[3]

---

[1] https://www.lawsociety.org.uk/support-services/research-trends/documents/law-society-lawtech-adoption-research-2019/.

[2] https://www.pwc.co.uk/industries/law-firms/pwc-law-firms-survey-report-2018-final.pdf.

[3] 2019 Global Legal Department Benchmarking Report: https://www.acc.com/sites/default/files/2019-06/ACC_Benchmark_062019.pdf.

Radiant Law has been collecting data through its benchmark tool on what in-house law departments have actually achieved.[4] Their conclusion is that "everyone thinks that they are behind, but the reality is that little has been done across the board". Based on data from over 60 companies, from the largest banks to high-growth tech companies, "processes are generally manual, data is not being used to improve performance and improvements generally are ad-hoc".

The general position that law firms have led the way is backed up by the Law Society who state: "While a large portion of legal work takes place outside law firms, LawTech has not yet engaged with in-house professionals directly in a way that is anywhere near comparable with activity among the large B2B law firms."

This is concerning, if you, like me, believe that technology has the potential to change the way legal business is executed. Unless more in-house teams increase the effective adoption of legal technology, they will not be able to leverage the technology to their advantage to change the way they deliver services to their internal clients and address any concerns with how they receive legal advice from their panel law firms and increasingly from legal service providers.

Why Do Many In-House Teams Lag Behind?

Frequently cited barriers to LegalTech adoption are those catch-22 situations of a lack of time, budget or resources to assess and implement available options. Others cite a lack of interoperability of technology solutions or difficulty demonstrating return on investment, which legal vendors are starting to address.

Some General Counsels have been burnt by complex systems that took months or years to implement with little adoption, while others may simply fear that AI and blockchain hype won't live up to reality.

The reason for these negative implementations is a failure to target technology to particular pain points and the poor user experience of some legal technology. This is perhaps not surprising given that many of the available solutions have been designed for the early demand from law firms rather than the specific needs of in-house teams. This is now changing with a new wave of legal technology providers building functional solutions to change the way legal services are actually delivered, rather than simply replicating ways of working from analogue to digital or adding a layer of digital bureaucracy.

The Business Case for LegalTech

In-house lawyers face issues that are exactly the challenges that legal technology vendors claim their solutions address: demonstrating value through operational efficiencies, managing budgets, streamlining and adding value to commercial transactions, or compliance and risk assessment processes. Without a data platform, the General Counsel and chief executive officers or chief financial officers often struggle to identify actionable key performance indicators to measure the legal team's impact.

Those teams that do deploy legal technologies can achieve impressive results if the technology is well integrated and designed to tackle specific problems. The ACC have identified that "High-performing departments with a more comprehensive state of technology are more likely to be working closely with business leadership and consulted on the company's risk exposure early on in business deals".[5] Lexis Nexus found that 57% of General Counsels believe that technology investments have already

---

[4] https://radiantlaw.com/benchmark.

[5] ACC Law Department Management 2016 Report.

increased their efficiency, while 60% believe technology will improve their legal work over the next three to five years.[6]

There is every reason for more in-house teams to adopt LegalTech to the same levels or beyond their law firms and legal service providers.

Change on the Horizon!

In-house teams have become alive to these issues. A Thomson Reuters survey found that the top priorities for in-house teams were controlling outside counsel costs, followed by using technology to simplify workflow and manual processes.[7] Gartner surveyed 61 companies and found that over 40% expect spending on LegalTech to increase by 10% or more over the next three years, outstripping the rise in spend on legal personnel, while over 70% predict outside counsel spend will remain flat or reduce.[8]

Law firms can counter these trends using legal technology to improve margins and client relationships. For in-house teams with increasing workloads, operational efficiencies will need to be found to achieve these ambitious goals. Alongside process re-evaluation and change management, for many teams, legal technology will form part of the solution.

There are an increasing number of law firms and legal service providers offering technology solutions alongside or as part of legal services, helping in-house teams uncover legal technology. However, Law Society respondents highlighted that in-house lawyers still do not feel law firms are client centric and law firms' technology solutions can fail to translate well to in-house scenarios. In-house counsels expect their law firms to use technology and pass on the benefits, including lower fees, improved quality and faster turnaround times. However, in 2017, *The Lawyer* found that cost savings were not being passed on in line with these expectations. Fifty per cent of respondents said they had experienced 0% cost savings.[9]

In-house teams will need to implement their own systems in collaboration with one of the new vendors focused on their needs and their law firms/legal service providers to tackle future challenges. If more in-house teams do take the initiative with legal technology, they can create the systems to do more work in-house and build stronger integrations with their outside providers for more flexible work overflow and responsive advice. If the goal is improved legal service and working relationships with business clients, then now is a good time to evaluate and invest in legal technology.

---

[6] https://www.newlawjournal.co.uk/content/legal-technology-looking-past-hype.

[7] https://www.thomsonreuters.com/en/press-releases/2018/february/corporate-legal-departments-seeing-greater-value-from-their-outside-counsel-says-2018-state-of-corporate-law-departments-report.html.

[8] Gartner 2018 Legal Technology and Analytics Benchmarking Report.

[9] https://www.thelawyer.com/legal-technology-litigation-law-firms-top-50/.

The Role of LegalTech in Financial Services: A Case Study

Brie Lam
Founder and Regulatory Compliance Consultant, Brie Lam
Regulatory Advisory Services

Background

No discussion of the shifts in the leveraging of technology for legal application is complete without reference to the explosive growth of legal document automation. Document automation refers to the technology that assists in the assembly of electronic documents. As applied to the legal industry, the term refers to software, typically accessed online, that enables a user to autogenerate legal contracts following a series of targeted and relevant questions. According to IBISWORLD, the online legal services industry – of which document automation represents a significant component – generates US$8 billion in revenue per annum in the US,[1] up sharply from US$4.1 billion in 2014.[2]

Such application has seen widespread adoption with the retail and small business customer bases. For those customers, online legal technology providers like LegalZoom and Rocket Lawyer will within seconds generate a partnership agreement, a non-disclosure agreement or any number of other legal documents that a small business may require. One need only input responses to a few simple questions to produce an agreement. Businesses are opting to use its machine-generated documents for routine legal needs; LegalZoom estimates that it has served more than 4 million customers in the US and UK since its formation in 2001.[3] LegalZoom's valuation may be an additional indicator of healthy consumer appetite for such services: in its most recent July 2018 round of funding, the firm was valued at $2 billion (£1.6 billion), with revenue increasing at about 20% per annum and profit margins above 20%.[4]

The success of businesses like LegalZoom underscores the fact that consumers of legal services have come to realize that many of the repetitive tasks around documentation that have been traditionally performed by lawyers don't have to be performed by lawyers. Research backs that thinking: in January 2017, the McKinsey Global Institute published a study estimating that 23% of a lawyer's tasks can be automated with existing technology, as reported by *The New York Times*.[5]

Legal Document Automation in Financial Services

As quickly as retail segments have embraced document automation, wholesale sectors have done so with even greater

---

[1] IBISWORLD, "Online Legal Services Industry in the US – Market Research Report": https://www.ibisworld.com/industry-trends/specialized-market-research-reports/advisory-financial-services/legal/online-legal-services.html (accessed 18 September 2019).

[2] Issues Paper Concerning Unregulated LSP Entities, ABA Comm. on the Future of Legal Services 5. 31 March 2016: https://www.americanbar.org/content/dam/aba/images/office_president/final_unregulated_lsp_entities_issues_paper.pdf (citing Will McKitterick, IBISWORLD Industry Report OD5638: Online Legal Services in the U.S. 4, 2014).

[3] Lawpath, "LawPath Partners with LegalZoom to Expand Legal Services throughout Australia": https://lawpath.com.au/press-release-july-10-2018 (10 July 2018).

[4] Gerrit de Vynck, "LegalZoom Gains $2 Billion Valuation in Funding Round", Bloomberg, 31 July 2018: https://www.bloomberg.com/news/articles/2018-07-31/legalzoom-gains-2-billion-valuation-in-latest-funding-round (accessed 18 September 2019).

[5] Steve Lohr, "A.I. is Doing Legal Work. But it Won't Replace Lawyers, Yet", *New York Times*, 19 March 2017: https://www.nytimes.com/2017/03/19/technology/lawyers-artificial-intelligence.html (accessed 18 September 2019).

haste. One specific industry had good reason to lead the shift to adopt modernized document assembly processes, that of the wholesale financial services sector. For financial services firms that survived the global financial crisis of 2007–2009, adoption of document automation was a necessity rather than a choice. A specific use case is the context of derivatives, an area in which the unlikely progenitor of the global financial crisis created the perfect environment for the growth of document automation.

Much writing has been devoted to the blame directed at the derivatives industry for spreading contagion that began as a US housing crisis into the global economy. In the aftermath of the crisis, global regulators put in place widespread reforms targeted at how over-the-counter derivative products were traded by financial firms. These reforms resulted in trading counterparties having to negotiate and execute documentation compliant with new regulations to replace older, obsolete document iterations.

Case Study

Bank Alpha is dealing derivatives with 5000 trading counterparties with whom it has to replace non-compliant Agreement A with compliant Agreement B, as a result of the regulatory changes. The project has an allocated budget of £x. Bank Alpha wants to allocate a greater percentage of that budget to high-value tasks that cannot be automated – like bespoke terms negotiation – and to spend less on tasks that can be automated away in order to maximize the outcome of their total expenditure. This was exactly the situation that derivatives dealers found themselves in.

A Problem of Scale

Not only was there a clear use case, but this was further compounded by the dearth of legal talent with the background and expertise to handle this specific type of negotiation, as all the players scrambled to put in place their new obligations. As dealers of derivative products found themselves in the midst

of the "repapering" drive, it became clear that the available talent was not going to be able to cover the demand. CEO Scott O'Malia of the International Swaps and Derivatives Association (ISDA) summed up the industry conundrum in a late 2018 speech addressing upcoming regulation borne of the financial crisis, "The pressure on resources across the industry will also be severe, potentially leading to disruption in the non-cleared derivatives market … there are only so many lawyers available to negotiate the documentation."[6] Derivatives dealers recognized that without innovative ways of leveraging automation and scalability for the document assembly component of repapering, without reserving lawyers' efforts for higher-value requirements that are not easily automated with existing technology, mandatory repapering deadlines would not be met. O'Malia continued, "ISDA has been working to raise awareness of the issue, and to develop solutions to help firms with implementation." They certainly have. At the start of 2019, ISDA and law firm Linklaters LLP launched ISDA Create, an online solution that automates the process of producing and agreeing collateral documentation central to derivatives trading. Having standardized a widely adopted framework of legal documents that facilitate such trading, the evolution into automating components of that framework seems like a natural one for ISDA.

Risk Mitigation

The most obvious advantage to leveraging technology in the legal industry is moving lawyers away from rote processes to higher value work. However, an equally important advantage is the risk mitigation afforded by document automation. Quality control tightens as decreased manual interaction decreases – reducing the chance of human input error. The legal name of a corporate

---

[6] ISDA, "ISDA Europe Regional Conference, CEO Opening Remarks – Scott O'Malia": http://www.isda.org/a/mevEE/CEO-Remarks-ISDA-Europe-Conference-Sept-2018.pdf (26 September 2018).

entity, for example, can be sourced from a single field stored on the back end, and inserted into agreements with consistency not only throughout the document, but across the firm. Field validation can be built into processes, rejecting erroneous inputs known as fat finger errors, particularly where numerical values of price and quantity are concerned, which in financial services can be an expensive mistake.[7] In December 2005, an employee of Mizuho Securities Co. sold 610,000 shares of a company's stock for one yen, rather than one share for 610,000 yen.[8] The mistake cost the firm 40.5 billion yen (£313 million). In another instance, in February 2009, a trader working in the Japanese unit of UBS erroneously ordered £22 billion of Capcom convertible bonds with the intention of ordering bonds with a value of £220,000. Fortunately for UBS, the trade was executed out of trading hours and was cancelled at no cost to the bank.

Document automation brings with it a related advantage of seamless downstream processing, as an additional layer of risk mitigation. Today's solutions can store contractual data elements as structured data and send them downstream in a defined schema. This negates the need for the rekeying of fields from a legal agreement into processing systems, such as sending terms from a mortgage agreement to feed a bank's system that generates mortgage statements.

What the Future Holds

Given a compelling post-crisis need for mass legal documentation replacement – termed "repapering" – coupled with a need for risk mitigation, it is little wonder that global banks led and continue to lead the charge in making the upfront investment in document automation in order to access longer-term benefits. We fast forward to the present day, and every major financial institution is leveraging documentation automation solutions. Necessity was the mother of invention here. Without post-financial crisis outcomes, document automation solutions might not enjoy the same innovative momentum that they do today. A similar wave of adoption, at the same scale, has yet to be seen in the legal sector and the jury is still out as to whether a crisis is an essential catalyst.

---

[7] Eric Lam, "A Brief History of Some of the Market's Worst Fat Fingers", Bloomberg, 23 January 2019: https://www.bloomberg.com/news/articles/2019-01-24/oops-a-brief-history-of-some-of-the-market-s-worst-fat-fingers (accessed 18 September 2019).

[8] David McNeill, " 'Fat Finger' Trade Costs Tokyo Shares Boss his Job", *The Independent*, 21 December 2005: https://www.independent.co.uk/news/world/asia/fat-finger-trade-costs-tokyo-shares-boss-his-job-520283.html (accessed 18 September 2019).

How Artificial Intelligence Is Transforming the Legal Profession

Laura Stoskute
Independent Researcher

Gone are the days when artificial intelligence (AI) was merely a notion used in science fiction. Although companies have already begun to embrace technological advancements to some degree,[1] AI impact on legal services is still in its infancy.

The Changing Face of the Legal Profession

The changes in workforce, client demands[2] and disruptive technology[3] are just a few factors impacting the legal industry and the way many traditional firm lawyers work. Ten years ago the legal profession was concerned with file security; today's challenge is how to deploy AI and machine learning (ML) algorithms and natural language processing to assist with due diligence and disclosure exercises.[4] Businesses need to take effective action today to stay current.

Drivers of Technological Advancement in the Legal Industry

Although the legal industry has been known as rather slow and reluctant to adopt any technological automation, many lawyers now recognize the importance of technological and AI advancements in their daily work. According to some legal experts,[5] there are two fundamental reasons for that.

- Growing pressures on lawyers to cut down fees.

Historically, there was no great necessity for both lawyers and law firms to enhance the efficiency of their work as clients were willing to pay on the basis of the billable hour. In such cases, why would one bother to adopt technologies? However, in recent years the situation has changed and become more intense – clients are putting pressure on lawyers to reduce not only the hourly fees but also the total amount of hours spent on various tasks.

- AI applications are able to deliver volume and quality, compared to humans.

Previous technologies generally replaced clerical and supporting staff, but modern ML-based applications can deliver tasks such as due diligence checks with greater speed and accuracy and ultimately lead to lower costs and better service for clients.

---

[1] A report, "Capturing Technological Innovation in Legal Services" produced by The Law Society, 2017.

[2] An article, "Legal Tech in 2018: Threats and Opportunities" in The Law Society by Alex Heshmaty, 2018.

[3] A report, "The Future of Law and Innovation in the Profession" produced by The Law Society of New South Wales, 2017.

[4] An article, "Legal Tech Uses AI to Help Business to Help Itself" in *Financial Times* by Cat R. Pooley, 2018.

---

[5] A lecture, "Artificial Intelligence and Law – an Overview and History" at The Stanford Center for Legal Informatics. Professor Harry Surden on 3 April 2018. Also, a keynote "Artificial Intelligence, Technology and the Future of Law" at the University of Toronto Faculty of Law. Professor Dana Remus on 25 March 2017.

How Is AI Revolutionizing the Legal Field?

It is a very exciting time as legal services are on the verge of a revolution, driven by the availability of AI and ML-based technologies. A few examples of the types of solutions already available include:

- Document review and legal research. The efficiency of document analysis can be significantly improved by using AI-powered applications. Machines can sort through documents much faster, providing between a 40 and 80% efficiency saving on human time for the same amount of work.[6]

- Due diligence. With the help of AI tools a few big law firms are aiming to reduce the time spent on traditional due diligence methods, yet providing even more accurate facts that uncover the background information on behalf of their clients.

- Natural language processing (NLP). NLP technology is unique in a way that it allows computers and humans to interact via voice or text. One popular example today is a chatbot, which is commonly used for customer care, such as answering questions or even booking appointments.

- E-Discovery. E-Discovery applications are helping law firms to search, locate and secure data for the purpose of using it as evidence in a legal case.

How Should Legal Departments Be Prepared for the AI Revolution?

It is quite clear that legal departments need to be prepared for and adapt to the upcoming technological change swiftly in order to stay competitive in the market. Here are a few things to consider according to the American Bar Association.[7]

1. Acquiring the right talent.

As the legal landscape will continue to develop, young attorneys will need to become more proficient in understanding AI applications and how they can benefit their daily work. It will not be enough just to understand the client's business – it will be necessary to comprehend different software tools and be able to discuss their advantages and drawbacks with "techies" – i.e. developers. A superior knowledge of AI tools will help a lawyer not only satisfy the client needs but also stand out in a competitive legal market.

2. Have a clear strategy.

Legal departments need to understand that AI has to serve a client's needs. ML algorithms will shortly be capable of replacing a valuable and unique specialization that a lawyer developed over 20 years of practice. Therefore, understanding the underlying needs of a client and being able to foresee the issues that might arise, and developing the strategy that could relate the client's goals to the machine's tasks, will undoubtedly become the benchmark of adequate and valuable legal work.

3. Become more "business-savvy"

It has always been common for a lawyer to be specialized in one specific area of law. However, a changing legal scene will create a new legal culture where the breadth of knowledge will be more praised than its depth. In order to be able to better apply AI to client business and legal needs, lawyers will need to understand

---

[6] A report, "Capturing Technological Innovation in Legal Services" produced by The Law Society, 2017.

[7] An article, "AI and the Young Attorney: What to Prepare for and How to Prepare" in the American Bar Association by Kurt Watkins and Rachel E. Simon, 2019.

the evolving world of business and markets. By embracing the business, decision-making attorneys would go beyond what has been long considered as a "conventional legal scope of work".

What are the Implications of AI in the Legal Industry?

Given that AI applications will continue to develop at a fast pace, the legal industry will face some meaningful implications.[8]

- Decreasing number of lower-grade legal jobs.

It is estimated that around 100,000 jobs in the legal sector have a high chance of being automated by 2036.[9] Over the next decade we will have fewer people doing routine work and instead focusing on highly skilled and complex tasks, such as helping clients with business advice or representing them in court.

- Increasing new legal skill sets.

Young lawyers entering a job market will need to have not only a new set of skills such as contract management and e-discovery but also business acumen in order to be successful. In addition, we are likely to see the emergence of wholly new roles, such as AI legal analysts, suggests Harry Surden, Associate Professor of Law at the University of Colorado Law School.[10]

- Greater number of blended educational programmes.

Law firms will not only need to invest in new software programs and AI tools, but also they might want to look for talent with both legal and computer science skills. That being said, AI topics are being introduced into the curriculum of many universities. Harvard, Stanford, Oxford, and other leading law and business schools are launching AI courses that will give students a perspective and the tools necessary to be successful in the legal market.

- Lower costs – higher market outreach.

By replacing some tasks and humans with machines, law firms could reduce service costs, which could have a positive impact on the market – boosting a demand for legal services from people who could not afford it previously.

Conclusion

In a decade or two the legal profession will be completely different. Advancing technology, shifting client demands and employee expectations will transform the nature of the legal profession and the skills required. AI technology has a potential to eliminate the drudge and rote work from lawyers in the near future. And even though AI might not be able to negotiate an agreement and become a trusted legal advisor, its underlying potential lies in helping lawyers become better professionals in the process.[11]

---

[8] A report, "Artificial Intelligence and the Legal Profession" produced by The Law Society, 2017.

[9] A report, "Developing Legal Talent. Stepping into the Future Law Firm" by Deloitte, 2016.

[10] A lecture, "Artificial Intelligence and Law – an Overview and History" at The Stanford Center for Legal Informatics. Professor Harry Surden on 3 April 2018.

---

[11] Keynote, "Artificial Intelligence, Technology and the Future of Law" at the University of Toronto Faculty of Law. Professor Dana Remus on 25 March 2017.

Can the Law Keep Up with the Growth of AI?

Charlotte Gerrish
Founding Lawyer, Gerrish Legal

and Lily Morrison
Legal Consultant, Gerrish Legal

The development of artificial intelligence (AI) is changing our everyday lives. Companies are increasingly using algorithms and machine learning-based tools to improve their business offerings, whether to enable strategy decisions or deliver services, and lawmakers in our connected societies are attempting to adapt to this changing landscape. As the digital world advances, is the law able to adapt to this ever-changing environment whilst supporting and driving innovation?

Big Data, Text and Data Mining – Can the Law Keep Up?

Text and data mining (TDM) is a key process underpinning AI. TDM processes generally include access, extraction and, crucially, reproduction of big data by non-human means. The process requires unfettered access to big data to be able to attain the most useful results, which help us to drive innovation in AI and technology generally. Two commonly engaged categories of data in the process provide a useful illustration of the tensions that exist between the law and the drive for innovation: personal data and copyrighted data. Both are likely to be captured in big data sets, and both are subject to complex legal regimes, which can be problematic for innovators.

AI vs Privacy Laws

The GDPR[1] overhauled the European privacy framework in 2018 and set out obligations for companies handling personal data. Its aim is to respect individual privacy rights,[2] with its roots coming from the EU Charter for Fundamental Rights.[3] The GDPR cements rights such as the "right to be forgotten", giving data subjects more control over how their personal information is processed.[4]

Many software as a service (SaaS) and other analytics technologies rely on big data, which is analysed by AI processing either to provide core services or to improve their underlying technology. Providers of these solutions often need to retain data for long periods (or indefinitely) for effective machine learning. Similarly, blockchain provides certainty since information can never be deleted. Yet, when these solutions process *personal data*, both blockchain and data analytics providers find their technologies are in conflict with the GDPR's data minimization principles.

Furthermore, AI analytics tools often perform profiling and automated decision-making. Under the GDPR, when these practices are capable of producing a legal or similar effect on data subjects, clear consent is required. It must also be possible to review such decisions by human means.[5] The ability to obtain consent from data subjects pursuant to GDPR requirements can be difficult, and it can be hard for fully automated processes to integrate human intervention. Whilst the law should be applauded for protecting individual rights, especially given several high-profile privacy scandals, it is arguable that the GDPR's strict requirements already fall behind technological advances creating hurdles for innovators – an example of law not keeping up with AI.

Of course, innovation in any setting can never be an unencumbered process; throughout history there has always been, and will always be, protective rules in place to prohibit or limit the

---

[1] The General Data Protection Regulation (EU/2016/679).

[2] The General Data Protection Regulation (EU/2016/679) Article 4.

[3] The Charter of Fundamental Rights of the EU 2012/c 326/02: https://eur-lex.europa.eu/legal-content/EN/TXT/PDF/?uri=CELEX:12012P/TXT&from=EN.

[4] The General Data Protection Regulation (EU/2016/679) Article 17.

[5] The General Data Protection Regulation (EU/2016/679) Article 22.

degree of potential harm. Whilst legislation may seem prohibitive at times, it endeavours to safeguard our world. Perhaps the real issue is not so much that the law has fallen behind and is *no longer* fit for purpose, but that the law was *never adapted* to this purpose to begin with. The technological boom was impossible for legislators to predict and has forcefully presented a dilemma to be deciphered: do we care more about protecting our rights or promoting innovation? Those in the tech industry might search for opportunities to develop new ideas; however, public fear of data breaches show that we are also increasingly concerned about who is using our personal information, and why. It therefore falls to innovators not only to invent new processes, but also to dream up ways in which these processes can exist harmoniously in our regulated world.

TDM vs Copyright Laws

When TDM is used to analyse data sets for patterns and trends, the conclusions produced can often include not only facts but also the reproduction of copyrighted works contained within the mined data such as quotes of the work, for example. Copyright laws, on the other hand, confer a right on copyright holders enabling them to control how their work is reproduced, and to oppose unauthorized acts.[6]

It should be pointed out that TDM processes big data where the copyrighted expression of work is not perceived by a human, so it is arguable that copyright infringement by TDM is less damaging than by traditional means (i.e. unlawful file sharing). In reality, there is little value to be gained from TDM carried out on one single piece of work; the value comes from the insights that can be gained from thousands of extracts when mined as a whole.

Despite this, the legal view tends to be that *any* reproduction (including through TDM) of a protected work can trigger copyright infringement unless a valid limitation or exception applies, such as the right to undertake temporary acts of reproduction for network transmissions (i.e. to allow broadcasting) or for freedom of press or for political speeches, public lectures, criticisms and reviews (as, for example, set out in Article 5 of InfoSoc). In the absence of a TDM-specific limitation or exception, TDM carried out by innovators on big data containing protected works brings with it a high risk of mass-scale copyright infringement. The US attempts to combat this by relying on the fair use doctrine which, whilst providing more flexibility, is fraught with issues given that the criteria must be satisfied as a defence rather than a permission. Europe's DSM Directive[7] attempted to solve the issue by creating TDM-specific exceptions and limitations to copyright infringement.[8] Unfortunately, the provisions are heavily caveated and far too restrictive for the use and development of commercial TDM. Here, again, the law has not only failed to keep up with AI but was arguably not fit for purpose in the first place. The struggle shows how the law can be misaligned with the realities of technological advances and innovator requirements.

A Global Concern

The responsibility for ensuring that law keeps up with AI is a global one; however, the response has in general been national, or at best regional – as in the case of the EU. In Europe, for example, the focus seems to be on individual rights holders, creating an arguably tougher environment for innovators. In other jurisdictions, however, the focus on individual privacy rights is less of a primary concern.

---

[6] Directive 2001/29/EC of the European Parliament and of the Council of 22 May 2001 on the harmonization of certain aspects of copyright and related rights in the information society ("InfoSoc"), Articles 2, 3 and 4.

---

[7] Directive (EU) 2019/790 on copyright and related rights in the Digital Single Market.

[8] Articles 3 and 4 of Directive (EU) 2019/790 on copyright and related rights in the Digital Single Market.

Through its recent legislation, the EU has effectively enforced a static list of limitations and exceptions to the monopoly on the intellectual property right of copyright, which the courts have made a habit of reading narrowly and which the Advocate General has instructed should be interpreted restrictively.[9] This restricted approach also falls in line with settled Court of Justice of the European Union case law, in which the judges have systematically confirmed that exceptions and limitations to copyright should be interpreted narrowly.[10] Whilst a narrow application of copyright exceptions and limitations provides certainty for creators of original content, this is arguably hindering the EU's competitiveness in the global race to AI in comparison to other countries, where it is recognized that AI-powered solutions must include vigorous support for TDM. Such countries include the US and China, amongst others, where TDM is permitted and effectively encouraged through the more accommodating practices described below.

The results of this can be seen in practice. While there is less overall AI talent in the US than in the EU, studies show that the talent in the US is more elite.[11] For example, while the US produces less scholarly papers on AI than the EU, it produces papers of the highest standard on average.[12] This may be driven by the more flexible fair use doctrine allowing TDM users to develop their research more freely than they can in the EU, which in turn attracts talent to work in an environment which has a more favourable legal framework governing their core activities. Similarly, it is arguable that researchers in China have more access to data than those in the EU and its larger venture capital ecosystem suggests that the EU could stagnate while China innovates. By way of example, in China 53% of businesses adopted AI and 32% began piloting AI systems in 2018, whereas the EU saw only 26% of businesses piloting AI and only 18% actually adopting AI that same year.[13]

However, the success of a region's innovation appears not only to be based on a favourable legal environment which keeps up with the development of AI, but is also related to several factors present, such as government funding, private company incentives and the ability to attract a high-quality talent base. A territory's lack of growth in terms of tech, innovation and AI, therefore, cannot solely be attributed to regulatory measures. Nonetheless, it has been noted that in order to thrive in the field of innovation, the EU should create exceptions for digital-based business models to ensure that the law keeps up with the growth of AI, for example by adapting competition laws, pre-empting the requirement for adapted regulations in our digital economy and fostering political support[14] – and perhaps crucially – "leading a dialogue which explores adopting an innovation principle, rather than a precautionary principle, when dealing with AI and other new technologies".[15]

---

[9] For example, *Pelham GmbH, Moses Pelham, Martin Haas v Ralf Hütter, Florian Schneider-Esleben* C-476/17, Opinion of Advocate General Szpunar delivered on 12 December 2018.

[10] See Case C-476/01 *Kapper* [2004] ECR I-5205, para 72, and Case C-36/05 *Commission v Spain* [2006] ECR I-10313, para 31, and judgment in Case C-5/08 *Infopaq*, para. 56.

[11] Castro, D., McLaughlin, M. and Chivot, E., "Who is Winning the AI Race: China, the EU or the United States?", 2019. Available at: http://www2.datainnovation.org/2019-china-eu-us-ai.pdf (accessed 13 September 2019).

[12] Elsevier, "Artificial Intelligence: How Knowledge is Created, Transferred, and Used", 2018: https://www.elsevier.com/research-intelligence/resource-library/ai-report (accessed 19 September 2019).

[13] D. Castro, M, McLaughlin and E. Chivot, "Who is Winning the AI Race: China, the EU or the United States?", 2019. Available at: http://www2.datainnovation.org/2019-china-eu-us-ai.pdf (accessed 13 September 2019).

[14] Robert D. Atkinson and Stephen Ezell, "Promoting European Growth, Productivity, and Competitiveness by Taking Advantage of the Next Digital Technology Wave", ITIF, March 2019: http://www2.itif.org/2019-europe- digital-age.pdf in D. Castro, M. McLaughlin and E. Chivot, "Who is Winning the AI Race: China, the EU or the United States?", 2019. Available at: http://www2.datainnovation.org/2019-china-eu-us-ai.pdf (accessed 13 September 2019).

[15] Ibid.

It therefore goes without saying that the legal environment does nonetheless impact on a country's ability to innovate. For example, other dominant countries in this competitive market include Singapore, Canada and Australia, which are continuously focusing on improving their copyright laws to better accommodate TDM.[16] Interestingly, Canada is following the US' aforementioned approach of the fair use doctrine, and through its recent jurisprudence is dissociating itself with the more confined version of the fair use doctrine found in almost all (the exception being the US) common law countries.[17]

Indeed, Japan was the first jurisdiction to legislate for TDM,[18] creating an exception to copyright holders' exclusive rights for certain TDM operations. Effectively, Japan has ensured that copyright will no longer be an obstacle for the development of AI.[19] Feeling increasing pressure from the serious competition and ambitious goals of China, and with concerns from stakeholders that innovators could find themselves operating in a redundant framework, Japan ensured its legislative background is fully supporting its AI ambitions by updating its laws in January 2019. Japanese legislators have afforded TDM users a robust exception, extending the law specifically to permit analysis of copyrighted works for machine learning, amongst others, without risk of infringement.[20] This has led to Japan boasting a higher amount

of all-time leaders in AI patent fields when compared with the EU,[21] and demonstrates how law *can* keep up with AI, provided innovators and lawmakers collaborate.

Alternative Solutions: Innovation-Friendly Laws

Soft-law guidance

When hard black letter law fails to keep up with AI, it falls to practitioners and authorities to fill in the gaps with more flexible guidelines and laws. For example, in July 2019 the think tank of the European Union released a study into the conflict between the requirements of data deletion, data retention periods and data modification contained in the GDPR, suggesting that developments should be supported by case-by-case codes of conduct and research funding,[22] and acknowledging that the traditional legislative process cannot keep up, so soft-law options must pave the way. Perhaps, as is so often the case, the most effective way of responding to fast-paced developments in AI is through a combination of soft law (guidance, standards, codes of conduct) and hard law.

In some areas, guidance is forthcoming, such as the above-mentioned think-tank guidance which acknowledged that the GDPR purposefully renders the unilateral modification of data onerous in order to ensure data integrity and an increase in trust

---

[16] The Global AI Race. Available at: http://eare.eu/assets/uploads/2018/06/Global-AI-Race.pdf (accessed 13 September 2019).

[17] Ibid.

[18] Copyright Law of Japan 2009, Article 47, *Reproduction, etc. for information analysis.*

[19] Japan amends its copyright legislation to meet future demands in AI and Big Data, European Alliance for Research Excellence, 3 September 2018. Available at: http://eare.eu/japan-amends-tdm-exception-copyright/ (accessed 13 September 2019).

[20] Japan amends its copyright legislation to meet future demands in AI and Big Data, European Alliance for Research Excellence, 3 September 2018. Available at: http://eare.eu/japan-amends-tdm-exception-copyright/ (accessed 27 April 2019).

[21] D. Castro, M. McLaughlin and E. Chivot, "Who is Winning the AI Race: China, the EU or the United States?", 2019. Available at: http://www2.datainnovation.org/2019-china-eu-us-ai.pdf (accessed 13 September 2019).

[22] European Parliament, "Blockchain and the General Data Protection Regulation", July 2019. Available at: https://www.europarl.europa.eu/RegData/etudes/STUD/2019/634445/EPRS_STU(2019)634445_EN.pdf (accessed 12 August 2019).

in the systems.[23] The World Economic Forum has issued a wealth of guidance related to AI governance, such as a white paper discussing how to implement ethics into AI,[24] and the OECD has issued AI principles, one of which expressly states that "AI systems should be designed in a way that respects the rule of law, human rights, democratic values and diversity, and they should include appropriate safeguards – for example, enabling human intervention where necessary – to ensure a fair and just society".[25] As international organizations work together and recognize the importance of the law keeping up with AI, we are hopefully paving the way for workable solutions with further innovation with respect to the applicable legal frameworks.

Technological Solutions

The use of technological solutions themselves can also ensure that the law keeps up with AI. "Virtual machines" running in isolation can be used in AI to contain data breaches and ensure new technologies remain GDPR compliant. Furthermore, anonymizing personal data, as recommended by the Article 29 Working Party in 2017,[26] can overcome the application of stringent privacy laws, which are sometimes in conflict with machine learning and AI. However, research has found that AI machines are capable of eventually de-anonymizing anonymized information, meaning that even the most sophisticated techniques may fall foul of

the GDPR.[27] Furthermore, the implementation of such solutions can be prohibitively expensive or onerous, meaning that they are not workable for startups or independent developers.

Given the complex social and policy objectives legislators need to balance, as well as ensuring that law, binding on companies and individuals, is created pursuant to fair and democratic processes, it is in actuality unreasonable to expect hard law to keep up with AI as they develop at contrasting paces. Whilst sometimes behind AI, laws are created to protect society's wider interests. This may have the knock-on effect of increasing the regulatory burden for some, but it does also provide the stimulus for growth, gained from the development of a cohesive and clear regulatory framework – albeit slowly.

In the meantime, the lawyer plays a crucial role. Lawyers can both ensure that their clients' AI technologies fall within the relevant frameworks and feed into the policymaking process the insights they have gained from working with their clients. This is more likely to lead to an informed framework with a better chance of balancing the competing needs of innovation and protection of rights. Developers should protect their interests by applying a "law-by-design" approach to ensure that their innovations are responsible and sustainable and engage with lawmakers at the beginning rather than the end of the innovation cycle. Equally, it is incumbent on the lawmakers to engage with stakeholders, listening to their concerns and reviewing legislation accordingly when it is in danger of becoming redundant.

The responsibility of ensuring that the law keeps up with the growth of AI therefore falls on all actors – lawmakers, lawyers, and developers themselves – to ensure that their growth, development and use of AI remains innovative while responsible.

---

[23] Study: Blockchain and the General Data Protection Regulation, Can Distributed Ledgers be Squared with European Data Protection Law? European Parliament Think Tank, Panel for the Future of Science and Technology, EPRS, European Parliamentary Research Service, Scientific Foresight Unit (STOA), PE 634.445 – July 2019.

[24] AI Governance: A Holistic Approach to Implement Ethics into AI, World Economic Forum, Report, 3 May 2019.

[25] Artificial Intelligence – OECD Principles on AI. Available at: https://www.oecd.org/going-digital/ai/principles/ (accessed 13 September 2019).

[26] Article 29 Data Protection Working Party, "Opinion 05/2014 on Anonymisation Techniques", 10 April 2014. Available at: https://www.pdpjournals.com/docs/88197.pdf (accessed 12 August 2019).

---

[27] L. Rocher, J. Hendrickx and Y. Montjoye, "Estimating the success of re-identifications in incomplete data sets using generative models", 2019, 10(3069), Nature Communications.

Fairness, Accountability and Transparency – Trust in AI and Machine Learning

Cemile Cakir
Teaching Fellow, The University of Law

A fair, transparent and ethical legal system is a fundamental organ in a well-functioning, democratic society. Maintaining the fine balance between the rights of the individual and the interests of the state has long been the pursuit of the English legal system, cultivating deep-rooted guiding principles and conventions. The rule of law and the Human Rights Act are the core of legal practice, setting the parameters to keep the powers of the ultimate authority in check and balance.

Within the midst of the evolution of legal practice, a new force has evolved: artificial intelligence (AI) and machine learning, enabling the fusion of technology with law. These advancements present new opportunities for efficiency and effectiveness, realizing benefits to public services, businesses and clients.[1] Machine learning, commonly referred to as AI, has enabled progress from mere automation to decision-making capabilities by employing sophisticated algorithms to identify information relevant for the future. Despite a lack of mainstream understanding in the working of these technologies, they are routinely entrusted to make choices in people's lives. As they become more prominent in significant legal and public affairs, however, caution is urged against complacency. The mechanics behind how technology generates information and how it is used has the potential for much good or great harm.[2]

These innovative technologies are currently created within a free state in the absence of regulation, ethical codes and guidance. Housed within the domains of computer science, engineering and technology, these processes often bypass the interrogation expected of legal processes. In the guise of statistical and technological objectivity, the outcomes from these machines are not subjected to the scrutiny expected of the legal domain, giving coders a licence and discretion to play architect to the morality of the bot. As law keepers grapple with their proficiency to challenge the authority of a machine, both in their omission to substantiate its findings and in their execution based on the results of the algorithms, there is the peril of injustice. Potential threats demand proactive lawyering and ingenuity to preserve and negotiate terrain. Increasingly, there are calls for this domain to be better understood and safeguards put in place.[3]

Privacy – A Trade-off for Access

Big data fuels the development and innovation of these technologies, which are gathered via technology surveillance practices. Whilst GDPR has made strides in protecting individuals from unscrupulous data harvesters, technology surveillance practices continue and concerns surrounding their legitimacy remain. "Privacy fatigue"[4] has meant that people are unwilling to read the lengthy and complex privacy notices used to impart key information when obtaining consent for the processing of their personal data and has rendered the tick box "I have read and agree to the terms and conditions" "the biggest lie on the web".[5]

---

[1] The Law Society, "Lawtech Adoption Research", 2019: https://www.lawsociety.org.uk/support-services/research-trends/lawtech-adoption-report/.

[2] EPIC, "Algorithms in the Criminal Justice System", 2017, 1 Electronic Privacy Information Center: https://epic.org/algorithmic-transparency/crim-justice/.

[3] Ibid.

[4] Seizing Opportunities and Preserving Values, "Big Data: Seizing Opportunities, Preserving Values", in *Big Data: An Exploration of Opportunities, Values, and Privacy Issues*, by C. Agnellutti, 2014, 1.

[5] Information Commissioner's Office, "Big Data, Artificial Intelligence, Machine Learning and Data Protection", 2017, Data Protection Act and General Data Protection Regulation, 144: https://ico.org.uk/media/for-organisations/documents/2013559/big-data-ai-ml-and-data-protection.pdf.

Time constraints, practicality and difficulty in explaining the data analytics often means it is not apparent to people when their data is being collected and/or how it is being processed. Consequently, the concept of "meaningful consent" becomes redundant and a trade-off between privacy and access.

Surveillance Capitalism and Threats to Democracy

Whilst data collection is necessary for supporting technology, much of the data is repurposed. Data is of great value to advertisers who target individuals to grow their business. However, it has also been used to manipulate user behaviours via social media, search engines and other internet services.[6] This is of great concern when the public's faith in the technology's neutrality exposes them to manipulation and has the capability to threaten democracy, such as the Cambridge Analytica scandal.[7]

State Surveillance and Enforcement

The Snowden revelations have caused "widespread wariness" about being spied on by governments and organizations.[8] As the benefits of technology are explored, such as the use of social media to detect crime,[9] recent cases against the UK concerning the bulk interceptions of communications, and the obtaining of communications data from communications service providers, found breaches of the European Convention of Human Rights.[10]

"Mobile device extraction" or "digital stop and search", facial recognition technologies and other law enforcement practices in policing raise concerns over unjustified infringements to individuals' rights.[11] Extraction of such sensitive personal data from citizens who may not have been charged with an offence or be aware that personal information has been taken is an invasion of fundamental rights.

Bias/Unfairness

Neither mathematical basis nor technology absolves the outputs of AI from bias. Data quality determines the quality of results: "garbage in, garbage out". Insufficient data sets that generate inconclusive or discriminatory results, which are assumed to be credible, can lead to unjustifiable actions.[12]

Further, the design and functionality of the algorithm will reflect the values and choices of its author.[13] Given the intrusive effect of profiling upon individuals, these decisions ought not to be

---

[6] Wu Youyou, Michal Kosinski and David Stillwell, "Computer-Based Personality Judgments Are More Accurate than Those Made by Humans", 2015, 112 *Proceedings of the National Academy of Sciences of the United States of America*, 1036.

[7] Hannah Jane Parkinson and Hilary Osborne "Cambridge Analytica Scandal: The Biggest Revelations So Far", *The Guardian*, 2018: https://www.theguardian.com/uk-news/2018/mar/22/cambridge-analytica-scandal-the-biggest-revelations-so-far (accessed 19 August 2019).

[8] Information Commissioner's Office (n. 5).

[9] Matthew L. Williams, Pete Burnap and Luke Sloan, "Crime Sensing with Big Data: The Affordances and Limitations of Using Open-Source Communications to Estimate Crime Patterns", 2017, 57 *British Journal of Criminology*, 320.

[10] The Court, "Some Aspects of UK Surveillance Regimes Violate Convention, Complaints, Procedure and Composition of the Court, Decision of the Court, Admissibility, 2018, 299, 1.

[11] EPIC (n. 2).

[12] Brent Daniel Mittelstadt and others, "The Ethics of Algorithms: Mapping the Debate", 2016, 3 *Big Data & Society*, 205395171667967.

[13] Felicitas Kraemer, Kees van Overveld and Martin Peterson, "Is There an Ethics of Algorithms?", 2011, 13 *Ethics and Information Technology*, 251.

determined unilaterally, without debate or in silo. When checking for algorithmic bias, prominent factors, such as gender and race, may be more visible.[14] Latent biases, however, are not so detectable and of concern. Even if mathematical probabilities reflect real-world bias, institutions' reliance on AI may perpetuate them in code. Whilst precedent and consistency are fundamental, so too is the common law's ability to respond to the complexity of individual cases to ensure fair outcomes.

Transparency

Machine learning generates outputs from the algorithm's observations of patterns or ability to draw inferences from feedback to achieve a result. In this way, machines can generate new solutions[15] beyond the human observer and can be a mystery to the most advanced of computer specialists. The lack of transparency makes them difficult to check, correct or control.[16]

Decisions based on opaque and inscrutable algorithms[17] do not align with the adversarial framework, due process and legal reasoning,[18] particularly if the decision-maker feels restricted in their autonomy when reaching a decision.[19] Yet algorithms are used to support predictive hotspot policing, whether offenders are released via an "out of court disposal", and to assess the prospects of reoffending.[20] Such profiling and predictive analytics can reinforce discrimination and be difficult to challenge.

Accountability

GDPR has done much to promote accountability. The "right to an explanation" does not, however, resolve the opacity of a "black box". The safeguards affording the right to human intervention and meaningful information also have limitations[21] as these rights are only applicable to "solely" automated processes and decisions with "significant" effects. Given that the discriminatory effects of algorithms are not known until after the individuals have suffered the effects, retrospective resolutions are insufficient, advocating the need for the development of robust, accurate technologies that factor ethics[22] and human impact by design.[23]

What Next?

There is a responsibility within the legal profession to consider how the law will accommodate these new developments and how it can maintain authority over a black box. Foresight of the challenges ahead relating to trust, accountability and transparency is a lawyer's call to action, to employ their talents to ensure the advancement of legal practice whilst preserving faith in the legal system.

---

[14] Latanya Sweeney, "Discrimination in Online Ad Delivery" – 1071-1.Pdf: http://dataprivacylab.org/projects/onlineads/1071-1.pdf.

[15] Nikolaos Aletras and others, "Predicting Judicial Decisions of the European Court of Human Rights: A Natural Language Processing Perspective", 2016, *PeerJ*, 1.

[16] Mittelstadt and others (n. 12).

[17] Jenna Burrell, "How the Machine 'Thinks': Understanding Opacity in Machine Learning Algorithms", 2016, 3 *Big Data & Society*, 205395171562251.

[18] Reuben Binns and others, "'It's Reducing a Human Being to a Percentage'; Perceptions of Justice in Algorithmic Decisions", 2018, April Conference on Human Factors in Computing Systems – Proceedings.

[19] Aletras and others (n. 15).

---

[20] Alexander Babuta, "Innocent Until Predicted Guilty? Artificial Intelligence and Police Decision-Making", 2018, RUSI Newsbrief 38, 2: https://rusi.org/sites/default/files/20180329_rusi_newsbrief_vol.38_no.2_babuta_web.pdf.

[21] Lilian Edwards and Michael Veale, "Enslaving the Algorithm: From a 'Right to an Explanation' to a 'Right to Better Decisions'?", 2018, 16 *IEEE Security and Privacy*, 46.

[22] Kraemer, van Overveld and Peterson (n. 13).

[23] Edwards and Veale (n. 21).

The Chiron Imperative – A Framework of Six Human-in-the-Loop Paradigms to Create Wise and Just AI-Human Centaurs

Brian Tang
Founder, ACMI and LITE Lab@HKU

Artificial intelligence (AI) and machine learning (ML) can tremendously assist humans with perception, analysis, prediction and decision-making. The concept of autonomous machines has a long tradition in science fiction. Today, lethal autonomous weapons are rightfully a cause for concern, with numerous calls for bans worldwide.[1] At the same time, companies like Honda, Lyft, Uber, Google, Nuro and Waymo are at or approaching Level 4 of US National Highway Traffic Safety Administration's six levels of car autonomy,[2] with some casualties on the road to progress.[3] Today, the main public triumph of autonomous machines is with games of defined rules and rewards (such as chess, Atari, Go and poker), with mahjong being the latest frontier.[4]

And so, while there is no "robot lawyer" yet, concerns along the lines of Nick Bostrom's Paperclip Maximizer thought experiment and human existential risk[5] remain.

---

[1] See, e.g., "Autonomous Weapons that Kill Must Be Banned, Urges UN Chief", *United Nations News*, March 2019.

[2] US National Highway Traffic Safety Administration, "Automated Vehicles for Safety".

[3] See, e.g., "The Stark Traffic Safety Divide", CityLab, March 2019.

[4] See Microsoft, "More Than a Game: Mastering Mahjong with AI and Machine Learning", August 2019.

[5] See, e.g., the work of the Future of Life Institute and Oxford University's Future of Humanity Centre for Governance of AI.

Human-in-the-loop (HITL) is an increasingly common AI and ML refrain.[6] After chessmaster Garry Kasparov lost to IBM's Deep Blue in the first major Human vs Machine Battle, he coined the phrase Centaur Chess when he demonstrated how both working together are better than either alone.[7]

LawTech (defined broadly) relates to technology that assists law service providers, citizens, regulators and governments. This chapter briefly outlines a framework of the six HITL paradigms that AI policymakers, LawTech AI solution providers and users should address to design human-centred AI to better embody Chiron, whom Homer called that "wisest and justest of all centaurs".[8]

Human as AI Trainer

ML relies on good data sets. Bias data sets have already proven problematic.[9]

A good data set is critical especially for supervised or semi-supervised ML in computer vision, natural language processing, text, audio and speech and has resulted in a new industry of data trainers and labellers who engage in data annotation, enrichment and integration.

---

[6] E.g., Workshop on Human Interpretability is now known as Workshop on Human In the Loop Learning (HILL); IBM's Almaden Lab has recently proposed an HITL interactive dictionary expansion using neural language models (HumL): see "Interactive Dictionary Expansion using Neural Language Model", IBM Research Almaden; "HumL: Better Text Intelligence with Humans in the Loop", Towards Data Science, September 2018.

[7] See, e.g., "How to Become a Centaur", *Journal of Design and Science*, January 2018.

[8] Homer, Illiad, xi, 831. In Greek mythology, Chiron, Chieron or Kheiron was centaur teacher of classical heroes such as Herakles (Hercules), Achilles, healer Asclepius and Argonaut Jason.

[9] See, e.g., "When it Comes to Gorillas, Google Photos Remains Blind", *Wired*, January 2018.

Many companies engaged in active learning[10] and transfer learning[11] use crowd mini-tasking services such as Amazon's Mechanical Turk,[12] while their equivalents in China rely on data farms or factories.[13]

Some tasks require experts (such as for medical imaging, legal and music[14] categorization), and firms like Figure Eight even market under www.humansintheloop.org and create specialized data sets for training data as a service.[15] This is a core HITL paradigm, which makes reports of Mechanical Turks using bots particularly disconcerting.[16] The use of automated labelling software[17] and synthetic data[18] also requires greater scrutiny.

Human as AI User-Trainer

As we use AI-powered recommenders as customers, we are in fact training them, often unconsciously revealing our psychological identity through our questions and searches.

Many chatbots have been deployed to interact with and learn from the world. Famously, Microsoft's Tay "learned" within a day on Twitter to be racist due to mischievous intent,[19] while Facebook and YouTube attribute offensive autocomplete suggestions to popular usage by users.[20] In China, Microsoft's XiaoIce is incredibly popular with reportedly 660 million registered users.[21]

With the global proliferation of data protection and privacy laws and concerns about online freedom of expression, the debate over digital rights and their enforcement (as counterparts to the responsibilities and obligations of technologists gathering, using and otherwise monetarizing such data) is expected to rise.

Human as AI Quality Control and Governance

The growth of AI and ML development in private corporations has led to the introduction of independent review boards for AI governance at companies such as Axon and SAP to review whether and to what extent AI should be used.[22] Axon's decision

[10] See "A Window into How YouTube Trains AI to Moderate Videos", *Wired*, March 2018; note complaints of inconsistency: "YouTube Does not Know Where its Own Line is", Wired, March 2018.

[11] See, e.g., Robert Munro, "Human-In-The-Loop Machine Learning", Manning, forthcoming.

[12] Some already argue for more equitable approaches to compensate the humans who contribute to AI: see, e.g., Fabio Massimo Zanzotto, "Human In The Loop Artificial Intelligence", October 2017.

[13] See, e.g., "Data Labelling: The Human Power Behind Artificial Intelligence", XinhuaNet, January 2019; "'AI Farms' are at the Forefront of China's Global Ambitions", *Time*, February 2019; "Tiling the Data Farms of Guizhou", Sixth Tone, May 2018.

[14] See "The Feedback Loop: AI, Machine Learning and the Human in the Middle", Venture Beat on YouTube, July 2017.

[15] See, e.g., "Humans in the Loop: Machine Learning and AI for the People", ZDNet, May 2018. Figure Eight has partnered with Google Cloud and AWS. See also https://youtu.be/EM6LZ0xD2qc.

[16] See "A Bot Panic Hits Amazon's Mechanical Turk", *Wired*, August 2018; "People Fear Mechanical Turk has a Bot Problem, Which is Bad for AI", Architecht, August 2018.

[17] See, e.g., "A Pickax for the AI Gold Rush: LabelBox Sells Training Data Software", TechCrunch, July 2018.

[18] See, e.g., "Some Startups use Fake Data to Train AI", *Wired*, April 2018.

[19] See, e.g., "Tay, Microsoft's AI Chatbot, Gets a Crash Course in Racism from Twitter", *The Guardian*, March 2016.

[20] See "Facebook and YouTube Should Have Learned from Microsoft's Racist Chatbot", CNBC, March 2018.

[21] See "This Chatbot has Over 660 Million Users – and Wants to be Their Best Friend", Singularity Hub, July 2019.

[22] See Brian Tang, "Independent AI Ethics Committees and ESG Corporate Reporting on AI as Emerging Corporate and AI Governance Trends", *The AI Book*, Wiley, 2020. Note that establishing such boards can be challenging, as seen by Google's experience: "Google Dissolves AI Ethics Board Just One Week after Forming it", *The Verge*, April 2019.

to decline introducing facial recognition in their police bodycams shows such boards can have impact.[23]

Similarly, in the complex area of content moderation, the limitations of relying solely on humans[24] or AI has been recognized,[25] with multistakeholder gatekeepers like Facebook's Oversight Board being proposed.[26]

Human as AI Explainer or Interpreter

To promote transparency and trust, cutting-edge AI projects promote explainable[27] and interpretable[28] AI as well as techniques like counterfactuals[29] for black boxes.

In the meantime, the General Data Protection Regulation is often argued to bestow a "right to explanation" to citizens for automated decision-making, including profiling.[30]

While it is debated whether this means meaningful information about the model for interpretability[31] and/or algorithmic explainability, it is a human that must ultimately do so and be responsible, whether to a consumer, regulator or a court of law.[32]

Human as AI Creator

In all cases (currently), human programmers, mathematicians and entrepreneurs remain the creators of the AI code and algorithmic and business models. AI ethics initiatives worldwide led by multistakeholder initiatives[33] and many national data privacy commissioners[34] focus on values and responsibilities of such creators.[35]

---

[23] See, e.g., "Taser Maker Won't Use Facial Recognition in Bodycams", *Wired*, June 2019.

[24] See, e.g., "Why Thousands of Human Moderators Won't Fix Toxic Content on Social Media", *Fortune*, March 2018.

[25] See "AI Won't Relieve the Misery of Facebook's Human Moderators", *The Verge*, February 2019; "Human Help Wanted: Why AI Is Terrible at Content Moderation", PC Reviews, July 2019.

[26] See "Global Feedback and Input on the Facebook Oversight Board for Content Decisions", Facebook, June 2019.

[27] See, e.g., "Inside DARPA's Effort to Create Explainable Artificial Intelligence", TechTalks, January 2019.

[28] E.g., "Creating AI Glass Boxes – Open Sourcing a Library to Enable Intelligible Machine Learning", Microsoft, May 2019, introducing IntepretML.

[29] See Sandra Wachter, Brent Mittlestadt and Chris Russell, "Counterfactual Explanations Without Opening the Black Box: Automated Decisions and the GDPR", *Harvard Journal of Law & Technology*, Spring 2018.

[30] See, e.g., "GDPR and AI: Friends, Foes or Something in Between?", SAS Europe; "Towards Accountable AI in Europe", Alan Turing Institute, July 2017.

[31] See "Machine Learning Explanability vs. Interpretability: Two Concepts that Could Help Restore Trust in AI", KDnuggets, December 2018; "Interpreting Machine Learning Models", Towards Data Science, February 2018.

[32] See, e.g., Brian Tang, "Forging a Responsibility and Liability Framework in the AI Era for Regtech", in The RegTech Book, J. Barberis, D.W. Arner and R.P. Buckley (eds), Wiley, 2019.

[33] See, e.g., Partnership on AI, European Commission High-Level Expert Group on Artificial Intelligence, "Ethics Guidelines for Trustworthy Artificial Intelligence", April 2019.

[34] See, e.g., "Declaration on Ethics and Data Protection in Artificial Intelligence", 40th International Conference of Data Protection & Privacy Commissioners, October 2018; "A Proposed Model: Artificial Intelligence Governance Framework", Singapore Personal Data Protection Commission, January 2019.

[35] See, e.g., IEEE Global Initiative on Ethics of Autonomous and Intelligent Systems; Asilomar AI Principles.

This approach is especially important as more unsupervised ML models emerge,[36] such as the powerful generative adversarial networks (GANs) and generative models promoted by OpenAI[37] used to "extend creativity":[38] these same models are used to create deepfakes[39] and synthetic media.[40]

Human as Customer-User of AI Products and Services

With AI's pervasive power in perception and data gathering, a menacing narrative has emerged – for whom is the data gathered and for what purpose? And is the data collected fit for purpose regarding how they are used? Already, bans on the use of facial recognition have been introduced[41] due to concerns relating to inaccuracy and personal privacy intrusion,[42] and the European Union is also reportedly considering "sweeping regulation".[43]

At the same time, there are grave concerns about the malicious misuse of GANs to create deepfakes that could have a devastating impact on our democratic processes and national and global security.[44] To that end, OpenAI recently thought that its new unsupervised text writer GPT2 was "too dangerous to release"[45] and conducted a staged release and partnership sharing model.[46]

---

[36] See "Unsupervised Learning: The Curious Pupil", DeepMind, June 2019.

[37] See "Generative Models", Open AI, June 2016.

[38] See "Generative Deep Learning: Let's Seek How AI Extending, not Replacing Creative Process" Towards Data Science, September 2018.

[39] See "GANs and Deepfakes Could Revolutionize the Fashion Industry", Forbes, May 2019; "Generative Adversarial Networks: The Tech Behind DeepFake and FaceApp", Interesting Engineering, August 2019; "New AI Generates Freakishly Realistic People Who Don't Actually Exist", Science Alert, February 2019.

[40] Separately, Facebook's chatbot created a new language from talking to another chatbot: see "AI is Investing Languages Humans Can't Understand. Should We Stop It?", Fast Company, July 2017; "Facebook's Artificial Intelligence Robots Shut Down after They Start Talking to Each Other in Own Language", Independent, July 2017.

[41] See "Facial Recognition Ban: Coming to a City Near You", Daily Beast, July 2019); https://www.vice.com/en_us/article/bj93z5/ai-has-made-video-surveillance-automated-and-terrifying.

---

[42] See American Civil Liberties Union, "The Dawn of Robot Surveillance: AI, Video Analytics and Privacy", June 2019; "The Strange Politics of Facial Recognition", Wired, June 2019.

[43] See "EU Plans Sweeping Regulation of Facial Recognition", Financial Times, August 2019. The current trade war complicates matters, with the US considering banning Chinese company Hikvision: "US Takes Aim at Chinese Surveillance as the Trade War Becomes a Tech War", CNBC, May 2019. See also "Facebook Exposed for Listening to Users Alongside its Big Tech Peers", Morning Brew, August 2019.

[44] See Robert Chesney and Danielle Keats Citron, "Deep Fakes: A Looming Challenge for Privacy, Democracy and National Security", 107 California Law Review, 2019, who also introduce the concept of the liar's dividend; "The Malicious Use of Artificial Intelligence: Forecasting, Prevention and Mitigation", February 2018.

[45] See "New AI Fake Text Generator May Be too Dangerous to Release, say Creators", The Guardian, February 2019.

[46] See "GPT-2: 6 Month Follow-up", OpenAI, August 2019. It is interesting to note that in DeepMind's "Unsupervised Learning: The Curious Pupil", June 2019, while it did not specifically mention the importance of AI ethics and governance, it did express such concerns, with suggestions such as using statistical techniques to help detect synthetic media and verify authentic media; raising public awareness; using generative models themselves to detect synthetic media and anomalous data (see "GROVER: A GAN that Fights Neural Fake News, as Long as it Creates Said News", Packt, June 2019; and limiting the availability of trained generative models (which is what OpenAI did). This approach has analogies with the Treaty on Non-Proliferation of Nuclear Weapons (1968), but with complications that in AI, non-state and commercial actors are at the forefront of AI and ML technology.

Embodying Chiron as the Ideal AI Centaur

The concept of AI-human centaurs creates a hopeful vision that traces back to JCR Lickliter's Man-Computer Symbiosis in 1960[47] and is part of a trend known as intelligence augmentation:[48] humans augmented through the increased analytical, perception and predictive tools that AI and ML bestow.

Humans are flawed and we have our own bias. Yet, we have unique rational and moral insights that currently cannot be replaced by machines alone.[49] AI can help humans make better decisions, and can help us better understand ourselves. But as the stakes increase beyond shopping recommendations when used by professionals like lawyers, doctors, bankers and insurance agents, HITL remains critical for licensing, liability and responsibility considerations. While our generation is still willing to disagree with such machine-generated recommendations, will the digital native generation of lawyers and doctors raised on Google search engines be?[50] What sets of decision-making are appropriate to wholly delegate to machines through automation? And how will insurers deal with all of this?

In the backdrop of nations creating AI strategies[51] and a seeming race to establish AI standards,[52] we are already witnessing centaurs (users and misusers; private and public) battling in areas like cybersecurity, personal privacy, deep fakes and national security. Even worse, deep fakes could threaten our core worldviews regarding reality and trust in "seeing is believing",[53] and introduce a darker world of scepticism and mistrust. Addressing each of the six HITL paradigms is imperative to enable us to better attain a Chiron-like centaur relationship with AI. Together, we can better strive for Chiron's wisdom and justice.

---

[47] See J.C.R. Licklider, "Man-Computer Symbiosis", Ire Transactions on Human Factors in Electronics, 1960.

[48] IBM uses the marketing phrase augmented intelligence for AI.

[49] For example, humans have counterfactual reasoning, can imagine parallel universe and can conduct generalizations of untried policies.

[50] See, e.g., Academy of Medical Royal Colleges, Artificial Intelligence in Healthcare, January 2019; "Who's to Blame When a Machine Botches Your Surgery?", Quartz, September 2018.

[51] See, e.g., Centre for Data Innovation, "Who is Winning the AI Race: China, the EU or the United States?", August 2019; Kai-Fu Lee, *AI Superpowers: China, Silicon Valley and the New World Order*, Houghton Mifflin Harcourt, 2018.

[52] See, e.g., US National Institute of Standards and Technology, "US Leadership in AI: A Plan for Federal Engagement in Developing Technical Standards and Related Tools", August 2019; China Electronic Standardization Institute, Artificial Intelligence Standardization White paper (January 2018 – unofficial translation); ISO/IEC JTC 1/SC 42 Artificial Intelligence; "Standards for AI Governance: International Standards to Enable Global Coordination in AI Research and Development", Centre for the Governance of AI, Future of Humanity, Oxford University, April 2019.

[53] See, e.g., "Why You can't Remove Humans from AI Training Loops", Mighty AI, May 2017; "Q&A: Philip Isola on the Art and Science of Generative Models", MIT News, May 2019; "From Faces to Kitties to Apartments: GAN Fakes the World", Synced, February 2019; "You Thought Fake News was Bad? Deep Fakes are Where Truth Goes to Die", *The Guardian*, November 2018.

Lawyers' Ethical Responsibility to Leverage AI in the Practice of Law

Laura van Wyngaarden
COO, Diligen

Lawyers are well versed in the ethical responsibilities of their profession, but what does ethical responsibility look like when it comes to new technologies, such as machine learning and artificial intelligence (AI)?

Consider some of the technologies that preceded these newcomers – email, cloud computing, electronic case organization and eDiscovery. At one time each of these seemed like risky new tools, yet now they are part of the responsible practice of law. But what about AI?

AI-powered LegalTech has the power to help lawyers do faster, more thorough and more cost-effective legal work. If we can do this work better and more efficiently for our clients – do we have a responsibility to do so? While leveraging AI may not be considered an ethical obligation at the moment, I suspect this is a conversation we will be having many more times in the years ahead.

Lawyers are well aware of their ethical responsibilities. Those responsibilities permeate relationships with clients and extend to every aspect of lawyers' professional lives – including the technology they use.

AI's Black Box

For AI's use in the legal profession, one of the most notable issues is dealing with the so-called "black box". A lawyer submits a query to an AI-powered tool, it goes into a black box, and the AI-based solution provides an answer. How much does a lawyer need to know about what goes on inside that black box? This black box can pose a significant obstacle. Even though a computer is processing the information, and the computer is making a recommendation, it does not have the final say. That responsibility falls on a human decision-maker, and this person is held responsible for any negative consequences.

Lawyers are not necessarily computer scientists or technologists, and nobody would expect them to be experts in the algorithm-level workings of AI systems. But at the same time, one could argue that they must have some basic understanding of how the tools they utilize work.

Despite all of the hype, AI is not currently intended to replace human decision-making but rather help humans make better decisions. And it can do so powerfully. But if people do not trust the decision-making capabilities of AI systems, these technologies will fall short of widespread adoption. To a large extent, that trust will be earned through consistent high performance over time (getting the answer right) by AI systems. Transparency into the inner workings of these systems on the part of their creators as well as educated and informed use on the part of those that leverage them will also be important.

Duties of Competence … and Supervision

It's been seven years since the American Bar Association (ABA) updated Model Rule 1.1[1] (competent representation) to state that lawyers have an ethical responsibility to "keep abreast of changes in the law and its practice, including the benefits and risks associated with relevant technology". This signified a sea change in the legal

---

[1] ABA Model Rules of Professional Conduct Rule 1.1: Competence, Client-Lawyer Relationship: https://www.americanbar.org/groups/professional_responsibility/publications/model_rules_of_professional_conduct/rule_1_1_competence/.

professions. As of August 2019, 36 states have updated their rules to follow suit and the Canadian bar is debating revising its Code of Professional Conduct to include technical competency.

AI is most definitely "relevant technology". Indeed, as Erik Brynjolfsson and Andrew McAfee wrote in a cover story for the *Harvard Business Review*,[2] AI is "the most important general-purpose technology of our era".

Competence is a key principle for the trustworthy adoption of AI in the law. However, this does not require attorneys to be AI technology experts. It's as much about personal education as it is knowing one's limits, educating internal and external stakeholders about the possibilities and limitations of AI, as well as demanding more transparency and guidance from AI software developers.

Depending on who (or what) a lawyer works with, the duty of competence also includes a duty of supervision. If a lawyer delegates something, there's an ethical duty to make sure the work has been done competently. And this duty, arguably, extends to AI-based tools – meaning that the lawyer who reviews and signs off on AI-assisted work has appropriately "supervised" the AI.

Equally, just as there are certain tasks lawyers cannot delegate, there are some processes that cannot yet be appropriately handled by AI – and legal professionals must know how to tell them apart.

Global AI Ethics

AI ethics and best practices are serious business globally across a variety of vertical markets, including the legal profession. To what extent are AI ethics discussions and guidelines consistent across geographies? Where do they vary? Leading law firms are helping provide clarity around ethics-related AI policies and guidelines. Following the release of the "Artificial Intelligence: Governance and Leadership" white paper by the Australian Human Rights Commission in January 2019, a discussion paper to boost conversation about AI ethics in Australia emerged. Core principles of the AI ethics discussion paper, which draws upon international approaches, as well as those developed by companies such as Google and Microsoft, focus on "fairness", "accountability", "regulatory and legal compliance", "privacy protection" and "transparency", among others. The EU, having established a High-Level Expert Group comprised of 52 AI experts, recently published its Ethics Guidelines for Trustworthy AI. Like Australia's Discussion Paper, the EU Guidelines highlight the importance of non-discrimination, promoting societal and environmental well-being, privacy, accountability and transparency. Although the EU guidelines are not binding, they are informed by the EU Charter of Fundamental Rights.

Governments globally are equally working hand in hand with the technology sector on the complexities of AI ethics issues. Stateside, AI policy-focused initiatives such as the San Francisco-based "Partnership on AI" includes the tech sector's "big four". Facebook in collaboration with the Technical University of Munich recently announced funding for an independent AI ethics research centre, while Amazon is working with the National Science Foundation to fund research into AI ethics and fairness. The list of "ethics in AI" initiatives across the globe goes on.[3] In May 2019, the World Economic Forum announced the formation of six separate fourth industrial revolution councils, designed to develop new technology policy guidance, best policy practices, strategic guidelines and to help regulate technology under six domains, including AI. Similarly, the Organization for Economic Co-operation and Development (OECD) created a global reference point for

---

[2] The Business of Artificial Intelligence: What it Can – and Cannot – Do for Your Organization: https://hbr.org/cover-story/2017/07/the-business-of-artificial-intelligence. By Erik Byrnjolfson and Andrew Mcafee, *Harvard Business Review*, 2017, July issue.

[3] Global Initiatives to Support AI Governance and Ethics: https://blog.ecosystm360.com/global-initiatives-ai-governance-ethics/. Ecosystem blog, 19 June 19 2019.

AI adoption "value-based" principles and recommendations for governments of countries across the world.

Likewise, the Personal Data Protection Commission in Singapore presented the first edition of a Proposed Model AI Governance Framework to facilitate the discussions around harnessing AI in a responsible way.

AI and Ethics: Hand in Hand

The ABA addresses lawyers' "duties of competence" and their ethical responsibility to "keep abreast of changes in the law and its practice, including the benefits and risks associated with relevant technology". This loosely includes new technology like AI and machine learning but still leaves room for interpretation and practical application. With that being said, legal professionals cannot afford to avoid the "AI and ethics" conversation as AI acceptance and adoption increases. While requiring a PhD in AI is exaggerated, today's law firms need to understand how AI can help them and their clients as well as comprehending ethical, technical and practical limitations that come along with "doing AI". Today's legal AI ecosystem is thriving and the future looks even brighter. Increasingly, legal professionals will be key stakeholders in the ongoing AI and ethics debate, whether that be broadly or within the domain of their own professional responsibilities.

Dispute Resolution 2.0: The Era of BIG Data, AI and Analytics

Paula Hodges QC
Partner, Head of Global Arbitration Practice, Herbert Smith Freehills LLP

and Charlie Morgan
Digital Law Lead (UK), Senior Associate (International Arbitration), Herbert Smith Freehills LLP

The digitization of products and services is nothing new. However, the speed of that process has increased exponentially in the last 10 years. This acceleration has in large part been driven by the development and widespread reach of smartphones since Apple launched the iPhone in 2007. However, many technologists still consider that society's journey towards the digitization of assets and communications is still in its infancy.

The increasing adoption of technologies such as machine learning, natural language processing, augmented analytics, distributed ledger technology (aka blockchain) and, looking further ahead, quantum computing stands to convert an ever-greater number of physical goods and services into bits (i.e. 1s and 0s).

Building on this digital revolution, business practices in every industry are changing quicker than ever. Companies are increasingly monetizing raw and analysed data, as well as leveraging data to improve customer experiences, reach new markets, make employees and processes more productive, and create new sources of competitive advantage. In the era of Big Data, the ways that disputes arise and need to be resolved are also changing at unprecedented speeds.

Digitizing the Dispute Resolution Process

"Basic" forms of technology such as electronic communication, e-filing and online document review are pervasive in large commercial arbitrations and litigation today. However, the focus on and investment in disruptive technologies within the legal sector remains slow, compared to other industries.

This is starting to change, as legal practitioners increasingly recognize that having the right digital infrastructure and business practices, which go well beyond technology alone, is essential for keeping pace with clients' needs and the realities of how business is being done (and will increasingly be done in the future).

In this context, law firms and in-house legal teams are increasingly looking to develop, invest in and use software tools which can help convert repetitive processes (traditionally performed manually) into software.

AI in Dispute Resolution

The focus of investment in artificially intelligent technology within the dispute resolution context has been confined primarily to software which can, based on a seed set of documents that is manually reviewed, scan and tag large quantities of documents which it would be impossible or inefficient for human reviewers to analyse manually within the necessary timeframes of budgets. These AI tools are already saving time for dispute resolution practitioners, and saving money for clients. However, as software tools continue to become "smarter", they stand to transform the dispute resolution process more fundamentally.

At the Transactional Stage

AI tools can be relevant to dispute resolution well before a dispute has arisen. For instance, machine learning could be used at the transactional stage to guide the drafting of bespoke dispute resolution provisions, taking into consideration factors such as the place of performance, application of mandatory laws under the governing law of the contract, location of assets and parties' priorities and risk appetite. Such tools could help significantly to reduce the number of defective dispute resolution clauses and, as a consequence, the likelihood of procedural disputes or delay to substantive proceedings arising out of such clauses.

As more sophisticated software becomes available and more detailed data analysis is performed by legal teams, that software will be able to make more tailored and specific recommendations to reflect clients' preferences and past experiences of relevant dispute resolution methods or jurisdictions.

More advanced data-recording practices within firms and in-house teams will fuel further improvements in software performance and the ability to develop off-the-shelf software which can automatically raise red flags or highlight inadequate drafting in transactional documents.

At the Time of Breach or Failed Performance

Businesses are increasingly able to generate and monitor their operational data in real time. This enables parties to identify (and be automatically notified of) even small operational issues as soon as they occur. The ability to do so helps parties to nip problems in the bud, thereby avoiding potential issues of contractual performance. For example,

Internet of Things devices, which automatically feed real-time data about the functioning of an industrial plant back to a contract management software, may identify that a scheduled maintenance plan has not been completed. This issue can then immediately be raised between the parties to the contract to avoid the issue of delayed maintenance escalating into a larger and more complex dispute.

Alternatively, by enabling parties better to understand the context, reasons and impact of a breach of contract, legal teams can help their clients (whether internal or external) to narrow the scope of disputes, save unnecessary cost and focus on the real (generally more complex) issues between the parties. In turn, this increases the probability of amicable settlements, because parties' expectations are likely to be more realistic at an early stage in the dispute.

Where disputes cannot readily be settled, however, the substantial increase in the volume of data that businesses are generating (and the multitude of data sources and repositories) can make dispute resolution more complex and costly. Indeed, electronic communication channels and repositories (which are often owned and controlled by third parties) are increasingly numerous and varied. This can pose challenges for and increase the costs of data preservation, retention and analysis once a dispute arises.

Document Review

Machine learning tools help lawyers to digest data more quickly and efficiently.

At the early stages of a dispute, these tools can suggest salient repositories or files to review (AI tools can cluster groups of documents in unstructured data or identify files with specific characteristics). This can help lawyers to develop initial case strategies at lower cost than would be possible if a preliminary manual review of entire data sets was required.

If the dispute continues beyond the early stages, machine learning software can also extrapolate to a large volume of data human decisions made in relation to a smaller seed set of documents. Again, this saves time and gives legal teams and their clients greater certainty than a human manual review which, realistically, could only digest a proportion of the overall volume of data.

Intelligent software may also be needed in the future to help verify the authenticity of data. With deepfakes becoming increasingly prevalent and more realistic, it may no longer be possible for the human eye to identify and confirm authenticity. A decision-maker will likely need to call upon digital forensic scientists as experts (who, in turn, will rely on software to test and probe the evidence being challenged) to verify the authenticity of evidence more often in the future.

Looking further ahead, AI will combine with distributed ledger technology (blockchain) and smart legal contracts (SLCs, being a contract whose natural language provisions have been fully or partially translated into computer code thereby creating a digital contract that is able to call upon external data sources and perform digital actions based on the data that it receives). These technologies will revolutionize the process of contract management yet further and, therefore, the way in which disputes arise and are resolved. For example, a codified contractual delivery requirement may automatically generate and issue a notice of breach if the delivery deadline is not met (or suggest to the delivery recipient to send a dispute notice if retention of an intermediate human step is preferred).

Innovative "on-chain" and "off-chain" dispute resolution options are being developed and tested. These range from automated non-binding decision-making on data-based questions to automated digital enforcement of judgments and awards using digital assets (cryptocurrencies or other tokenised assets). While there are a number of technical and legal obstacles to overcome

before these tools are capable of widespread adoption, blockchain and SLCs continue to represent a very exciting area of evolving law and practice.

Legal Research

Another area where AI tools are currently impacting upon the disputes landscape is legal research. Most research tools no longer rely on simple keyword searches. Instead, they can apply complex functionality to understand the context of search terms, remember user preferences and habits, and connect or cluster information thematically. This helps a researcher to focus more quickly on relevant results, albeit that there is a need to understand the functionality of the software and any limitations which require further manual review (e.g. when looking for an outlier case or a decision which may have been made outside the usual context).

Machine learning tools are also increasingly being used to predict the outcome of cases. This enables lawyers to manage expectations, give their clients more robust advice on their options and ultimately promote a win–win settlement.

Bundling and Administrative Tasks

Considerable human time has traditionally been spent on tasks such as bundling and summarizing documents. AI tools have helped to automate and streamline these tasks, and they will only continue to get better at doing so. This frees up junior lawyers to deal with more substantive issues or to learn the new legal and technical skills they will need in preparing for the next wave of digitization.

Trials

Trials are also likely to look rather different in years to come. As video conferencing technology continues to improve and societies move to 5G, more hearings are likely to take place remotely. Real-time automated transcription and translation of witness testimony may also dispense with the need for court reporters. This would save costs and make the trial process less cumbersome and more efficient.

Another interesting avenue for research has been in the use of artificially intelligent decision-makers (i.e. a computer/software which processes the parties' data, analyses relevant case law or submissions and generates a judgment or order). We are already seeing the increasing use of online dispute resolution programmes for settlement of small claims, and parties are keen to identify cheaper and faster solutions for resolving their larger cases too. An algorithmic decision could help to meet that need; however, it is unlikely that a binding dispute resolution process could be entirely automated in the near future because there remain several ethical and legal issues around enforceability of a computer-generated order.

That being said, there is no doubt that human decision-makers are likely to be much more dependent on technology in the future.

Why All LegalTech Roads "Point" to a Platform Strategy

Ben Stoneham
Founder and CEO, Autologyx

Our consumer experiences shape our expectations of the technology we use. We bring these expectations to work with us every day: the ease of use, the joined-up use of data and the ability to seamlessly deliver valuable services.

LegalTech promises the same universal benefits, but on the face of it struggles to deliver the same experience as its consumer cousins. This chapter will touch on the "point solution" market; the growing cry for interconnectivity and platforms; the pursuit of artificial intelligence (AI); and provide useful context and pointers along the way. The benefits of technology are being brought to bear in legal at an unprecedented pace and scale – so much so, it is unlikely the market at the time of writing will be the same by the time you are reading this.

How Did We Get Here?

Arguably the only technology to universally impact legal has been the introduction of email and electronic word processing. This spark combined with faster internet speeds ignited an explosion of transformation from paper to digital, with downstream impacts in all areas. Take, for example, the hard copy due diligence data room, a room full of files once the staple of corporate transactions. If your documents can be in digital format, and storage made available with fast, secure access, it isn't long before a tech company offers a far more efficient "virtual" data room online, accessible anywhere. Afterwards, one by one came more LegalTech applications: electronic billing, e-Discovery platforms, contract databases, document generation, legal project management, analytics and more. At the point of writing, there are over 2000

LegalTech companies,[1] leading to what we describe as our market of "point solutions": technology designed to tackle single areas well.

Today we therefore have new opportunities, new challenges and an ever-evolving landscape. Businesses are working out what "digitization" means for them, transforming how they organize and use data, and the products they sell. Legal delivery itself is evolving with new models, processes and uses for technology. Finally, the technology itself is changing: introduction of cloud, the rise of platform economics and the promise of AI. So where are we going?

Digital Operations, Data and Platforms

"Digital operations" is a term that Gartner coined to describe a key capability underpinning an organization's competitive edge, defined by its ability to leverage technology and data to react to opportunity, innovate, solve problems and drive new products and services. It is the ability to harness the new digital world we are in.

Inherent in the term is the smart use of data and interoperability between components of our business. Silos, a drag on efficiency and speed of business, exist both in business processes and supporting technology. We have all experienced tasks repeated across a business which could be done just once: for example, entry of contract details into a template, negotiation and re-entry into fields in a contract management system, appended with an often unreadable PDF scan of the signed contract. Further contracts with the same parties or similar terms follow without leveraging what has gone before. These contracts will inevitably be reviewed in the future to extract the same key terms. And so,

---

[1] See AngelList 1800+ companies under "legal" search, or Stanford Codex List's curated 1150+.

our precious legal expertise is wasted repeating basic tasks made inevitable by siloed systems. Because of this, we cannot benefit from network effects and scaled effort: legal is stuck in a world of bespoke drills and screws.

This is where platforms enter: driving interoperability and standardized data between point solutions, eventually not just across legal, but the whole enterprise. Progress is being made on this front in a few areas. Application programming interfaces connecting point solutions are becoming more common "out of the box", which allows data to flow between applications. The use of "containerized" software deployment to provide "Amazon Web Services Market Place"-like features has also started to become popularized in legal, which will make management of the technology easier. Promises that it will eradicate or alleviate security concerns may be overblown, however, as containerized applications still need to be tested for security and don't inherently offer any data-driven interoperability between discreet software solutions.

Indeed, the last part is possibly the hardest: cross-industry efforts are required to promote common data models. Containerized platforms alone will not help this: the act of making technology more accessible to end users via a few market-dominant app stores will if nothing else highlight that very little of it works in unity. History tells us that pressure from customers focused on enterprise-wide digital operations capability may well be a key driver in forcing change.

Some barriers do exist: the non-legal skill sets required to understand and adopt these changes are growing, yet are still scarce in legal. Education, whether formal or via osmosis from collaborating with other business areas, on digital transformation and what it means for business and operating models, is key. The traditionally siloed nature of legal – from the business and even within areas of the profession itself – also does not facilitate digital development. Many of these silos are reinforced by the peculiar language of the industry.

The benefits of reduction of inefficiencies across business and legal processes caused by excessive bespoking and waste from repetition are too great to ignore. Theories on innovation predict that such standardization will drive further innovation. When legal stops reinventing the wheel across point solutions, our ability to focus on new products and services, and make best use of the resources we have, will dramatically increase.

The Promise of Artificial Intelligence

No conversation about legal technology is complete without mentioning AI. Scepticism of product marketing in so-called AI capabilities is sadly too often justified. AI, by definition, is an aspirational capability. We use machine learning (ML) techniques to try to achieve AI capabilities. The mathematics behind approaches used was around long before the computational power and available data caught up to enable us to start to put it into practice.

Legal technology uses this capability today to parse large quantities of data and highlight or extract specified terms – in essence its primary function is currently "search". The benefits of this have already been enormous, reducing effort in areas such as large-scale contract review, remediation and e-Discovery.

There are signs that new avenues could open up for this technology as data, critical for training and implementing algorithms, becomes more structured and well understood. This, coupled with increased automation of processes and data capture, will likely result in development of in-house ML capabilities bespoke to each business environment as the technology becomes more accessible.

The integrated "operationalizing" of ML outputs into real-time everyday business processes is the next natural step, enabling smarter automation which blends eventually into what we will come to think of as the organization's AI capability.

How Can We Keep Up?

There are some steps we can take to help transform our digital operations and enable use of technology such as ML. Data is clearly key. It must be structured, curated and be able to flow to the person, process or application which needs it at any given point in time to avoid inefficiencies and repetition. Legal, therefore, needs experts in data, coupled with the right subject matter expertise to bring the data science to bear. Legal departments and law firms/companies are already starting to invest in these capabilities.

Focus on defining and standardizing once-bespoke legal processes is already well under way, and will help drive both the data story and the requirements for technology to support them. Once a business' processes and data are well understood, ideally on an enterprise-wide level, use cases for technology become more obvious and parsing the multitude of technology providers becomes an easier task.

End customers and technology providers, both buy and sell sides, have a part to play in the evolution of digital operations. Platforms, use of AI technology and creation and benefits of standard data models are in our future; none of which will happen in a vacuum. Legal itself is becoming less of a silo, and we may find the next step in legal's journey is ultimately about the integration of legal capabilities, process and technology into the business.

An Introduction to the Internet of Things

Simon George
Associate Professor, The University of Law

What Is the IoT?

The Internet of Things (IoT) just may be the fastest-growing phenomenon on earth. Excluding mobile phones, landlines, laptops and tablets there were 7 billion IoT devices (and 17 billion connected devices) at the end of 2018. By 2025, that number is likely to be 22 billion IoT devices.[1]

McKinsey estimates the IoT market to be worth anywhere in the region of $4 trillion to $11 trillion in 2025.[2]

The potential applications for homeowners and businesses are incredible. In June 2019 an Indonesian shipping company, PT TKSolusindo, set sail with a number of devices, each slightly longer and thinner than a brick.[3] These devices can track GPS, record shock and motion, and check the humidity, temperature and any triggered alarms on refrigerated containers. If you combine a device like this with the immutability of a blockchain recording system, you have unprecedented amounts of real-time trustworthy data that interested parties can use to make operations safer, faster and more profitable.

---

[1] https://iot-analytics.com/state-of-the-iot-update-q1-q2-2018-number-of-iot-devices-now-7b/.

[2] McKinsey Global Institute. The Internet of Things: Mapping the Value Beyond the Hype, 2015.

[3] https://spectrum.ieee.org/tech-talk/telecom/internet/shipping-industry-bets-big-on-iot-in-bid-to-save-billions.

What Is an IoT Device?

It's normally spoken about as the extension of internet connectivity into objects, often everyday objects, that wouldn't normally have the internet. There is no universal definition, but a complete IoT system integrates four things: sensors – connectivity – data processing – and a user interface.

1. Sensors

There is always some kind of sensor that will collect data. It could be anything from a GPS location, a temperature or a video feed. Data is being collected from the environment by something.

2. Connectivity

The data collected by the sensor is then sent to the cloud. Connection to the cloud can be by a number of methods – like mobile networks or Wi-Fi. Some options use more power, or have a longer range than others, but they all get data to the cloud.

3. Data processing

When the data arrives, it has to be processed by some kind of software. The cloud is the ideal place to perform this processing, because the IoT device itself is often small with limited battery and processing power.

Processing could be simple and not require much power, such as checking that a temperature is above X degrees, or it might be very complex, such as facial recognition from a video feed.

4. User interface

We must put the data processing to some use in order to make the system work. There is no point in discovering that your house is too cold unless the device also turns on the heating, or at the very least tells you to do it.

Most IoT devices are small, might be located somewhere you can't get to it (like inside a shipping container) and generally not suited to having a large display or a keyboard. Often the user interface is located away from the IoT device itself; it's usually a phone or computer app.

The data processing could trigger something like a text/email/app notification. More advanced systems will make changes themselves like turning on the heating or recording something in a database without the need for user input.

Users might be able to monitor the system and even make changes via the interface. Mobile phone apps that control heating or video doorbells are classic examples of these – you can set desired heating times or change the motion detection area of your video doorbell via your phone.

The interface may even alert third parties such as emergency services, security firms or insurers when particular things are detected.[4]

Security of the IoT

Some IoT devices are very secure. However, the security of devices overall is currently very weak. Different manufacturers and different governments cannot agree any common standards. There are no mandatory standards that devices have to meet even though several influential organizations have made recommendations.[5]

---

[4] https://support.apple.com/en-gb/HT208944.

[5] The European Telecommunications Standards Institute released a cybersecurity standard for consumer Internet of Things devices in February 2019 (TS 103 645). Similarly, there is a code of practice for IoT security from the Department for Digital Culture Media and Sport, also a draft standard from the International Standards Organization 2018 – ISO/IEC 27030. None of these are mandatory.

The potential for crimes to be committed via the IoT (or at least made easier) is growing. Smart cameras may provide the homeowner with a live feed of their driveway, but if the camera can be accessed by a burglar they will know when the homeowner is out. In 2017, Germany banned the sale of certain children's smartwatches over privacy concerns due to poor security protocols.[6]

In 2010, the uncovering of the Stuxnet virus[7] showed the world that a new age of cyberattacks was here. Beyond just mere snooping and privacy concerns, the IoT had made cyberattacks on physical objects a grim reality. By controlling connected objects in a malicious way, hackers can cause damage in the physical world (in this case they made uranium centrifuges explode) – and with it comes the potential to hurt or kill people.

Blockchain

Blockchain may provide some of the answers to the security problems faced by the IoT.

Hashing is a blockchain technology that can verify an unlimited amount of information using encryption and only 256 characters. The system is essentially unhackable, takes almost no time or data to transmit and can be relied upon by third parties.

This could allow some interesting developments in IoT devices, such as verifying firmware updates, identifying devices – perhaps even giving each device a reliability score (like an eBay seller rating that can't be manipulated). Crucially, it can also verify that the information received on one device was the same as the information that was sent by another.

---

[6] https://www.bbc.co.uk/news/technology-4203010.

[7] https://www.mcafee.com/enterprise/en-gb/security-awareness/ransomware/what-is-stuxnet.html.

A lot of these things go towards making interoperability in the IoT a reality. It would provide a basis of trust that would make devices made from other manufactures trust each other and adopt common standards. Interoperability is a key barrier to the IoT at the present time.

The IoT and the Law

There is no doubt that the IoT will become an important area for legal advice in the next five years. The sheer size of the industry, combined with its ability to impact almost every area of modern business, will make it essential to understand.

There are complex legal questions that arise from the IoT, caused in part by the web of devices that interconnect together. When so many devices act together using a mix of software and hardware by different manufacturers, and information flows back and forth in various ways, there are complexities with even fundamental legal concepts like contract or tortious liability.

At the moment, there are more questions than answers. The issue of "are smart contracts legally binding contracts?" hasn't been fully resolved at this point.[8] And, as the IoT develops, it will likely rely heavily on smart contracts.

General Data Protection Regulation and data are also complicated areas. The IoT is fundamentally a giant data collection device with billions of sensors collecting information all over the planet. The Article 29 Working Party has raised a number of concerns regarding the IoT, including noting that a number of stakeholders in the IoT supply chain will constitute data controllers and that consent must be the principal basis for lawful processing of personal data – this consent must be freely given and individuals must be able to retain control over their personal data.[9]

Conclusion

There are several drawbacks and uncertainties surrounding the IoT but these have not slowed its growth. Businesses and consumers alike are fuelling the demand for IoT devices and the market will provide them, even if they are not secure or some of the legal elements remain uncertain. As is often the case with technology, regulation lags behind innovation, and we will do our best to make sense of it after the problem arises.

[8] The Law Tech Delivery panel set up a consultation in May 2019 to attempt to resolve the legal status of smart contracts among other things: https://www.lawsociety.org.uk/news/stories/cryptoassets-dlt-and-smart-contracts-ukjt-consultation/

[9] Opinion 8/2014.

Law and Data

2

"These are extraordinary times, but human rights law still applies. Indeed, the human rights framework is designed to ensure that different rights can be carefully balanced to protect individuals and wider societies. The decisions that governments make now to confront the pandemic will shape what the world looks like in the future"

Joint civil society statement, More than 100 human rights groups, April 2020

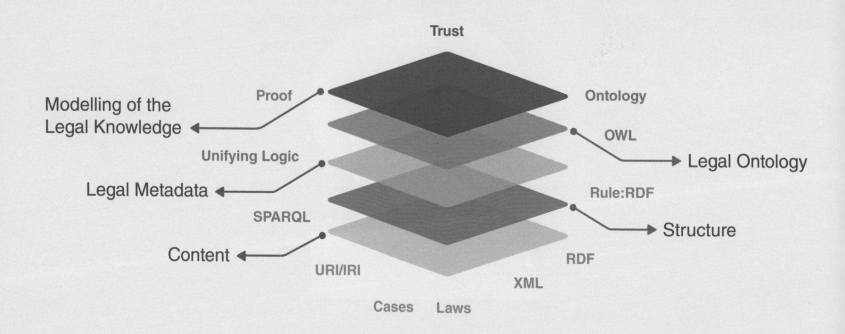

Executive Summary

In her introduction, Natasha McCarthy reviews the current, data-rich societal perspective and the challenges it represents in terms of regulation and governance.

Thomas Hyrkiel's chapter is a starting point given the governance concerns about content management systems and data quality. Legal data warehousing and legal platform interoperability are conditional on developing and supporting the legal domain and technical standards, therefore involving just about any business of law.

This is followed by Stevan Gostojić, since the legal informatics community has continued developing data and technical standards over the last few decades, well before LegalTech came into the spotlight.

From an outsider's perspective, the non-adoption of (linked) data standards to legal cases and laws and lack of open data are surprising. The existing legal corpus is still overwhelmingly "analogue", serially retyped, transcribed and thus just "repapered" at high cost.

Afsaneh Towhidi et al. present information extraction, one of the principal natural language processing (NLP) methods, and apply it to legal documents. Information extraction and other NLP tools are often integrated within most LegalTech platforms on the market.

Once digitized and machine readable, legal logic, argumentation and inference can be further explored and tested and still represent active academic research domains.

For several decades, legal expert systems have attempted to deliver automated legal inference and Clive Spenser describes a stand-alone platform that emulates the formal legal rules applicable to the rule-based compliance domain.

The compliance domain has entered public discourse through General Data Protection Regulation and internet privacy concerns, and three selected chapters by Rebecca Kelly, Charles Lombino and Asim Jusic address specific facets. Kelly reiterates the consent challenges, Lombino looks at the jurisprudence of web-captured data and Jusic discusses the linkage between data protection and blockchain technologies.

The plethora of legal and ethical concerns carries over to consent management, smart contracts and even corporate governance responsibility (environmental, social and governance – ESG).

Two visions of future AI-driven legal services are addressed by Christy Ng and Leyanda Purchase: top-down corporate governance and the client's bottom-up delivery, repectively. Ng builds upon the previous chapters on information extraction and decision trees to present a vision of legal (chat- and other) bots. Purchase takes an extra step in the ESG direction by adding an AI minute-taker to board meetings (repurposing court recorders, potentially checking compliance and even assigning corporate ESG ratings).

Technology and the Law – Data and the Law

Natasha McCarthy
Head of Policy, Data, The Royal Society

The step change in the volume of data that is being generated and collected, and the power of data analysis to draw insights from that data, creates a range of challenges for the law. These challenges include the potential mismatch between the pace of legal change, the rapidity with which data-enabled technologies are developed and the friction between the languages of law, technology and wider society. Building alignment between law and technology is central to enabling the rapid but safe use of data and the technologies that it fuels.

The Paces of Change

It is common to hear that technology moves ahead of the law – that the law cannot keep pace with the rate of technological change. This is especially so in the context of technologies driven by data and powerful data analysis. The development of data-powered businesses and innovation in particular is becoming increasingly rapid due to step changes in the volume of data generated and the power of analytics to derive insights from that data. New businesses harnessing the potential of specific data streams or creating business models that generate valuable data sets can be established rapidly and grow in scale and value at pace. Developing excessively detailed law and regulation might be perceived as chilling or slowing down this agility and entrepreneurship. In this context, where the acts of small teams or individuals can have global reach – but also globally negative impact – the law faces challenges in enabling this rapidity, while ensuring safe and lawful development of technology.

However, it is not so simple as to suggest that new uses of data are running ahead of legislative systems. In fact, the absence of a sound legal basis for accessing, sharing or trading data can be a limit on the ability to access data, tap into its value and use it as a basis for innovation. For example, companies in competition with each other might benefit from sharing data and drawing deeper insights into their markets or their methods, but the commercial sensitivity of that data can mean that the data is kept close to the companies that create it. Similarly, health data is critical to research that will inform new medicines and treatments, but the sensitivity of this data means that the right agreements must be in place to access it.

Legal tools are a key part of enabling the kinds of access to data that can enable research and innovation. The concept of a data trust has been explored as a potential legal basis for sharing and trading of data. According to the Open Data Institute, a data trust is an arrangement by which a trusted steward can make legally founded decisions on who can use and access data.[1] But this notion of a data trust is still in development, and its detail will likely depend crucially on the context of use. Developing this notion further and testing it in practice could unlock many beneficial applications and uses of data, which are currently limited by the absence of well-tested law.

Governance Beyond the Law

The law might be considered to sit above the tide of new technology, designed to enable new generations of technology. The General Data Protection Regulation (GDPR) established in 2018, for example, gave an update of data protection law for the new era of an abundance of data and the power to use it. This law is intended to be technologically neutral: "The GDPR is also technology neutral, meaning it protects personal data regardless of the technology used or how the personal data is stored"[2] on the basis that the law

---

[1] https://theodi.org/wp-content/uploads/2019/04/ODI-Data-Trusts-A4-Report-web-version.pdf.

[2] https://ec.europa.eu/commission/sites/beta-political/files/data-protection-factsheet-sme-obligations_en.pdf.

creates constancy and a foundation for decisions as technologies develop in potentially unpredictable ways.

However, technology not only changes *how* things are done with data, it also changes *what* is done, and with what kinds of data. GDPR is a law to protect personal data – but this is not the only data with value or with sensitivity. While this law is technologically neutral, it is data specific, which leaves potential gaps in the governance framework. In particular, where diverse data sets are brought together in analysis, or where data is combined in such a way that renders anonymous data personal, gaps in the legal framework may emerge.

When new applications of data outpace legislation, there are other means to enact control over how data is used, to protect against risk and enable benefits where they exist. The British Academy and Royal Society report *Data Management and Use* focused on a governance framework that included not only law but other forms of governance such as standards and codes of ethics, which can be agile and adaptive as new uses of technology emerge. Organizations such as Nesta are exploring forms of *anticipatory regulation* that seek to provide both the controls and the enablers to develop new technologies in the absence of detail about what these technologies can achieve. Can these broader forms of governance rapidly open up safe paths for new uses of data?[3]

Technology or Application?

The suitability of any form of governance to the oversight of technology depends on whether legislation and regulation, whether anticipatory or not, should focus on technologies themselves or on their use. Data-enabled technologies such as AI are often thought of as general-purpose technologies, permitting use in a wide variety of contexts and enabling the development of other technologies, with electricity being a paradigm case. While regulation of electrical systems may depend on their technical nature and the environment in which they are used, for other technologies *purpose* of use might be the focus.

In *Data Management and Use* the case was made for governance to focus on the *use* of data, rather than on the protection of data itself. When this focus is taken, it leads to a closer consideration of whether and where new legislation is needed. In many cases, the use of data may be well governed by regulations that apply in the field of application – from finance to health. The challenge of data governance is in assessing where new uses of data disrupt this sector-specific regulation.[4]

The Languages of Law, of Science and of Society

Developing legislation and regulation for digital technologies is also a challenge because of the mismatch between the potential of technology, the language of law and the explicit and tacit expectations we all have in everyday life. There is a challenge in the law meeting the expectations and concerns of the public if the framing of those concerns does not translate neatly into the legal terminology that is supposed to codify those expectations, and where neither conform neatly with the potential of technology itself.

The idea of "data ownership" gives an example of such a situation, where we might naturally express our expectations of the

---

[3] See https://www.nesta.org.uk/feature/innovation-methods/anticipatory-regulation/.

[4] The Royal Society's exploration of machine learning technologies also recommends an approach to governance focused on areas of application and context of use: https://royalsociety.org/-/media/policy/projects/machine-learning/publications/machine-learning-report.pdf.

obligations of companies handling our data in terms of language referring to "my data" or data "about me". However, the rights associated with ownership as set out in property law do not apply naturally to data. Data can be both given away and retained, or given to many different people, unlike physical property. Data "about me" might also be about others – be that family history or everyday patterns of behaviour – and the decision on who holds the rights to that data is complicated by that fact.[5]

Similar concerns challenge the idea of "consent", which is one of the founding blocks of GDPR. What is the extent of the consent one can give to the use of data, where data about oneself is also data about others – which is the case for genetic data? How can consent be meaningful when the insights that can be drawn from data might not yet be known?

Data for the Wider Good

Addressing some of these needs will be essential in striking the balance between making use of data and protecting the interests of those involved in its generation. It will involve a deeper understanding of both the rights that individuals and organizations have in relation to data, but also the responsibilities. The pace and language of law and technology may often be in tension, but innovation in both spheres will be crucial to flourishing in a data-enabled society.

References

British Academy and the Royal Society (2017) *Data Management and Use: Governance for the 21st Century*.
British Academy, Royal Society and techUK (2018) *Data Ownership, Rights and Controls*.
European Commission Data Protection Factsheet (2018).
Open Data Institute (2019) *Data Trusts (summary report)*.
Royal Society (2017) *Machine Learning: The Power and Promise of Machines that Learn by Example*.

---

[5] See *Data Ownership, Rights and Controls*: https://royalsociety.org/-/media/policy/projects/data-governance/data-ownership-rights-and-controls-October-2018.pdf.

I Make the Rules, Why Should I Care About LegalTech?

Thomas Hyrkiel
Head of Publishing, IFRS Foundation

Entities that make rules or set standards (rule-makers) play a vital role in the legal ecosystem. It is difficult to imagine any part of the global economy functioning without legislation, regulations, rules or standards that act as an underpinning framework.

A key driver of change (technology or otherwise) is competition. It is competition that is a driving force behind what we call LegalTech as innovators possessing superior technologies disrupt existing operating models.

But rule-makers are not usually exposed to competition (putting aside, for the sake of simplicity, interjurisdictional competition). Their position is secure because of the remit they have secured or been explicitly given. The absence of competition means that there is often little in the way of urgency and certainly no compulsion for these entities to leverage incipient technologies.

And yet it is important for them to do so in order to continue to create, manage and disseminate good rules efficiently.

For rule-makers, adopting the best possible tools to carry out their mission, using data to ensure that the rules remain relevant, and also ensuring that the rules remain accessible to all stakeholders irrespective of their sophistication or size, is not optional. The expectations of the legal ecosystem and its participants are shifting as LegalTech continues to develop and thrive and rule-makers have a responsibility to adapt.

A polemic for action is easy, but digital transformation, which is what a rule-maker needs to undertake in order to take advantage of everything that LegalTech offers, is hard. All too often digital transformation programmes do not deliver on their promise, which results not only in a loss of time and resources, but undermines confidence and morale and can even be reputationally damaging.

So, Where Do You Start in Order to Have the Best Shot at a Successful Digital Transformation?

This chapter focuses on leveraging technology to effectively manage content – more specifically the rules and any materials connected with them. The rules are, after all, at the heart of what a rule-maker does. Having an adequate content management system (CMS) in place to manage content is, for the rule-maker, the first, and probably the most important, step to leveraging the power of a fully integrated technology stack.

The chapter is intended for operational decision-makers as well as operational staff who are starting on the technology transformation journey or are embarking on an upgrade path as their existing technologies reach end-of-life.

Legacy CMS

Even if a fully-fledged CMS is in place, it is important to consider whether this is fit for purpose, whilst, and preferably before, considering a technology transformation programme.

Critical issues that require immediate action	• Lack of stability • Absence of adequate back-up facilities • Poor responsiveness • Poor security
Other reasons to proceed down a technology upgrade path	• Lack of flexibility/scalability • Inability to effectively integrate into a technology stack • Poor search functionality • Lack of a clear update/upgrade path • Absence of efficient output mechanisms

Investment in Technology or Outsourcing?

If permitted from a governance perspective, it is possible for a rule-maker to collaborate with an external party to deliver and administer the technology required to store its content. In such a set-up the writers draft the rules while the external party is responsible for the maintenance, management and administration of the systems in which these are authored and stored, and from which they are disseminated. Although a CMS owned and managed internally will almost always be the way forward, a discussion around outsourcing can be extremely useful in crystallizing what it is that the organization expects at a strategic level, not only from a new system, but from a digital transformation more broadly.

Bespoke or Off-the-Shelf?

The temptation for building a system internally is to be resisted. The cost of development is high and the timeframe is long (often far longer than initially estimated). Purchasing an off-the-shelf system is almost always the best way forward. Some customization of this will always be required, but it should be limited as much as possible. Extensive customization is to be avoided at all costs. A system that caters to all of the specialist needs of the underlying content will be more difficult to maintain and upgrade. Customizing the system also reduces the opportunity for normalizing data and rationalizing processes. In addition, an internally built or highly specialized system will have consequences for integration into a technology stack that includes external systems and, potentially, also be disadvantageous in terms of output options and the servicing of a user-facing website.

Content Delivery Methods to Consider

When working to identify the right solution and data architecture, consider carefully the formats required for dissemination to users. Print, PDF, Word, XML and HTML will all require at least some calibration efforts. Stylesheet alignment is key to ensuring consistency across formats. Content normalization should precede any stylesheet work as the latter can be expensive and involved. Ideally, a CMS should integrate a rendering engine that covers all of the outputs that the organization requires. In addition, output to a website whether directly from the CMS or by way of an API should be considered as part of the organization's wider content strategy.

Resourcing

The key asset to rule-making organizations are the specialists who write and create the rules. This resource is specialized, expensive and a challenge to find and retain. Technology can enable organizations to change rules effectively and efficiently, while also allowing them to focus limited resources in the right area of work. Therefore, consider the workflow and reporting capabilities of any new system and how they could improve the organization's use of resources. Low morale stemming from inadequate tools available to internal users can be a real drag on productivity. An ideal CMS is one that provides the following enabling features:

Workflows	Enables end-to-end authoring of content, with particular focus on formal review cycles and the recording of amendments
Collaboration	Facilitates communication between users on specific project work
Reporting (dashboards)	Allows users to monitor activity, productivity and identify workflow issues

Data Resilience and Security

A key advantage of modern technology infrastructure is its ability to address the risk of data and data integrity loss, as well as addressing the potential for the content to be compromised by internal users or external attackers. In selecting a CMS, consider the following:

- robustness of its security features

- underlying server infrastructure, including access to areas for maintenance and upgrading

- ability to deploy CMS to User Acceptance Testing or test servers in order to assess and test changes/upgrades

- back-up/disaster recovery server(s), including the frequency of back-ups and switching over or migrating data (its usefulness is compromised if the path to restoring is arduous)

Maintenance and Accessibility

Modern rules are often very complex, which reflects the complexity of the areas that they support. Complexity, compounded by unstructured data, which is data that lacks adequate organization, poses a serious challenge for the effective maintenance of rule sets. Potential maintenance problems include:

- errors

- omissions

- conflict/discrepancy

- inconsistency

- unintended ambiguity

One of the advantages of technology is the potential to make complexity more manageable. Good practice ensures that the writers of the standards and other specialists are able to efficiently navigate the rules in order to produce content that is more reliable. It also means that external users can more easily identify content that is relevant to them and assess its importance, even when the rules are complex or overlapping.

Capturing Useful Data

One of the persistent challenges for rule-makers is the relative paucity of data on how their rules are being applied and used in practice. A good CMS holding a well-structured data set is a key enabler in capturing usage statistics as well as enabling interactivity with, or the target of, end users.

Well-Defined and Structured Data Model

Organizing and storing content in a logical and consistent way is critical, as is ensuring that the information architecture is uncomplicated. Key challenges for a rule-maker in this context are:

Exceptions	Although complete uniformity is often out of the question, the more exceptions are made, the more complex the data model. A data model that is overly complex runs the risk of being incoherent, difficult to service in practice and difficult to distribute outside of the CMS.
Exclusion	The rules will always have primacy in a rule-maker's data set. However, it is important not to exclude content that is generated in support of the rules from the data model. Whether it is interpretation, commentary, rationale, etc. it is essential, in order to build a rich user experience, to be as inclusive as possible. This will significantly increase the ability to interconnect related content and will also help surface content to end users of the rules.

Granularity	A key advantage of a granular basic content unit (e.g. paragraph) is flexibility in terms of building content. A key disadvantage is the potential number of content units – which has consequences for organization as well as for output processing. The advantages of a more granular content unit will usually outweigh the disadvantages if the content is stored in a modern CMS that includes an adequate search capabilities.

Content Augmented with Metadata

The addition of metadata to content results in a content set that is no longer entirely flat. The key advantages of an enriched content set are:

- effective filtering
- improved searchability
- potential to optimize search

If starting out on a journey towards content enrichment, focusing on metadata that is essential is, at least, initially the best way forward. An extensive metadata set requires considerable resources in order to be adequately maintained, so keep things simple, at least to begin with. Essential metadata will almost always include:

- document type
- key dates
- exception/exemption information
- reference to things that change the content
- commentary/interpretation

In addition to metadata, consider incorporating a human-readable naming convention for the files storing your content. This is especially important in regards to generating error reports and troubleshooting problems.

Taxonomy

The classification of rules is important as it permits content to be organized in a way that is more useful to users. Once the content has been enriched with metadata, the development of a content taxonomy should be considered. A content taxonomy will usually be organized by theme and topic that is informative and practical. A possible starting point to a content taxonomy is a topical index of the rules if this is available. A reason why investment in taxonomy is rarely a wasted effort is the ability to use it in order to optimize search and filtering.

Data Migration and Testing

The migration of data of a large content set can be difficult because even slight imprecisions (in a transform script, for example) can lead to substantive errors in the content. Preparing a testing plan that includes automated tools to test content integrity as well as regression testing tools to ensure that the content behaves as expected will help mitigate this risk.

To Conclude

I hope that the practical focus on the management of content means that this chapter, although very brief, is useful to anyone helping a rule-maker in their LegalTech journey.

From Legal Documents to Legal Data

Stevan Gostojić
Associate Professor, University of Novi Sad, Faculty of
Technical Sciences

Introduction

Documents play a crucial role in law firms and legal departments. They are both inputs and outputs of legal transactions and a valuable source of knowledge in the case of sources of law.

The web revolutionized the way we work. The legal profession is not an exception. Legal reference websites were among the first websites on the internet. Over the years, the web has transitioned from the web of documents, through the dynamic web, to the web of linked data. However, the legal web did not follow trends.

This chapter reviews recent developments in the legal web – from standardized machine-readable document formats, metadata ontologies and citation schemas, through automatic extraction of data from text, to successful case studies of computer-assisted services.

Legal Documents

The legal informatics academic community specialized web standards, such as XML and RDF, to the legal domain. The most promising legal document format is LegalDocML sponsored by the OASIS standardization body. It provides an XML document format for parliamentary, legislative and judicial documents. LegalDocML enables the representation of document structure, references to legal sources and metadata.

The main advantages of using legal document formats, in comparison to generic document formats such as Microsoft Word, PDF and HTML, is the explicit specification of syntax and semantics and better interoperability.

The syntax and the semantics are specified explicitly. This facilitates automatic data extraction from text. Extracted data is used for automatic document processing and implementation of novel services.

Integration of legal information systems was not a simple task. This is becoming even truer as legal services are increasingly taking place in an international setting. Machine-readable document formats enable better interoperability between organizations at semantic and technical levels and easier integration of information systems.

There are several machine-readable legal citation mechanisms in use today. Some of them are specializations of URL and URN identification schemas. European Legislation Identifier provides a mechanism for the identification of legislative documents. European Case-Law Identifier provides a standard for the identification of court decisions. URN:LEX is another convention for identifying persistent resources in the legal domain.

Machine-readable legal citation schemas enable unambiguous citation of sources of law on the web, automatic resolution of citations and automatic retrieval of cited documents.

Legal Data

In the last decade, the availability of data and hardware enabled the proliferation of machine learning. However, most of the legal data is still trapped in textual documents. This data can be extracted either manually or automatically. An even better solution would be to create documents in a machine-readable format first.

W3C promotes a set of recommendations for knowledge graphs (RDF), knowledge graph schemas (RDFS and OWL) and a query language for querying knowledge graphs (SPARQL). There are also some community-driven initiatives (e.g. Schema.org).

The scale of the web of data has reached the same order of magnitude as the scale of the web of documents. Some of the better-known examples are the DBPedia (Wikimedia), the Open Graph (Facebook) and Knowledge Graph (Google). Linked legal data implements the web of data paradigm in the legal domain.

An ontology can informally be defined as a "knowledge graph schema" and a knowledge graph can be viewed as an "instance of an ontology". It represents knowledge using a formal language. Numerous legal ontologies have been developed: LKIF Core, FOLaw, LRI-Core, Judicial Ontology Library (JudO), CEN Metalex ontology, etc. Some of them are used to represent general legal knowledge and others to assign metadata to documents.

Publishing legal data as linked data promotes data reuse. Ontologies enable automatic inference of implicit knowledge from explicit knowledge (e.g. to implement legal knowledge-based systems).

Open Access

Another important development is open access to law movement. Legal sources can be published either publicly or for a fee. With the transition of legal documents from paper to electronic format, there are a growing number of organizations who advocate for and contribute to open access to law.

This creates new business opportunities by enabling the development of products and services that use documents previously unavailable or unaffordable.

Open data is defined as "data that can be freely used, re-used and redistributed by anyone – subject only, at most, to the requirement to attribute and share alike". Open data initiatives contributed to the increase in the quantity of open data. Data sets related to the law make an important part of this effort.

The main advantages of opening legal data are the increasing transparency and accountability of government, the increase in the efficiency and effectiveness of both data producers and consumers, and the creation of new business opportunities.

Natural Language Processing

Natural language processing (NLP) techniques offer many application opportunities in the legal domain.

Manual annotation of legal documents is a time-consuming and expensive effort. Many simple annotation tasks can be automated using NLP techniques. However, the precision and accuracy of those techniques have not reached the human level yet. Depending on the algorithm in use, they might also require human labour to annotate the training data set(s).

Automatic document classification is another possibility worth considering. This technique is usually used to find documents similar to a given document or to cluster documents.

One more technique to look out for is automatic document summarization. Although the technique also does not approach human-level performance, it can be quite useful when browsing through vast quantities of documents.

Case Studies

Among successful solutions that utilize legal web potential, several solutions are chosen from the profit, not-for-profit and public sectors.

LegisPro (Xcential) is a web-enabled software platform for legislative and regulatory drafting. It contains components for drafting, editing, amending, linking and publishing legal documents. LegisPro supports LegalDocML.

Legal Information Institute is a group linked to Cornell University that is a pioneer in free online legal information publishing. Its website uses XML and linked data to publish and help understand the law. Some of its services are also based on data extracted using NLP techniques.

Legislation.gov.uk uses a drafting, amending and publishing tool that is based on the LegalDocML predecessor. It also offers an application programming interface to access legislation in a machine-readable linked data format.

Conclusion

The legal informatics academic community has decades of experience in using information technology to tackle legal problems. This technology has matured during the years. Reusing their experience can help in the process of implementing LegalTech products and services.

As demonstrated by presented use cases, using legal document formats simplifies data extraction and fosters interoperability. Publishing legal data as linked data promotes data reuse. NLP techniques help in this process by automatic data extraction from text. Open access to legal information and data creates new business opportunities by providing information and data previously not available.

Those developments are a promising approach to bridging the gap between legal documents and legal data as a crucial step in the transition from the web of legal documents to the web of legal data. Full realization of the linked legal data potential will enable lawyers to spend less time and effort sifting through the vast quantities of legal information and focus on more intellectually challenging tasks.

Acquisitive Information Extraction Framework for Legal Domain

Mehran Kamkarhaghighi
NLP Data Scientist, Ontario Tech University

Afsaneh Towhidi
Graduate Research Assistant, Ontario Tech University

and Masoud Makrehchi
Associate Professor, Ontario Tech University

Introduction

Although text documents can be searched by regular expression search engines, fielded search, structured queries, data mining and decision support systems – all of them require information extraction (IE) techniques in order to work.[1] The task of IE is to find a fragment of a text document which contains the required concept of information.[2] Expressed simply, IE selectively structures and combines the identified data.[3] The objective function of an IE system is to extract specific data in natural language text. Some domains of application for IE include finance companies, publishers and governments.[3] Since its inception, different IE methods have been presented. An early approach was to develop manual rules by encoding patterns, but this approach has proved to be difficult and tedious due to the variety of contexts and forms. Supervised machine-learning approaches, which are trained on human-annotated corpuses, are the most successful. Alternative approaches include the use of automatically learned pattern-based extraction rules or the use of sequence labelling, which assigns a tag to the words in a document. This group of approaches may use the Hidden Markov Model[4] or Conditional Random Field[5] techniques for IE.

Named-entity is a term that is designated to a real-world entity and the purpose of named-entity recognition (NER) is to identify entities in a text and classify them into predefined categories, such as people, organizations, and locations. NER is fundamental in IE, because all other tasks use the inducted entities in this task.[6] The early solutions for NER were based on a hand-crafted pattern, an expensive option since it is time consuming and requires human expertise.[6] In rule-based systems, the text is compared with a set of rules; a rule is applied if the conditions satisfy.

In this study, the main focus of which is NER, a framework, known as the acquisitive information extraction framework (AIEF), is proposed as an approach to cover IE tasks.

Acquisitive Information Extraction Framework

Designing a system for IE tasks requires a group of experts in various domains such as natural language processing, machine learning, software engineering, and data science. Figure 1 illustrates the proposed framework for an expert-independent and task-adaptive system.

[1] A. McCallum, "Information Extraction: Distilling Structured Data from Unstructured Text", (2005), *Queue*, 3(9), 48–57.

[2] N. Kushmerick, E. Johnston and S. McGuinness, "Information Extraction by Text Classification", in In The IJCAI-2001 Workshop on Adaptive Text Extraction and Mining, 2001: Citeseer.

[3] J. Cowie and W. Lehnert, "Information Extraction", (1996), *Communications of the ACM*, 39(1), 80–91.

[4] L.E. Baum and T. Petrie, "Statistical Inference for Probabilistic Functions of Finite State Markov Chains", (1966), *The Annals of Mathematical Statistics*, 37(6), 1554–1563.

[5] J. Lafferty, A. McCallum and F.C. Pereira, "Conditional Random Fields: Probabilistic Models for Segmenting and Labeling Sequence Data", 2001.

[6] J. Jiang, "Information Extraction from Text", in *Mining Text Data*, Charu C. Aggarwal, and Cheng-Xiang Zhai (eds), Springer, 2012, pp. 11–41.

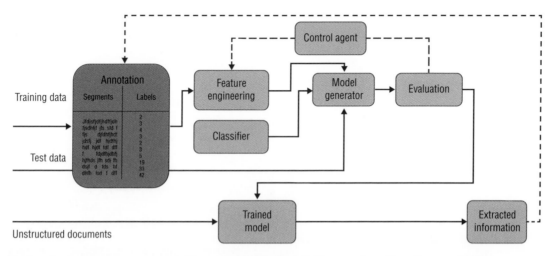

Figure 1: Multipurpose document representation-based information extraction framework

This architecture consists of six modules:

1. Annotation Module: The end users and domain experts, but not IE experts, annotate domain-interested segments of training data. This annotation is used for labelling the training data.

2. Feature Generation Module: A range of features will have been extracted from each segment of data. These document representation features benefit from methods such as bag-of-words, Word2Vec, GloVe, segment characteristics (location in document, length, number of punctuation marks, number of specific words/concepts) and previous and next segment assigned labels. The feature engineering process can be continuously updated.

3. Classification Models: Diverse kinds of classifiers, including naïve Bayes, SVM, decision tree, KNN, neural networks, logistic regression, and all of the deep learning-based solutions, including LSTM and CNN, can be considered in this module.

4. Model Generator: The main task of this module is to create different combinations of a feature-classifier for each training data.

5. Evaluation: In this module, the candidate combinations of the feature-classifier produced in the previous module are trained and evaluated. The best combination is selected and used as a final solution.

6. Control Agent: The main task of this module is feature engineering. This module controls the evaluation results and searches for an optimum combination of features.

This active learning-based system can improve its performance by obtaining continuous feedback from extracted information to the annotation module. Finally, the best trained model is selected and used to extract the information from unstructured or semi-structured documents.

Case Study: Named-Entity Recognition for Legal Documents

This case study is designed to evaluate the implemented framework in the domain of legal analytics. In this scenario, a new approach based on AIEF, known as the line classification-based (LC-based) method is presented and compared with off-the-shelf NER tools for the task of NER in case law documents from four Canadian courts. Figure 2 shows the different templates of the case law document for each court.

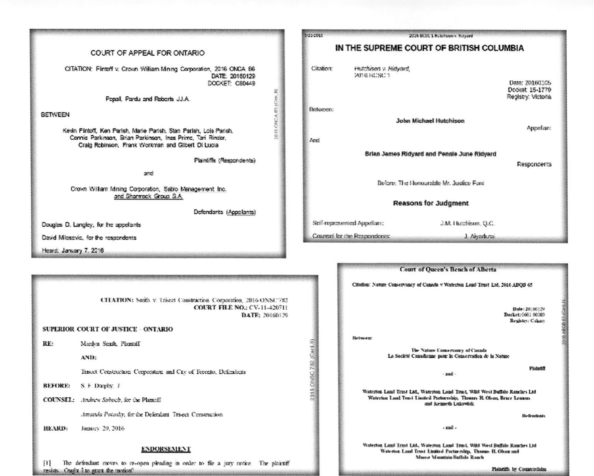

Figure 2: Different types of case law templates

For this case study, 25 cases from each court were randomly selected and named-entities were manually extracted by experts (annotation module). The LC-based approach has two phases: (1) line-by-line linear classification of legal documents based on textual features, and (2) pattern-based entity extraction based on the assigned class. In the first step, the following features were extracted from each line: (1) length of line; (2) number of words; (3) number of punctuation marks; (4) line number; (5) inclusion of month; and (6) presence of specific key words in the line, or previous or after lines. The keywords were selected based on a domain expert's opinion. The total number of extracted features from each line amounted to 48 (feature generation module).

According to the vast size of samples, a decision tree classifier model (classification model) is trained according to the training data for each court (model generator). For the second step of the proposed approach, an IE process at line level will apply to each line based on the result of the classification model. The candidate combination of features that are produced by the control agent module generates a model and is evaluated by a 10-fold cross-validation (evaluation module).

In this case study, according to the high computational cost of brute force search ($2^{48}-1$ combinations of features), the genetic algorithm approach is used to find the optimized combination of features (control agent).

Results and Discussion

The line classification step was applied to semi-structured legal documents in the designed case study. In the next step, a customized pattern-based entity extraction approach was applied to each line, based on the assigned class. Table 1 shows the evaluation results of each approach for each court and as an average.

Table 1: Evaluation of LC-based approach

	CQBA	SCBC	OCA	OSCJ	Average
Precision	0.6711	0.6865	0.7207	0.6611	0.6848
Recall	0.664	0.6865	0.5161	0.5025	0.5922
F-score	0.6675	0.6865	0.6015	0.571	0.6316

Acknowledgements

The authors would like to thank Mrs. Catherine Lee for her valuable comments and suggestions to improve the writing quality of this chapter.

Legal Expert Systems

Clive Spenser
Marketing Director, LPA\VisiRule

Many legal questions are sufficiently common and well understood that they can be readily encoded and automated. Advances in modern technology and the widespread availability of powerful personal devices means that hitherto isolated and computationally expensive previously abandoned technologies can now be re-examined and revisited. Neural networks were first implemented in the 1960s and 1970s and but had to wait almost thirty more years before attaining the popularity that they have now found as the basis for machine learning.

Legal expert systems provide the means of building intelligent legal advice systems in the same way that they have been used in other industries such as manufacturing and healthcare. Typically, they are delivered via interactive questionnaires which ask the user to provide answers to questions which are then used to evaluate some sort of conditional logic to arrive at a conclusion.

For example, VisiRule is a knowledge-based tool which allows lawyers to build complex, but logically robust, models in a no-code/low-code way and attach various layers of information which can later be used to help provide well-formed legal advice and guidance. No-code tools are attractive as they allow legal experts direct hands-on access and avoid the need to involve programmers to code the solutions.

Visual models are highly desirable as they can communicate complex ideas in a clear and transparent way to a wide group of stakeholders. Visual models are also able to support the extraction of knowledge from legal experts in a relatively painless and simple way.

Experts may know how to solve highly complex specialized problems, but don't always know how they do so! The process of having to instruct a computer as to how to do this task in itself forces people to question their own thinking and decision-making processes.

Relevancy of Questions

One of the benefits of using an intelligent tool with some artificial intelligence foundation is that the delivered solution only asks questions which are relevant, i.e. early answers help determine the path of the conversation and help ensure that the system asks only questions which are on that part of the decision-making path.

The questions may be presented as a set of web forms or as a conversational chatbot.

Explanations

The path taken during the computation can be used to help explain the basis for the advice. Ancillary explanation systems can piggy-back on the model and path and provide interactive chatbot-like access to explanations. This can include How a conclusion was reached, and Why a certain line of reasoning was taken.

Moreover, at run-time, the same information can be used to help explain Why a question is being asked, How we have reached a certain point in the conversation, What a certain term means and Insight into what assertions or internal inferences the system has been able to make so far. Hooks into knowledge-bases of existing FAQs can be integrated in a seamless way.

Links to relevant case law or legal texts can be provided which are sensitive to the path of reasoning taken and any internal inferences made. Links to helpful images or videos can help make the experience educationally rewarding as well as interesting.

In fact, sometimes the value, for some classes of users such as junior associates, is not so much in the final answer but in the process and route taken.

Intelligent systems which can make "smart" recommendations but can NOT provide insight into the basis for that decision are of limited value as they will struggle to gain people's trust.

Consider the following conversation:

User: Why was my claim rejected?

System: You failed to prove entitlement through any of the appropriate tests

User: What where they?

System: A (residency), B (authorized) and C (occupation)

User: Why did I fail B?

System: You answered that you were under the age of 18 and had not obtained authorization from your parents

It is very important for expert-based systems to develop to articulate all the logical combinations which it is able to handle. Given a set of answers, it should ALWAYS give the same result every time it is used. It may not be correct, but that is up to the author who creates the decision logic content. But it will be consistent and accountable. Contrast that to human decision-making, which is variable and affected by error, tiredness and random luck in the choice of agent or assessor.

Outputs can be in the form of simple answers, with or without some type of rationale, or be in the form of legal letters, or complex documents, or even draft contracts or agreements. This generally is implemented by pushing the answers given and inferences made into a suitably marked-up document template.

At the consumer end, such systems could help people who have little access to legal resources to, say, apply for a parking permit from a local authority or request permission to hold a fundraising event. Citizen access to legal systems is an emerging area in LegalTech – witness the success of DoNotPay.

Within various industries, automated legal advice can be provided on topics such as MiFID II or General Data Protection Regulation or intellectual property protection along with document templates that can be populated using the answers given by the respondent.

The same systems can be used to deploy their logic in a data-driven world, where, rather than ask a user to answer questions interactively, data is extracted from data sources to answer the questions.

Essentially, the same logic, but being applied to, say, documents or data points extracted from contracts by some other computer process. Prescriptive logic, which articulates what to do in certain situations, say, in the way of additional or alternate clauses, can be captured and deployed to help resolve problems in a fully or semi-automated way, and generate a full audit trail of the changes that it has made.

By incorporating logic-based reasoning with, say, robotic process automation or workflow technology, we can expect to see the reach of automated solutions expanded into many areas of legal practice currently serviced by expensive and often overworked employees and partners.

By delivering high-quality, consistent legal advice and guidance on a readily available and low-cost basis, tools such as VisiRule, Neota Logic and RainBird offer a way for legal practitioners to commoditizing some of the more tedious aspects of the workload, and so free themselves for the more intellectual aspects of the law.

Such systems can be enhanced downstream to capture reasoning both for and against a prognosis and hence provide the basis for argumentation systems, which again is a well-understood human activity.

In many cases, the aim of legal expert systems is not to automate all aspects of certain well-understood legal situations, but to deal with the 80% which are routine and repetitive and leave legal experts to help resolve the 20% which are truly difficult – and because such tools can explain their reasoning in the form of an internal audit trail and a chain of reasoning as executed by the internal inference engine, they stand a good chance of becoming popular.

Tech vs Law: Consent

Rebecca Kelly
Partner, gunnercooke LLP

The Issue

The notion of consent is one of the fundamental principles of the GDPR (or the General Data Protection Regulation (EU) 2016/679) to give its full title). The definition of consent in Article 4 of the GDPR states that for consent to be properly given it must be a:

> freely given, specific, informed and unambiguous indication of the data subject's wishes by which he or she, by a statement or by a clear affirmative action, signifies agreement to the processing of personal data relating to him or her.

However, given the multiple different data processing activities which occur when using even the simplest websites and web platforms, how can any data subject give truly informed consent to the manner in which their personal data is to be processed? For example, when personal data is processed on a social media platform (such as LinkedIn, Facebook, Twitter, Instagram, etc.), does every user whose data flows through that platform truly understand how and where their personal data is processed?

"Specific and Informed" Consent

The mammoth task of informing data subjects of the specific ways in which their personal data will be used usually falls to the legal, data protection and/or compliance teams employed by or acting for these organizations. It is their task to try to explain (in simple terms!) how and where personal data flows, and this is often done in the organizations' privacy statement or privacy policy. Such documents need to explain the types of personal data collected, where the data flows (often globally) and what companies are involved in the processing of that personal data. This list is generally extensive and will include suppliers providing hosting services, internet service providers, third party software providers and marketing agencies, to name a few. As someone who has drafted many of these documents, I know they can run to many pages in an attempt to "inform data subjects in a specific manner". But let's be completely honest – do the majority of people read these or even glance at them? I am under no illusion; they do not. These documents are ultimately a very dull read. Few individuals will feel compelled to read and fully digest the information included within them.

"Freely Given"

Is consent ever freely given? What happens if a data subject withholds their consent? If a data subject does not consent to their personal data being processed in the manner outlined to them, two things can happen; either they cannot use the relevant website or the website will attempt to rely on another justification to process that individual's personal data (such as legitimate interest, necessity, fulfilment of a contract, to name a few). For example, an individual wishing to use Facebook to its fullest extent will have to consent to the use of their personal data, otherwise, quite simply, they will not be able to "enjoy" the full Facebook experience. Similarly, if a user wishes to access wi-fi in a public area, it is likely they will be asked to agree to the wi-fi provider's terms and conditions (which will include details about how personal data will be used). Before a user accesses the wi-fi service, do they pore over those terms so they can fully understand how their personal data will be used? Or will the user simply tick a box to confirm they agree to the terms so they can use the wi-fi service? Generally, it is the latter.

In my opinion, the ability to give specific, informed, freely given consent is not a priority for the vast majority of internet users. It is without question important that users are informed as to how their personal data is processed. The right to privacy is a fundamental human right and accordingly individuals must have the opportunity to understand the manner in which their personal data is to be used by a company, website or web platform. Privacy policies will always be an important way of providing this information. However, it must be acknowledged that the vast majority of individuals will not read or consult these documents, so the concept of taking affirmative action to indicate consent is freely given, specific and informed is essentially redundant.

An Alternative Approach

If an individual is unhappy with how a website processes their personal data, they can (if they feel strongly enough) make the decision to stop using such website or web service. However, an alternative approach, which is pre-emptive instead of reactive, is to place more emphasis on other protections within data protection legislation, such as the right to be forgotten, the right to have data errors corrected and the right to limit the personal data which is processed.

I believe that individuals should be able to engage with a website in full knowledge that at any time they choose (and when their engagement with that website comes to an end), they can request that their personal data be corrected, limited or deleted, and they be completely forgotten. These rights would extend to any companies who had handled that individual's personal data, as a subprocessor of such website. This means that users will have assurance that their personal data will not be commoditized by that website (or any companies associated with it) now or in the future. A company's ability to commoditize the data would be significantly reduced, as at any time the individual could demand that their personal data be deleted.

By making it easy for a user to exercise their rights, individuals are empowered and their rights actually become effective. Forward-

thinking websites could take this further and offer users the ability to "freeze" their personal data on a website in a virtual private filing cabinet, which can only be accessed by that user. An individual could access the information in the virtual filing cabinet but it would be closed to other internet users.

The Way Forward

The notion of consent is a historic concept which was part of the Data Protection Act 1998. The concept was developed further in the GDPR. However, by the time the GDPR was implemented, the concept of consent (amongst other parts of the law) had, to some extent, been rendered redundant, due to the pace of technological developments. Technology is evolving at frightening speed. The time it takes to agree, pass and implement laws in a democratic society means that the law will, inevitably, be out of date in relation to the technology it seeks to regulate. However, the principles behind legislation will always be important. Practitioners and regulators can use these principles to interpret the law in a manner which enables it to adapt to the technology it seeks to regulate. The globe is becoming ever smaller due to technological advancements. As a result, the channels through which personal data ebbs and flows are becoming more complex and involved. Rather than try to explain all those channels to users (which may be incorrect or out of date from the moment they are written), let's focus on enforcing the other rights granted to web users more efficiently and effectively. If individuals can turn the use of their personal data "on and off" easily, the ability of companies to capitalize on the value of that data is significantly reduced. Furthermore, our fundamental human right to privacy is better protected.

New Privacy Laws Require Changed Operations on Commercial Websites

Charles Lombino

Attorney and Counselor, Lombino Law Studio

The Changing Landscape of Internet Data Privacy

The current frontier in internet law revolves around the right of users to the privacy of their data. In 2019, at least 45 states in the USA and Puerto Rico introduced or are considering legislation to deal with cybersecurity.[1] These new laws are affecting the way commercial enterprises do business on the web. These laws can be viewed as growing pains for the internet. The amount of legislation can also be viewed as strong consumer pushback to the way businesses are and have been handling consumer data. In a 2018 survey,[2] a huge 90% of those polled were very concerned about internet privacy.

The most significant pieces of legislation to date include the California Consumer Privacy Act of 2018 (CCPA) and Europe's General Data Protection Regulation (GDPR). Both mandate changes to the way companies conduct their internet operations. This chapter will focus on these two pieces of legislation. However, similar laws are being considered or rolled out in whole or in part by various other jurisdictions.

---

[1] See National Conference of State Legislatures Cybersecurity Legislation 2019: http://www.ncsl.org/research/telecommunications-and-information-technology/cybersecurity-legislation-2019.aspx, accessed 18 July 2019.

[2] Byer, "Internet Users Worry About Online Privacy but Feel Powerless to Do Much About It", *Entrepreneur*, 20 June 2018. See https://www.entrepreneur.com/article/314524.

Jurisprudence of Internet Data Privacy Regulation

A good way to approach internet data privacy regulation is to look at the underlying jurisprudence. The legislation creates a series of rights mostly residing in the consumer or individual. The CCPA creates several rights. The "right to know" concerns what information is being collected, whether it's being shared and with whom it is being shared. The "right to access" allows consumers to view personal data that is being processed and request its deletion and leads to issues around how malleable that data is to the consumer. The "right to say no" grants consumers the ability to formally opt out from the sale of personal information. The "right to equal service and price" grants consumers the ability to freely exercise privacy rights while still receiving equal service. The "right of deletion" concerns whether a consumer can assess their data and require personal data be deleted from a company's database. The "right of change" is a right that refers to whether a consumer can request that their data be changed and the extent to which they can request such changes. The "right of restriction of sale" addresses whether a consumer can demand that their information not be sold to another company.

The GDPR is more extensive than the CCPA and grants some additional rights. The "right of portability" allows data subjects to transfer their personal data between service providers. The "right of erasure" allows a data subject to direct a service provider to erase their personal data under certain circumstances.

To bring a website into compliance with internet data privacy laws, an understanding of the various rights granted and their implementation is needed. The ability of the consumer to exercise their rights in managing their personal data under these rights is key to an understanding of the legislation. An understanding of the procedures for regulation, which in turn concerns what data and processes are required, is also needed. Additionally, an understanding of penalties and enforcement of data rules are key for a processor to establish processes by which to conduct internet business.

The California Consumer Privacy Act of 2018

The CCPA was designed to enhance the digital privacy rights of Californians.[3] Most national business concerns will have to comply with the CCPA if they are involved in commerce in California.

Under the CCPA a consumer has the right to request and receive the categories and specific pieces of information a business has collected, along with the reasons for their collection.[4] Businesses must inform consumers at the point of collection the categories of personal information to be collected and the purposes for which it shall be used.[5] A consumer has the right to request that a business delete any personal information about the consumer that the business has collected.[6] The consumer has the right to know what personal information is being sold to third parties.[7] Third parties that receive such data are not allowed to resell it without notice to the consumer and a chance for the consumer to opt out.[8] The consumer has the right to opt out and prevent the business from selling personal data.[9] If the business has actual knowledge that the consumer is less than 16 years of age, the business may not sell the personal information without a parent's consent.[10] Businesses cannot discriminate against the consumer for the consumer exercising their rights under the CCPA, but a business may charge a different rate reflecting the value of the consumer's data.[11] Businesses that are required to comply with the

opt-out provisions of the CCPA are required to provide a clear and conspicuous link on the business' homepage, titled "Do Not Sell My Personal Information".[12]

The CCPA is applicable to any business, partnership, company, corporation or legal entity that operates for the purpose of profiting as well as collects consumer's personal information from the state of California. Additionally, a business must satisfy at least one of the following requirements:

- it has a gross annual revenue of $50 million or more;
- it annually sells personal information of at least 100,000 consumers; and
- it acquires 50% or more of its annual revenue from selling consumer information.

The CCPA is far more complex than the information presented here portrays. The scope of this chapter does not allow an in-depth review of the CCPA. Any business which is required to comply with the CCPA should consult an experienced attorney to aid in complying with the CCPA.

European Union's General Data Protection Regulation

For those doing business in Europe or processing the data of a European resident, the GDPR is even more complex. The GDPR views data protection as a fundamental right (GDPR, Article 1). And unlike the CCPA, the GDPR applies to all processors and collectors of data.[13]

The GDPR requires the consent of subjects for data processing.[14] It requires certain processors to anonymize collected data to

---

[3] See Cal. Civ. Code sections 1798.100 through 1798.199.

[4] See Cal. Civ. Code section 1798.100.

[5] See Cal. Civ. Code section 1798.100.

[6] See Cal. Civ. Code section 1798.105.

[7] See Cal. Civ. Code sections 1798.110–1798.115.

[8] See Cal. Civ. Code section 1798.115.

[9] See Cal. Civ. Code section 1798.120.

[10] See Cal. Civ. Code section 1798.120.

[11] See Cal. Civ. Code section 1798.125.

[12] See Cal. Civ. Code section 1798.135.

[13] See GDPR Art. 2, subsection 1.

[14] See GDPR Art. 6.

protect privacy.[15] It requires data breach notifications.[16] It requires safely handling the transfer of data across borders.[17] It requires that data collected be transparent as to what is collected and how it is used, and processors must establish time limits for keeping personal data.[18] The GDPR also requires that processors take every reasonable step to ensure that personal data is accurate.[19]

Articles 17 and 18 of the GDPR give data subjects more control over personal data that is processed automatically. The result is that data subjects may direct a controller to erase their personal data under certain circumstances. Articles 23, 30 and 32 require companies to implement reasonable data protection measures to protect consumers' personal data and privacy against loss or exposure. The GDPR requires notifications of data breach.[20]

Article 37 requires that certain companies appoint data protection officers. Specifically, any company that processes data revealing a subject's genetic data, health, racial or ethnic origin, religious beliefs, etc. must designate a data protection officer; these officers serve to advise companies about compliance with the regulation and act as a point of contact with the supervisory authorities. Some companies may be subjected to this aspect of the GDPR simply because they collect personal information about their employees as part of human resources processes.

The entire GDPR contains eleven chapters and 99 articles of multiple subparts. It is not within the scope of this chapter to address every provision of the GDPR.

Comparison of Two Seminal Laws

The CCPA is loosely based on the prior-enacted GDPR. However, the GDPR is more extensive. Furthermore, the California law is not just a US version of the European law. Basic to the differences is that the EU views data protection as a fundamental right, whereas the California law breaks down into a number of less extensive rights, as set forth above.

The scope of the laws is quite different. The GDPR protects individuals in the EU and outside the EU when a company sells products or services to individuals inside the EU or when EU individuals are targeted or monitored.[21] The CCPA protects consumers who are residents of California, including households and individuals.[22]

The GDPR applies both to data "controllers" and data "processors" irrespective of size and is hence very broad.[23] The CCPA applies to companies that do business in California and (1) have annual gross income of $25 million; or (2) alone or in combination, annually buy, receive for commercial purposes, sell or share for commercial purposes the personal information of 50,000 or more consumers, households or devices; or (iii) derive 50% or more of their annual revenues from selling consumers' personal information.[24]

The GDPR focuses on personal data, defined as any information relating to an identified or identifiable natural person, including publicly available data. It encourages pseudonymization of information that could be attributed to a person.[25] The CCPA

---

[15] See GDPR Art. 25.

[16] See GDPR Arts 33 and 34.

[17] See GDPR Art. 44

[18] See GDPR Art. 12.

[19] See GDPR Art. 5.

[20] GDPR Arts 33 and 34.

---

[21] GDPR Arts 2 and 3.

[22] Cal. Civ. Code section 1798.140.

[23] GDPR Art. 4.

[24] Cal. Civ. Code section 1798.140.

[25] GDPR Arts 2–4.

addresses information that relates to, or could reasonably be linked, indirectly or directly, with a consumer or household.[26]

As to the GDPR, the deletion right applies to all data concerning the data subject.[27] The CCPA deletion right applies only to data collected from the consumer. Under the GDPR, data processors must delete data in a number of specific instances, including (1) if the data is no longer necessary for the purposes collected; (2) if the data subject protests; (3) if the processing of data was subject to consent and no other legal grounds for processing exist; (4) if the data has been unlawfully processed; or (5) if the data was collected from a child.[28] Controllers don't need to erase data if it's necessary for (1) exercising the right of freedom of expression and information; (2) compliance with a legal obligation; (3) for reasons of public health and medicine; or (4) for archiving, scientific, historical research or statistical purposes.[29] Under the CCPA, consumers have a right to deletion of the personal information, and have the business direct any service providers to delete the consumer's personal information, except when it is necessary to (1) complete the transaction for which it was provided; (2) detect and prevent against malicious, deceptive, fraudulent or illegal activity; (3) exercise free speech or other rights (of the business and the consumer); (4) comply with the California Electronic Communications Privacy Act; (5) engage in public or peer-reviewed research in the public interest; or (6) comply with another legal obligation, among other instances.[30]

The GDPR requires businesses inform consumers of the rights at the point of collection.[31] The CCPA requires consumers to be informed at or before the point of collection, but only as to the categories of personal information to be collected and the purposes for which the personal information will be used, the business or commercial purpose for collecting or selling personal information, the categories of third parties with whom the business shares the personal information, and the specific pieces of personal information collected about that consumer.[32] Under the CCPA a third party may not sell personal information about a consumer unless the consumer has received explicit notice and the right to opt out.[33] Under both the GDPR and the CCPA, businesses are not required to retain personal information about a consumer.[34]

The GDPR provides that data subjects have the right to request access to the personal data.[35] A data controller which has made personal data public must take reasonable steps to inform other data processors that the data subject has requested erasure.[36] Under the CCPA, consumers have a right to request information about what personal information is collected, how it is processed, for what purposes it is processed and with whom it will be shared.[37]

The CCPA allows the consumer the right to opt out at any time from the sale of the consumer's personal information to third parties. Businesses must provide the consumer with notice of the opt-out right.[38] Under the GDPR, the data subject has the right to withdraw their consent at any time, or to object to processing at any time.[39]

---

[26] Cal. Civ. Code section 1798.140.

[27] GDPR Arts 7 and 16–18.

[28] GDPR Arts 17 and 18.

[29] GDPR Art. 17.

[30] Cal. Civ. Code section 1798.105.

[31] GDPR Art. 13.

[32] Cal. Civ. Code sections 1798.100 and 1798.110.

[33] Cal. Civ. Code section 1798.115.

[34] See, generally, GDPR Art. 14, Cal. Civ. Code sections 1798.100 and 1798.110.

[35] GDPR Art. 15.

[36] GDPR Arts 17 and 19.

[37] Cal. Civ. Code section 1798.100.

[38] Cal. Civ. Code section 1798.120.

[39] GDPR Arts 7 and 21.

The withdrawal is only effective if consent was the original grounds for using the personal information.[40]

Under the CCPA a business may not discriminate against the consumer because the consumer has exercised any of its rights under this CCPA.[41] The GDPR does not have a comparable provision.

The GDPR has a portability requirement that the CCPA lacks,[42] but under the CCPA a consumer can make a request for access to personal information which must be delivered in a readily usable format that can be easily transferred to another entity.[43]

Under the GDPR, data subjects may request that a controller restrict any type of data processing of personal data if (1) the accuracy of the data is contested; (2) the processing is unlawful; (3) the controller no longer needs the personal data; or (4) the data subject is subjected to processing pending verification of whether the controller can process on other legal grounds.[44] Under the CCPA consumers have the right to opt out of a sale of the personal information but not the collection or other uses. Businesses must provide notice of opt-out rights by providing a link that states "do not sell my personal information" on the homepage or California-specific homepage, and in any privacy policy, along with a description of opt-out rights.[45]

The GDPR requires data protection impact assessment for any processing likely to risk a data subject's rights,[46] whereas the CCPA (and the data privacy regime more generally in California) has no data protection impact assessment equivalent.

---

[40] GDPR Art. 7.

[41] Cal. Civ. Code section 1798.125.

[42] GDPR Art. 20.

[43] Cal. Civ. Code section 1798.100.

[44] GDPR Art. 18.

[45] Cal. Civ. Code section 1798.135.

[46] GDPR Art. 35.

Dealing with Tensions Between the Blockchain and the GDPR

Dr Asim Jusic
Attorney at Law, Law Office Jusic

Introduction

Regulators and stakeholders are at present debating whether – and how – the blockchain can be squared with the EU's General Data Protection Regulation (GDPR) (EU/2016/679).[1] Tensions between the blockchain and the GDPR persist because the two use different philosophies to achieve similar aims: empowering data subjects with control of their data and creating secure methods of data transfer. The GDPR primarily seeks to achieve these aims by relying on increases in the number and supervision of intermediaries, i.e. data controllers, processors and subprocessors. In contrast, relative disintermediation and decentralization are cornerstones of blockchain.

This chapter discusses the costs and benefits of using technological and legal methods for dealing with tensions between the permissionless and permissioned blockchain and smart contracts and the GDPR. It focuses on the points of tension that are most immediate in everyday practice, such as problems of identifying data controllers and processors on a blockchain, meaningful exercise of the right to erasure, liability of joint controllers, scope of the data protection impact assessment, data transfers, smart contracts and automated decision-making.

Problems of Identifying Data Controllers and Processors on the Blockchain

The GDPR rests on the interaction of two categories: data intermediaries, i.e. data controllers, processors and subprocessors – each with their own specific obligations – and data owners. Applying this categorization to the blockchain is complex. The French Data Protection Authority, for example, suggests that those writing the data on the blockchain and submitting it for validation, as well as commercial entities using the blockchain for commercial purposes, could be treated as "data controllers". Actors validating blockchain entries, however, could be treated as "data processors".[2]

This classification would be hard to implement on a fully decentralized permissionless blockchain, since, depending on the situation, one and the same entity could simultaneously be the data controller, processor and data subject. Complying with the GDPR and determining precisely who data intermediaries are is more easily done on the permissioned blockchain. Determination should not be rigid, but should be based on the nature of the relationships between actors in the blockchain. Even then the classification of data intermediaries and their corresponding obligations should be performed on a case-by-case basis.

The Right to Erasure on the Blockchain

The GDPR grants data subjects the right to erasure of data, whereas near immutability is considered to be the blockchain's

---

[1] European Parliament, "Distributed Ledger Technologies and Blockchains: Building Trust with Disintermediation", 2018: http://www.europarl.europa.eu/doceo/document/TA-8-2018-0373_EN.html; Dylan J. Yaga, Peter M. Mell, Nik Roby and Karen Scarfone, "Blockchain Technology Overview", National Institute for Standards and Technology US Department of Commerce, 2018: https://www.nist.gov/publications/blockchain-technology-overview; Commission Nationale Informatique & Libertes, "Premiers éléments d'analyse de la CNIL: Blockchain", 2018: https://www.cnil.fr/sites/default/files/atoms/files/la_blockchain.pdf; Tom Lyons, Ludovic Courcelas and Ken Timsit, "Blockchain and the GDPR", The EU European Union Blockchain Observatory Forum, 2018: https://www.eublockchainforum.eu/sites/default/files/reports/20181016_report_gdpr.pdf.

[2] Commission Nationale Informatique & Libertes, 2018, 2.

primary virtue.[3] The tension between the right to erasure and immutability is often considered as the main discrepancy between the GDPR and the blockchain, further complicated by the fact that the GDPR does not clearly define what "erasure" means.[4]

This tension is perhaps irresolvable in the case of the public permissionless blockchain, in which erasing blocks must be approved by all participants in the blockchain. Nevertheless, techniques such as chameleon hashes, private channels and pruning have been proposed as methods for dealing with this issue.[5] Furthermore, the GDPR allows flexibility in determining what constitutes an erasure of data, i.e. some legal systems consider the data erased if the mode of storage makes the actual physical deletion of data impossible.[6]

Liability of Joint Controllers on the Blockchain

If several participants collectively determine the purposes and means of data processing, GDPR Art. 26 considers these participants "joint controllers" (JCs). JCs must arrange and "clearly allocate" their responsibility towards the data subject, with **each**

joint controller being liable for the entirety of the damage towards the data subjects. The French Data Protection Authority suggests that JCs can allocate their responsibilities using two types of arrangements. First, the JCs can create a new, separate legal entity that would act as a controller. Second, the JCs could designate one of the controllers as a lead controller, which makes the data protection decisions for all JCs and acts as a contact point for data subject(s).[7]

Both arrangements noted above entail cost and legal risks. If JCs create a separate legal entity or designate one lead controller, they would be likely to need to perform a data protection impact assessment (DPIA) beforehand and implement a data protection management system.[8] Furthermore, if JCs appoint one lead controller amongst themselves, non-lead JCs should request contractual assurances that the lead controller's decisions will not harm other controllers.

The Scope of the DPIA on the Blockchain Network

It is not entirely clear whether it is necessary to perform a DPIA when using the blockchain network. Some stakeholders argue that a DPIA is always necessary; others hold that a DPIA is needed only if other processing factors raise risks of the data processing to an elevated level.[9] The former opinion seems more in line with the spirit of GDPR Art. 35, since, as an example, the blockchain containing the data on shipped cars does not pose a high risk for individuals.

[3] Asim Jusic, "Practical Guidance: Data Transfers – Gulf Region", Bloomberg Law, 2018, 2.

[4] Matthias Berberich and Malgorzata Steiner, "Blockchain Technology and the GDPR – How to Reconcile Privacy and Distributed Ledgers", *European Data Protection Law Review (EDPL)*, 2016, 2, 426.

[5] Grant Thornton, "GDPR & Blockchain", 2018: https://blockchain. grantthornton.es/en/blockchain-gdpr-2/; Finck, Michèle, "Blockchain and the General Data Protection Regulation", European Parliamentary Research Service, 2019, 34 and 35: https://www.europarl.europa.eu/ RegData/etudes/STUD/2019/634445/EPRS_STU(2019)634445_EN.pdf.

[6] Michèle Finck, "Law and Autonomous Systems Series: Blockchains and the Right to Be Forgotten", Oxford Law Faculty, 20 April 2018: https://www.law.ox.ac.uk/business-law-blog/blog/2018/04/law-and-autonomous-systems-series-blockchains-and-right-be-forgotten.

[7] Commission Nationale Informatique & Libertes, 2018, 4.

[8] Paul Voigt and Axel von dem Bussche, *The EU General Data Protection Regulation (GDPR): A Practical Guide.* 1st ed. Springer International Publishing, 2017, 36.

[9] Tamás Bereczki and Ádám Liber, "Blockchain and the GDPR: Addressing the Compliance Challenge", 2018: https://www.lexology.com/library/detail. aspx?g=571106ac-1aaf-4db9-b1a0-0152848fd040.

Conducting a DPIA for a permissionless blockchain is cumbersome and especially impractical if a large-scale public permissionless blockchain is being created. Private companies should therefore use a permissioned blockchain and conduct the DPIA in the first phases of designing the permissioned blockchain. Such a DPIA should determine the relevance of data being processed, estimate the level of risk data processing might pose to one or more individuals and specify measures for reducing or eliminating such risks.

Data Transfers

GDPR allows the transfer of data to third countries or international organizations and onward transfers only in limited circumstances: if there exists an EU adequacy decision; if mechanisms used for the data transfer provide adequate safeguards for protecting rights of data subjects; in case of "derogations"; and if relevant international agreements apply.[10]

Applying the GDPR's data transfer requirements to a permissionless blockchain consisting of a decentralized network of nodes intercommunicating for the purposes of data transfer is unrealistic. Alternatively, the data transfer can be done using the permissioned blockchain and the GDPR's mechanisms such as standard contractual clauses, binding corporate rules, codes of conduct or certification mechanisms.[11] Caution is still necessary, however: for example, the designers of a permissioned blockchain could find sectoral methods of self-regulation like codes of conduct and certifications attractive means of proving "compliance with the GDPR". Nevertheless, certifications and codes of conduct for the blockchain are as yet insufficiently developed and do not constitute full proof of compliance, but rather a partial defense against liability.[12]

Smart Contracts and Automated Decision-Making

Contemporary smart contracts are essentially coded protocols that complete the contract if the pre-agreed event(s) occurs or condition(s) is met and that without the third-party confirmation.[13] Hence, smart contracts are a form of automated decision-making (ADM), i.e. decisions made by technological means without human involvement.[14] Art. 22 of the GDPR prohibits ADM unless it is necessary for entering into or performance of a contract between the data subject and a controller, or is based on the data subject's explicit consent, or authorized by the EU or Member State law applicable to the data controller who is responsible for safeguarding the data subject's rights.[15]

This suggests that smart contracts are not per se in high tension with the GDPR. The legal effects of decisions made using smart contracts will determine the method of compliance with the GDPR. As a rule of thumb, if the smart contract is likely to pose a high risk for one or more individuals performing the DPIA before deployment of smart contracts is advisable.[16] An upstream system of control should be set in place in order to secure meaningful exercise of the right to human intervention and a right to be informed.[17]

---

[10] Jusic, 2018, 7.

[11] Sonia Daoui, Thomas Fleinert-Jensen and Marc Lempérière, "GDPR, Blockchain and the French Data Protection Authority: Many Answers but Some Remaining Questions", 2019: https://stanford-jblp.pubpub.org/pub/gdpr-blockchain-france.

[12] Voigt and Bussche, 2017, 69–79.

---

[13] Aaron Wright and Primavera de Filippi, "Decentralized Blockchain Technology and the Rise of Lex Cryptographia", 2015, 10 and 11: https://papers.ssrn.com/abstract=2580664.

[14] Article 29 Working Party, "Article 29 Working Party: Guidelines on Automated Individual Decision-Making and Profiling for the Purposes of Regulation 2016/679", 2018, 8.

[15] Finck, 2019, 83 and 84.

[16] Article 29 Working Party, 2018, 20 and 21.

[17] Commission Nationale Informatique & Libertes, 2018, 10.

Conclusion

Tensions between the blockchain and the GDPR persist because the two use different philosophies to empower data subjects with an increased control of their data and create secure methods of data transfer. Creators and users of blockchain should combine technological and legal methods to resolve these tensions. As this chapter showed, using the permissioned blockchain assists with this and makes compliance with the GDPR less burdensome. Continuous experimentation, design thinking and agility are necessary, since both the blockchain and GDPR are a work in progress.

Rise of the Legalbots: How In-House Teams and Business Lines Benefit

Christy C.L. Ng
Consultant, D2 Legal Technology LLP

In the twenty-first century, the role of a lawyer, either in-house or in private practice, has evolved and will continue to evolve. Lawyers are frequently overwhelmed by the scale and quantum of legal enquiries they receive today, which can serve to obfuscate those issues that require serious legal judgment.

This chapter explores what has changed in the industry and how the use of chatbots – and in due course legalbots – can represent an opportunity for industry participants to enhance business value and not get left behind.

What Has Changed

The world has changed, some simple facts to consider:

- **Fact A** – Financial lawyers are facing challenges keeping up with the voluminous requests precipitated by the fallout of the global financial crisis. It is frequently difficult to differentiate between the issues and prioritize which issues justify urgent focus.

- **Fact B** – Some of the tasks lawyers perform today are not an effective use of a lawyer's time, e.g. opining on the same vanilla issue multiple times – it was estimated in a US survey in 2016 that at least 22% of a lawyer's job can be automated.[1]

---

[1] McKinsey report, Is Technology About to Decimate White-Collar Work?: https://www.technologyreview.com/s/609337/is-technology-about-to-decimate-white-collar-work/

- **Fact C** – The technology now exists to dramatically enhance the legal operating model, for example artificial intelligence (AI)-powered document discovery tools have been very effective and we are all now accustomed to using technology whether through our smartphone or tablet. Chatbots and legalbots are another core tool in this technological toolkit.

- **Fact D** – This technology is being embraced by disruptors in any event, so organizations need to invest the time to consider how this new toolkit can be employed or there is a risk of being left behind.

In the near future, the lawyers who will become indispensable to business will be the ones who can effectively harness technological solutions with their legal expertise.

The Legalbot – What Is It and What Can It Do for You?

At the very basic level, it all started in the 1950s with the advent of computers and a chase to see how a computer can become intelligent and replace humans.

Alan Turing developed an approach to determine whether a computer was intelligent and, though rudimentary, has been widely employed as a yardstick of progress.

The test is a type of imitation game and requires individuals (the judge) to interface with a computer and ask questions, and yet behind the computer screen will be a combination of humans and chatbots. Can the chatbot trick the judge into thinking that it is a real human?

Even today it is doubtful that there are many examples of chatbots successfully passing the test, but what we can see is massive technological advancement in the world of chatbots.

The chatbot itself particularly gained notoriety in the 1990s and was a computer software program with a user-friendly interface that conversed with users and assisted them to perform tasks of varying complexity – no real attempt at this stage to pass off for humans but rather to provide technological assistance. These have, through their evolution since the late 1990s, been adopted at a steady pace by financial institutions and businesses to deal with high volumes of general customer enquiries. The earliest versions of chatbot were only programmed to provide predefined answers to exact questions. The legal industry embraced the notion and "chatbots" became "legalbots" when addressing the challenges of the legal industry.

The evolution can be seen on two levels: (1) optimization of workflow and (2) extension to AI and machine learning.

1. Optimization of workflow

The science around developing an efficient operating model for a legal function, or indeed any other function, is predicated on an understanding of the activities that need to be performed by that function. Similarly, an analysis will include the complexity and frequency of the performance of those functions. A legalbot is a tool at its most simple that can facilitate a differentiated workflow for mass frequency simple tasks and the less frequent more complex matters. Legalbots have therefore been used as effective workflow filters with decision trees and escalation profiles.

Effective ticketing systems are typically available with legalbots where users can log their issue, being allocated a case reference number which is recorded along with the user's question. From there, system administrators can sift through the questions and allocate each question accordingly to the appropriate lawyer. This ensures that there is an orderly process to answering other departments' questions and that the questions will be allocated to the legal personnel with the most relevant expertise to answer them.

It is therefore commonplace to develop some form of bot at the very least to answer regular questions in a consistent, efficient and auditable manner. However, the potential is far greater.

2. Extension to AI and machine learning

On a technical level, chatbots have evolved to act as a neural network based on deep learning from data, with increased accuracy using natural language processing (NLP) and algorithms that evaluate the context of the user question to provide more targeted answers to stakeholders. This is achieved through the development of a comprehensive cloud or local data centre knowledge repository that is maintained and developed.

So, in practical terms, the bot will improve through usage and analysis and will through a combination of human intervention and AI become more accomplished at addressing the concerns of a legal function. This is where we are beginning to approach the Turing hypothesis.

In fact, it is possible for the bot to pull up targeted sections of text in legal documents and webpages. Bots can also provide alternative options if the answer is not satisfactory to the user, such as referring the user to the personnel best placed to answer the question (this might be based on expertise/knowledge, or workload and capacity to assist), or giving the user options to explore other topics related to the original question.

As an intelligent chat service, legalbots will be able to assist with the provision of legal advice once the knowledge content (and its ability to connect this to the relevant presented fact patterns – based on the use of business ontologies and taxonomies) is connected to the legalbot's repository. The legalbot will be trained on the questions it is likely to encounter and the correct customer journeys to lead the users to the appropriate resolution of their questions. With NLP and AI learning capability, the legalbot will be able to ensure that high volumes of lower-importance queries are dealt with by an automating advice for commonly asked questions about standard documents, therefore affording lawyers more time to focus on strategic priorities.

Bots are continuing to evolve and whilst starting with a relatively simple, predefined Q&A set, they are constantly leveraging learning capability to enhance their offering in a way no standard list of Q&As could ever perform.

Conclusion: Legalbots – An Opportunity or a Threat?

It is abundantly clear that legal functions are suffering under the weight of expectations of stakeholders, including regulators and clients, and irrespective of any scepticism of AI and machine learning, an effective legalbot can optimize workflow.

However, once an organization has embraced a legalbot and then opened its mind to leveraging new technology, the process should become more efficient and insightful and that can take legal functions to a different level.

Naturally, this represents an opportunity but if ignored can become a threat as not only disruptive but also mainstream organizations begin to reap the benefits. They offer a great channel through which to unlock business value through legal technology and innovation.

AI Is Changing Boardroom Dynamics

Dr Leyanda Purchase
National Programme Director – Academic Master's in Law,
The University of Law

Artificial intelligence (AI) in its simplest form is nothing new to those with smartphones who embrace the likes of Siri, Cortana and Google Assist. However, the use of AI in boardrooms is starting to have an impact on the way boards operate, how they reach decisions and, in some instances, has a direct impact on board composition. In its simplest form, directors, and in particular non-executive directors, are increasingly turning to social media platforms to conduct pre-meetings[1] – away from the potentially corruptible company email and towards more secure communication platforms. We have already seen the use of board portals replacing the creation of board packs across all sectors. Such software enables a level of automation when it comes to the collation and dissemination of board papers.[2] The next step, which is well on the way to becoming a reality, is more automation of the data within the portal.[3]

More advanced forms of machine learning solutions are also being used by boards for tasks such as minute taking and instant language translation.[4] Whilst instant language translation could have a real impact for global firms where language barriers have the potential to cause delays and miscommunication, it is the use of AI for minute taking that is potentially game changing.[5] Whilst the software might not be perfect, the very nature of machine learning means that it will get better the more it tunes into the rhythm of the company.[6] At the moment, the technology is limited to providing a record of what was said verbally by way of recording and transcription. Of course, words alone do not always paint the full picture of what happened at a meeting and individuals may change the way they contribute if full verbatims are the new norm in minute taking. That aside, use of this technology could pave the way for company secretaries to be more engaged with the substance of the meeting, thereby enabling them to better engage with governance monitoring and acting as a trusted advisor to the board during the meeting itself.[7]

AI is also being explored in relation to board member communications such as the use of audio, and visual communications platforms such as Skype and the use of facial recognition and virtual reality (VR) software. Holding board meetings by Skype would have been unheard of when the technology first existed, but it is now presented as a viable alternative when it is either impossible or impracticable for all board members to be

---

[1] Examples include Yammer and Trello. See D. Venus, "Futureproofing: Technological Innovation, the Company Secretary and Implications for Corporate Governance", ICSA Publishing, 2018.

[2] See, for example, Diligent Boards: https://diligent.com/en-gb/company-secretary-software/ (last accessed 30/08/2019) and Praxonomy: https://www.praxonomy.com (last accessed 30/08/2019).

[3] For example, Diligent already provides board evaluation software, which assesses whether companies are following governance best practice. Available at: https://diligent.com/en-gb/board-evaluation-tool/ (last accessed 30/08/2019).

[4] At the start of 2019, Google launched its "interpreter mode", which enables users to be able to hear and see the translated conversation in real time. See D. Seifert, "Google Assistant's Interpreter Mode is Now Available", *The Verge*, 5 February 2019. Available at: https://www.theverge.com/2019/2/5/18212383/google-assistant-interpreter-mode-available-roll-out-home-smart-speaker-smart-display (last accessed 30/08/2019).

[5] See, for example, Otter: https://otter.ai/ (last accessed 30/08/2019).

[6] Otter is powered by Ambient Voice Intelligence, meaning it can be trained to recognize voices and learn specialized terminology.

[7] See, for example, H. Matthews, Tom Morrison Essay Prize Second Place Essay, 2019. Available at: https://www.icsa.org.uk/assets/files/marketing/essays/tmep2019runnerupessay.pdf (last accessed 30/08/2019).

physically present in the same space.[8] In the future, VR technology could become the new norm, simulating physical attendance in a virtual space. Of course, VR technology is already being used as a tool by some boards to take virtual tours of key sites or play the role of corporate stakeholders in a bid to make better decisions.[9]

Whilst the above provide some interesting developments in the way boards operate as a result of emerging technology, they are not the biggest driving force behind the current changing dynamics. The biggest changes come as a result of directorial appointments and decision-making. We have already seen companies sit up and take notice of the tech agenda by appointing known tech leaders to boards of non-tech companies.[10] Some companies have gone further by appointing "AI entities" as directors themselves.[11] In 2014, the algorithm known as "Vital"

was appointed to the board of Deep Knowledge Ventures, a Hong Kong venture capitalist fund.[12] Managing partner Dmitry Kaminskiy credits Vital with having saved the firm from going under as without it they would have invested in "overhyped projects".[13] The use of AI directors is currently limited, but it is easy to see the potential attraction for shareholders who could appoint an "AI entity" programmed to safeguard their interests, thereby partially negating the effects of the agency conflict.[14]

Another way AI is impacting the selection of directors is through the use of algorithms to determine who is best suited to the board. The research on this area has demonstrated that algorithms are better placed to determine director suitability than the company's existing directors and that AI simultaneously increases diversity at board level.[15] Despite advances in board level diversification, the research "confirm[s] an observation that dates back over two hundred years: the board selection process leads to directors who often are not the best choices to serve shareholder interests."[16] Naturally, the algorithm is only as good as the data that it is given to work with and so could inherit directors' biases.[17]

Rather than appoint AI entities to the board, many more companies have taken a more conservative approach to machine learning decision-making and are using algorithms to analyse data to

---

[8] Virtual board meetings are not new but how they are conducted and the frequency of use are both changing. In July 2016, Jimmy Choo PLC held the first electronic AGM. For an analysis see Ashfords, "Are Virtual Meetings the Way Forward", 29 November 2017. Available at: https://www.ashfords.co.uk/news-and-media/general/are-virtual-meetings-the-way-forward (last accessed 30/08/2019).

[9] For an explanation see B. Ashwell, "How Virtual Reality Can be Used in the Boardroom", *Corporate Secretary*, 22 August 2017. Available at: https://www.corporatesecretary.com/articles/technology-social-media/30832/how-virtual-reality-can-be-used-boardroom (last accessed 30/08/2019) and D. Lancefield and C. Gagliardi, "Reimagining the Boardroom for an Age of Virtual Reality and AI", *Harvard Business Review*, 3 April 2015. Available at:https://hbr.org/2015/04/reimagining-the-boardroom-for-an-age-of-virtual-reality-and-ai (last accessed 30/08/2019).

[10] See K. Kark, C. Brown and J. Lewris, "Bridging the Boardroom's Technology Gap", Deloitte Insights Article, 29 June 2017. Available at: https://www2.deloitte.com/us/en/insights/focus/cio-insider-business-insights/bridging-boardroom-technology-gap.html (last accessed 30/08/2019).

[11] For more on this see W. Pugh, "Why not Appoint an Algorithm to Your Corporate Board?", *Slate*, 24 March 2019. Available at: https://slate.com/technology/2019/03/artificial-intelligence-corporate-board-algorithm.html (last accessed 30/08/2019). AI entities are known as decentralized autonomous organizations.

[12] See, for example, BBC, "Algorithm Appointed Board Director", 16 May 2014. Available at: https://www.bbc.co.uk/news/technology-27426942 (last accessed 30/08/2019).

[13] See N. Burridge, "Artificial Intelligence Gets a Seat in the Boardroom", *Nikkei Asian Review*, 10 May 2017. Available at: https://asia.nikkei.com/Business/Artificial-intelligence-gets-a-seat-in-the-boardroom (last accessed 30/08/2019).

[14] For a classic study, see A. Shleifer and R. Vishny, "A Survey of Corporate Governance", *Journal of Finance*, 1997, 52, pp. 737.

[15] I. Erel et al., "Selecting Directors Using Machine Learning", SSRN Electronic Journal, 2018, 10.2139/ssrn.3144080.

[16] Ibid, page 28.

[17] Ibid, page 27.

better inform them when they come to make their own decisions.[18] Understanding this tech and how it impacts decision-making is vital for boards as shareholders are also embracing AI in order to determine where to invest. The fastest-growing use of this form of machine learning is in relation to environmental, social and governance (ESG) performance data.[19] For example, Ecofi Investissements, Ossiam and Nordea Asset Management are all actively using machine learning to analyse ESG data to determine future investments.[20]

The use of AI in boardrooms at present is very sporadic and consequently the extent to which boards are being changed by

AI can only be answered on an individual basis. What is clear, however, is that AI is starting to change the way boards operate, make decisions and is changing board composition for the better. These changes will only increase over time as these algorithms become more widely available and applications such as minute taking and translation tech become more accurate. What seems too far away at present is any real inroad into the use of RegTech to assist with corporate governance and risk management. While there is certainly potential to incorporate some of these tools at present, there are accessibility, cost, third-party risks, potential bias and the potential for misuse.[21]

---

[18] A. Agrawal et al., "Exploring the Impact of Artificial Intelligence: Prediction versus Judgment", Working Paper, 2016. Available at: https://www.aeaweb.org/conference/2017/preliminary/1426?page=2&per-page=50 (last accessed 30/08/2019).

[19] See, for example, Morningstar, "How AI Can Help Find ESG Opportunities", 4 July 2019: http://www.morningstar.co.uk/uk/news/193882/how-ai-can-help-find-esg-opportunities.aspx (last accessed 20/09/2019).

[20] See Introduction to ESG at Nordea: https://www.nordea.com/en/sustainability/sustainable-finance/news/2015/06-02-2015-introduction-to-esg-at-nordea.html (last accessed /09/2019).

---

[21] See N. Packlin, "Is RegTech the Answer to Corporate Governance and Risk Management Issues?", *Forbes*, 8 February 2019. Available at: https://www.forbes.com/sites/nizangpackin/2019/02/08/is-regtech-the-answer-to-corporate-governance-and-risk-management-issues/ (last accessed 20/09/2019).

Cloud Computing Contracts

Dr Sam De Silva
Partner, CMS Cameron McKenna Nabarro Olswang LLP

Similar to cloud computing models, cloud computing contracts appear in a wide variety of forms. These can range from simple standardized click-wrap agreements to framework and multilayered sets of terms and conditions. However, there is a set of core contractual issues that customers should consider in any cloud computing contract as part of a procurement exercise.

The purpose of this chapter is to assist customers to navigate through the typical contractual issues in cloud computing contracts. Some of these issues should be familiar to those who deal regularly with information technology contracts. However, even with respect to those issues, the nature of cloud computing can create new or different risks and customers may need to consider those issues afresh in the cloud computing context.

Data protection issues are also relevant for cloud computing. However, given the complexity of the subject matter and the coverage which would be required to explain the issues, a detailed examination of data protection is beyond the scope of this chapter.

In this chapter the cloud service providers that are providing the cloud services are referred to as service providers and the organization that is procuring the cloud computing services from the cloud provider is referred to as the customer.

The following sets out a brief summary of the key contractual issues that can arise in contracts with service providers for cloud computing services. Most of these issues are ultimately business ones, requiring business decisions, but they are "legal" in the sense that they either are embedded in the contract (typically in a way that favours the service provider) or should be dealt with in the contract (to ensure that the service provider's actions are appropriately constrained and that the service provider is accountable for its actions).

The customer should check that all of the following issues are covered in a cloud computing contract or the customer's internal governance policies (or at least considered and dismissed). It may be appropriate to accept greater risks for the service or cost benefits.

Issue	Comments
Automatic renewal	Is there a provision where the contract renews automatically for an additional period of time unless the customer gives prior written notice?
	The customer should have an internal process to remind itself when it needs to make a decision about renewal and give notice of any termination. Ideally, the contract would renew automatically (so the customer does not have to renegotiate every time), but also allow termination for convenience on some reasonably short period of notice.
Responsibility for end users	Is there a provision where the contract requires the customer to "ensure" that any end users (i.e. its employees, etc.) comply with the service provider's acceptable use policy (AUP), terms of service (ToS) or similar provisions, or (better from the customer's perspective, though still problematic) to use "best efforts" or "commercially reasonable" efforts to do so?

Issue	Comments
	This approach may be appropriate in relation to employees for whom the customer is vicariously liable, but the more preferable approach is to provide that the customer will "inform" its end users, for whom the customer is not vicariously liable and over whom the customer has minimal control, of their obligation to do so.[1]
	An alternative would be to provide that the service provider may require end users to agree directly with the service provider to comply with any such provisions.
Unauthorized or inappropriate use	Does the contract attempt to make the customer responsible for affirmatively preventing any "unauthorized" or "inappropriate" use of the service provider's service by others, or perhaps to use "best efforts" or "commercially reasonable efforts" to do so? Given that these services are "in the cloud" and therefore largely outside the customer's control, it may be better to provide only that the customer will not "authorize" or "knowingly allow" such uses.
	The contract also may require the customer to notify the service provider of "all" unauthorized or inappropriate uses of which the customer becomes aware. In relation to service providers with broadly stated AUPs or ToS, such expansive obligations could be burdensome and unnecessary. An option to consider is to replace "all" with "material" or some similar, higher threshold.
Suspension of end-user accounts	Does the contract permit the service provider to retain the right to suspend the customer's end users for breaches of the service provider's AUP or ToS? If so, such provisions are broadly drafted so the service provider will have an almost open-ended authority to suspend the customer's users. An option to consider is to limit any such rights to a more restrictive standard, perhaps only "material" breaches, or breaches that "significantly" threaten the security or integrity of the service provider's system.
Emergency security issues	Is there a provision which allows the service provider to have the right to "immediately" suspend an "offending use" and possibly the service altogether, in the event of an "emergency" issue? If so, the standard for what constitutes an emergency should: • be clearly defined; • not give the service provider much, if any, discretion or flexibility in its application; and • incorporate a "materiality" or similar threshold.

[1] Vicarious liability is a common law principle of strict, no-fault liability for wrongs committed by another person, in effect a form of secondary liability. Vicarious liability most often occurs in employment relationships but it may also arise in other areas, including partnerships. In an employment relationship, it involves an employer being liable for the wrongs committed by an employee where there is a sufficient connection between those wrongs and the employee's employment such that it would be fair to hold the employer to be vicariously liable. It does not matter that the employer itself has committed no wrong.

Issue	Comments
Suspension and termination of service	Does the contract give the service provider the right to suspend the service or to terminate it altogether upon certain events or conditions? Such provisions are not unreasonable in the abstract, but they should:
	• be limited in scope to only truly significant matters;
	• provide for an opportunity for the customer to remedy the alleged breach or some form of escalation rather than instantaneous implementation (except in the case of true emergencies); and
	• give the customer adequate time to make alternative arrangements for its data or service.
	The customer should also have assurance that the data will continue to be available in a usable format, for at least a specified period post-termination (or, if the service provider is unwilling to commit to a specific length, a "commercially reasonable" period of time), as well as that the service provider will return or destroy any copies of the customer's data once disengagement is complete.
Ownership of data	The contract should expressly make it clear that all data belongs to the customer (and/or its users) and that the service provider acquires no rights or licences to such data. It also may be useful to provide that the service provider does not acquire and may not claim any security interest in the customer's data.
Publicity	Does the contract allow the service provider the right to use customer's names, logos and trademarks for purposes of the service provider's own publicity? If such provisions (which are of generally no benefit to the customer) cannot be removed in their entirety, they should be modified to require prior review and approval (perhaps "which may not unreasonably be withheld"), or at least limit use to the inclusion of the customer's names (but not logos or trademarks) on a customer list, in a manner that does not state or imply an endorsement.
Service level agreements	The amount of guaranteed "uptime", the process and timeline for dealing with "downtime" and the consequences for any failures to meet those requirements should be set out clearly.
Disclaimer of warranty	Does the contract disclaim essentially all warranties except for any warranty that the service provider's service does not infringe third-party intellectual property rights? At a minimum, the contract should warrant that the service complies with and will perform in accordance with its specifications (which should themselves be as detailed as possible, to avoid misunderstandings and disagreements) and that it does not infringe any third-party intellectual property rights.
	Without these two warranties, there is minimal assurance for a customer that the service will in fact do what the service provider's marketing people claim it will do or that the service provider even has the right to provide the services to the customer.
Indemnification by customer	Is the customer required to indemnify the service provider not only for its own actions (which is not necessarily unreasonable), but also those of its end users, including users for whom the customer may not otherwise be vicariously liable? It is preferable not to voluntarily accept that liability. If the indemnity is accepted by the customer then the scope of such indemnity needs to be considered carefully – for example, is it an unlimited indemnity?

Issue	Comments
Indemnification by service provider	The contract is not likely to include any form of indemnification benefiting customers. However, such protection is important in at least two key areas:
	• infringement of third-party intellectual property rights; and
	• inappropriate disclosure or data breach, both of which are largely, if not entirely, in the service provider's sole control, and both of which can be extremely costly to defend and remedy.
	If a service provider refuses to accept liability for either of these issues, the customer needs to view this as a warning about the service provider's lack of confidence in its own service. Effectively what the service provider is really saying is that it expects the customer to accept the risk of these liabilities.
Modifications to the contract	Does the service provider have the right to make modifications to its services unilaterally? While some form of right to make changes probably is necessary and appropriate (such as improvements), such an approach is risky from a customer perspective and does not provide the customer with any assurance that any such modifications will be beneficial, let alone acceptable. Limiting the service provider's right to "commercially reasonable modifications" would be better. Even better would be to add to that a qualification prohibiting "materially detrimental" modifications, perhaps something to the effect of "Service provider may make commercially reasonable modifications to the Service, provided that they do not materially diminish the nature, scope, or quality of the Service."
Incorporation into the contract of other documents via website links	Does the contract incorporate by reference additional terms and policies posted to the service provider's website? If so, such additional terms and policies are likely to be subject to the service provider's unilateral amendment, and those terms and policies may in turn incorporate by reference other terms and policies posted elsewhere on the service provider's websites, which also typically are subject to the service provider's unilateral amendment. The result is that the contract itself is incomplete; it may well contain provisions that are inconsistent or that conflict with the incorporated provisions, and it likely will be difficult or impossible to fully comprehend. It will also potentially be meaningless, because the service provider will have the right to amend it significantly at any time, and likely even without any more notice to us than posting the change to its website.
	While it may be reasonable to deal with technical standards and guidelines or other "non-legal" matters elsewhere, it is strongly preferable that all contractual terms be included in the contract itself. At the very least, the customer should attempt to require the service provider to provide direct, individual notice sufficiently in advance of the effective date of any amendments to incorporated terms, along with the right to terminate if such amendments are unacceptable or materially detrimental to the customer's interests.
Data protection/privacy	Some of the data will constitute "personal data" for the purposes of data protection legislation and the service provider will be a "data processor" for the purposes of such legislation. Given that the customer will be the data controller it will need to ensure that it complies with the data protection legislation, including imposing the appropriate contractual provisions in the contract with the service provider.

Issue	Comments
Data security	The service provider is likely to promise to provide only "reasonable" security for the customer's data, or perhaps to adhere to "industry standard" security practices. Whilst such promises sound good in the abstract, they are open to considerable debate. It is preferable to specify an actual, specific, independent security standard and require that it be updated, and perhaps audited, regularly.
	The contract should require the service provider to give the customer notice of any security/data breaches, and, to the extent that user notification is legally required, such notice should preferably be in advance of user notification (which should be the service provider's responsibility).
Location of data	Some contracts expressly reserve the right to store customer data in any country in which they do business. Others may not address the issue, but the service providers may follow similar practices nevertheless, on the (generally legitimate) theory that what is not expressly prohibited is thereby permitted. The data protection implications of any personal data transferred outside the European Economic Area need to be considered.
Access for data for e-Discovery or regulatory purposes	Although the contract probably will not (and probably need not) expressly address the issue, it is important to understand (ahead of time) the architecture of the service provider's system, how and in what format it keeps the customer's data and what tools are available to the customer to access its data so that it will be ready for any e-Discovery needs that may arise.
Governing law and jurisdiction	The contract is most likely to specify that it is governed by the law of the service provider's home state and grant the courts of that state exclusive jurisdiction over any disputes arising out of the contract.
	Better options for the customer to consider include:
	• specify the law and jurisdiction of the customer's own jurisdiction (large service providers likely operate in and are subject to all such jurisdictions, so it is no significant inconvenience for them);
	• provide that disputes must be brought in the defendant's jurisdiction (which is even-handed and tends to encourage informal resolution, as the claimant won't have the "home court" advantage); or
	• delete the provision and leave the question open for later argument and resolution if and when needed.

Technology vs Law

3

EMPOWERING THE LEGAL FUNCTION

... define what good looks like, by advising on what new productivity, agility and service improvements can be driven successfully from digital transformation.

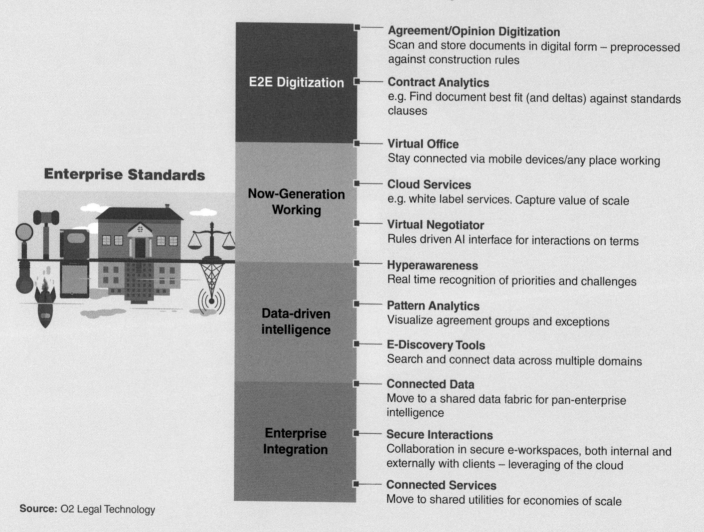

Enterprise Standards

E2E Digitization

Now-Generation Working

Data-driven intelligence

Enterprise Integration

Agreement/Opinion Digitization
Scan and store documents in digital form – preprocessed against construction rules

Contract Analytics
e.g. Find document best fit (and deltas) against standards clauses

Virtual Office
Stay connected via mobile devices/any place working

Cloud Services
e.g. white label services. Capture value of scale

Virtual Negotiator
Rules driven AI interface for interactions on terms

Hyperawareness
Real time recognition of priorities and challenges

Pattern Analytics
Visualize agreement groups and exceptions

E-Discovery Tools
Search and connect data across multiple domains

Connected Data
Move to a shared data fabric for pan-enterprise intelligence

Secure Interactions
Collaboration in secure e-workspaces, both internal and externally with clients – leveraging of the cloud

Connected Services
Move to shared utilities for economies of scale

Source: O2 Legal Technology

Executive Summary

Technology presents an opportunity to digitize the law, bringing home the benefits of efficiency gains and allowing us to embrace an increasingly popular agile workforce within the legal services industry. More importantly, it should allow us to support clients and unlock business value from new ways of approaching and solving business problems.

But are we looking at innovation through LegalTech, or is this, in the words of Clayton Christensen, "disruptive innovation"? Are we competing with market incumbents and the current status quo in the legal profession, or appealing to a new latent market, gaining revenue and new product offerings we could not even imagine before?

FinTech has dramatically changed clients' perception of payments by reducing transactional fees for moving money by 90% over the last decade. Can LegalTech ultimately deliver the same economic benefits and even unlock unrealized business opportunities?

With both innovation and disruption come challenges to the current frameworks we have in place. In the context of the law, these help us to manage and allocate liability in a way where the law helps society and commerce to flourish, balancing competing interests and promoting stability as well as social and economic considerations such as the creation of jobs and competition.

Reflecting changes in financial services regulation, would the competition authorities become increasingly concerned with current self-regulation and anti-competitive market behaviour, or would the better economics of alternative legal services make inroads into a historically closed profession?

This part considers all these factors, including looking at the very question of how we ought to regulate in the face of technology, encouraging innovation but without stifling the "fail-fast" attitude and rapid feedback loops it often needs to truly succeed and advance. In today's complex social and business environment, where change is the true constant, speed of execution is a lot more important than perfect execution – but does this work for something as fundamentally important as the law? This is the profession where mistakes are rarely tolerated.

Still, the "complexity of law" remains an open research and discussion area – is this simply an area too complex for automation? Therefore, beneficial margins and economies of scale generated by improved underlying technologies may not be passed to the end customers. Or have we simply failed thus far to create the standards and approaches needed to enable technology enablers that now exist and are used in everyday life.

It is over two decades since Sir Richard Susskind's "The End of Lawyers?", but if we are able to put the correct enabling frameworks in place, is this rather in fact their true rise and true beginning?

LegalTech in Our Daily Lives

D. Ann Brooks
President, Ann Brooks Law P.C.

I am one of those lawyers who starts presentations with a lawyer joke. Maybe this is gimmicky, but it goes to this: people loathe lawyers. So, with the advancement of LegalTech, should lawyer haters rejoice in the possibility of a lawyer extinction, or should we consider humanity's need to have people weigh the grey areas, to persuade, to make a case? If the uptake of LegalTech is inevitable, can it help lawyers be better?

Now, a disclaimer and words of caution – this discussion is for general information purposes only and is not intended to be and should not be taken as legal advice. You should contact your lawyer to obtain advice with respect to any particular issue or problem.

Let's examine some hypothetical situations (relating to employment, contract and then mergers and acquisitions) and how LegalTech solutions and a human lawyer might each evaluate the cases:

- **The employment case**: It is Friday afternoon, and the HR manager Rachel is upset because John, an employee working on new product development, secretly recorded a conversation with his manager Sally several months ago and is now using the recording as proof that Sally has denied his time-off request out of spite. Rachel and Sally want to fire John. By law, it's illegal to record conversations without consent, and the employee handbook clearly states that breaking the law is something that is a cause for dismissal.

There is software that can help companies recruit, onboard and assess people performance. These are functions that form the staple of business – human resources, sales and finance –

and we are seeing more and more software solutions that can automate tasks and analyse data for trends or expected performance and/or outcomes. Being data driven, we often view this as objective.

In a LegalTech-empowered HR solutions world, the Sally/John situation would be viewed as clear-cut. The algorithm walks HR through a decision tree of questions to arrive at what the law would say. Heck, it can even walk Sally through questions to advise her on what she could do, so HR can be eliminated. The question/answer steps would centre on the following facts:

- John reports to Sally
- John recorded a conversation without consent
- John put in a time-off request that was denied
- There is evidence (through the recording) that the time-off request was denied out of spite
- It is illegal to record conversations without the consent of the person being recorded
- The employee handbook states that breaking the law is a cause for dismissal

"Sally wins", and "the company wins" – because it didn't have to consult an expensive lawyer to arrive at this answer. Goodbye John.

But is that right? What might a flesh and blood lawyer ask? How about:

- What are the relevant company policies?
- Why did John feel like he needed to record his conversations?
- Was the company on notice about any sort of discrimination or other facts relating to the treatment of John (including by Sally) that might expose it to risk?

- What was on the recording?

- What is John's performance like?

- What impact would John's departure have on company innovation?

- If John is a regrettable loss, could he work for a competitor, and with what consequences?

- Finally: could he sue the company?

These questions are a great segue into what it is that makes a great lawyer. Is it simply understanding law? If anyone can pull up sample contracts and summaries of discrete points of law on the internet, an encyclopaedic mind regarding the law cannot be what makes a great lawyer. Is it cunningness; the ability to find loopholes; or a gift of the gab? A great lawyer is one who "adds value" – but what is value in the legal sense? Value may not just be about box-ticking of compliance checklists, being adversarial and a single-dimensional view of good and bad outcomes. Can expert-based systems or artificial intelligence (AI)-driven engines ever apply broader "judgment" and "wisdom" in the sense that we know it as humans?

- **The contractual breach case**: 123 has a long-standing relationship with ABC. Over the years, the contract has been liberally interpreted. ABC wasn't notified about the security breach because 123 caught the employee trying to sell the data – no harm, no foul, even if "technically" notice was required. But now, ABC has retained a startup that can upload the contract terms into a program and scan 123's emails for compliance with contract requirements.

Historically, document review was done by the entry-level lawyer, who sorted through dusty boxes full of musty documents, but now software can do this. Natural language processing (NLP) tools can scan hundreds of documents and flag relevant clauses. Applying such software to review agreements is far cheaper than having a

junior associate or in-house lawyer read thousands of pages of documents. And the tool just never gets bored or tired when asked to "burn the midnight oil". We can ensure compliance through such automated audits.

But our fact pattern describes a compliance audit – there is no dispute (yet). Let us assume this becomes a matter of litigation and one now needs to review a large number of documents as part of the document disclosure obligations. Software could be (and is today routinely) used as part of this exercise, not only as part of the e-Discovery process, but also assist with ensuring any privileged documents and emails are not inadvertently disclosed.

The technology is an enabler. Lawyers will still likely be required in the process of developing the tools, but they can now focus on activities that only lawyers can provide – the lawyering that distinguishes the good from the so-so. In our fact pattern, once ABC realizes that there was a breach that went unreported, 123 will want to meet with its lawyer to discuss options and what approach would work best – whether it is the risk appetite, the budget, the internal politics at 123 or many other "human elements".

- **The deal case**: The sales and purchase agreement is finally signed, but now the seller has gone off the deep end. Your client needs this deal salvaged.

Mergers and acquisitions are one area where lawyers cost a tremendous amount of money – but the stakes are high! Document review in a data room and drafting documents take time, and if the deal is complicated, specialist lawyers must be brought in. All of this increases legal costs.

Data rooms are one potential area of automation – a program could organize documents and scan them for relevance, materiality or red flags. If it could further churn out bespoke documents based on what it starts to see in the data room, even first drafts, can we reduce the legal costs involved?

But imagine now that the deal is in jeopardy because the seller has started to explore exit avenues other than the acquiring client. The indispensable lawyers in such cases now provide a different service – not just being an expert in the law but in (commercial!) counselling – listening and supporting the client's no doubt rollercoaster of emotions. LegalTech is not yet capable of providing such interaction, the ability which the client best needs and values.

Conclusion

As with other industries, the legal practice will become more automated, which frees up the lawyer to pursue higher-level tasks – analysis, advising, problem solving. It is those abilities that are valuable and distinguish the trusted advisors who are also licensed to practice law from lawyers who cannot provide such qualities and, at least for now, from enabling technologies, such as expert-based systems, NLP, AI and/or machine learning.

The Evolution of the Legal Marketplace

Ivy Wong

Product Manager, HighQ, a Thomson Reuters Company

Since the 2008 financial crisis, in-house legal teams have faced a "more-for-less" challenge: tightening legal budgets while having to solve more complicated legal issues. They are constantly searching for value for money and are no longer prepared to accept the traditional law firms' billable hours model.

At the same time, more and more lawyers are embracing remote working. These are often highly skilled workers that have left BigLaw for lifestyle reasons and wish to work flexibly and on their own terms.

As for the interaction between buyers and sellers of legal services, the industry has remained focused on traditional channels such as referrals or face-to-face networking. This contrasts with other industries such as retail, travel and hospitality, which have adopted increasingly advanced online marketplace models to deliver services with expanded reach, speed, convenience and efficiency.

These simultaneous developments have created the perfect conditions for the development of sophisticated online marketplaces within the legal services industry. This chapter will look at how far the model has developed in this industry and its future evolution.

The Evolution of the Legal Marketplace

Over the first few decades of the internet, marketplaces such as eBay, Airbnb and Uber have successfully reinvented their markets and revolutionized the way we do business. Their business models use technology to "connect people, organizations, and resources in an interactive ecosystem in which amazing amounts of value can be created and exchanged".[1] While this success has largely been restricted to marketplaces for goods, the marketplace business is set to reinvent the service economy, including the legal industry. This chapter will map the evolution of the legal marketplace model in three stages.

Stage One: The Marketplace

Many existing legal marketplaces have created efficiencies by simply matching buyers of legal services with sellers, i.e. lawyers. Matches are made based on a number of key attributes such as practice area, budget and jurisdiction. The marketplace then enables the exchange of information to help buyers evaluate, compare and instruct.

This is the marketplace as a lead generator: once a match is made, lawyers and clients communicate directly, and work is delivered off-platform. While this model works well for the most straightforward and simple advice, e.g. the drafting of a non-disclosure agreement or an employee handbook, it is less effective for more complex or higher-value transactions. The reasons for this include:

- the costs of hiring the wrong lawyer can be high – in high-stakes legal matters, clients naturally default to existing relationships or referrals, because lawyers are not interchangeable and there are serious trust barriers to be overcome. Issues with the work may not be immediately apparent, and may take many years to manifest themselves; and

- the quality of legal advice is subjective, making it difficult to judge success – the best lawyers are able to provide practical, commercial advice and put a client at ease, qualities that are hard to quantify in a simple marketplace.

---

[1] Geoffrey G. Parker, Marshall W. Van Alstyne and Sangeet Paul Choudary, *Platform Revolution: How Networked Markets Are Transforming the Economy – and How to Make Them Work for You*, (2016), W.W. Norton & Company, p. 3.

Stage Two: The Managed Platform

Some legal marketplaces have started maturing from interaction facilitators to managed platforms, providing more value-creating activities for clients and lawyers and enabling the delivery of complex, high-value legal advice. There are multiple ways to achieve this transition, including:

1. Greater transparency – enhanced matching and ratings

Trust and risk management are now table stakes in most marketplaces. In this next stage, clients make purchasing decisions based not simply on a lawyer's legal fees and reviews, but on a broader set of criteria designed to help them understand, on a deeper level, whether a lawyer is suitable for the job. Simple five-star ratings give way to nuanced metrics such as personality type, risk aversion and communication style.

Active curation means that clients can rely on the platform to vet lawyer quality and continually improve the service. Lawyers with below-standard ratings are filtered out, so clients can trust that they will consistently receive a high level of service.

On the other side of the marketplace, lawyers can build and develop their professional reputation on the platform, effectively differentiating themselves against their competitors. The platform can in turn provide an effective feedback loop by offering feedback to lawyers each time they lose a pitch or fail to win repeat instructions, helping them improve the quality of their proposals and client service over time.

2. Greater ease – access to value-creating tools

To capture the full client/lawyer interaction on the platform, the marketplace must offer value-creating tools to both clients

and lawyers. The parts that can be commoditized are handed over to the solution platform: given the economies of scale of a marketplace, this can significantly drive down price and standardize user experience, bringing consistency in a fragmented market.

Tools can be effectively introduced, at scale, to improve both the business and practice of law:

- *Business of law* – For lawyers, software as a service (SaaS) tools providing workflow support, such as e-billing, project management, and other back-office functions, will enable them to bring their whole practice online. For clients, user-friendly dashboards can help them track legal spend, supervise workflow and manage communications. Both sides will benefit from collaboration and sharing tools provided on a common platform.

- *Practice of law* – There are now a multitude of LegalTech tools designed to augment lawyers' practice so that they can better deliver legal advice. Not only can routine and standardized tasks be automated, more complex assignments such as legal research and contract review can be done with assistance from LegalTech solutions. Sole practitioners and boutique law firms, armed with these tools, will find themselves effectively competing with the largest players.

As such, a legal marketplace has the potential to democratize access to LegalTech and enable value creation for all participants. More importantly, these tools free up lawyers to focus on the areas they are trained for, such as exercising judgment, empathy and negotiation.

3. Greater networks – widening the market

The enhanced onboarding process within a managed platform should also remove any friction in referrals between lawyers, so that individual lawyers not restricted by the traditional firm structure can more easily build professional networks. Equally, clients can build flexible, expert, all-star legal teams based on these networks to help them achieve specific legal objectives.

Stage Three: Full Verticalization

In the final stage of the evolution, legal marketplaces will adopt data analytics to achieve standardization and customization, significantly improving the customer experience.

1. Standardization

Over time, platforms will be able to use data analytics to increase their ability to generate value for clients and lawyers. For example, based on data collected from similar matters, clients and lawyers can benchmark the staffing costs, length and outcome of each piece of work. Frameworks and models can be developed to standardize how legal service is delivered across different practice areas and matters.

2. Customization

Predictive analytics will enable the platform to anticipate clients' upcoming legal needs and risks, in each case proactively offering solutions in advance. Businesses will be able to streamline growth through timely legal input and neutralize legal problems before they become business-critical.

Multi-level supply options mean that a client can source solicitors, barristers, paralegals, contract lawyers and any support staff required for any piece of legal work through the marketplace. The matching algorithm would continue to learn from successful matches and outcomes, so that clients get the benefit of an increasingly curated marketplace and experience.

The Marketplace Evolution

The legal marketplace is democratizing access to quality legal services.

For clients, greater competition and technological advancement will drive down costs and ensure higher standards of delivery. The traditional barriers to entry will be increasingly broken down as clients gain access to highly qualified individuals that are cost effective, mobile and tech enabled. The marketplace model will provide the greatest improvement in user experience, as standardization and customization minimize the risks and uncertainty in purchasing legal services.

For lawyers, the marketplace model will level the playing field by allowing them to differentiate themselves against their competitors and build their practice on the basis of solid reviews, rather than word-of-mouth referrals and traditional marketing. Lawyers that were priced out of enterprise technology will gain access to LegalTech tools via the marketplace, and entire firms and professional networks can be built and run online.

The largest law firms will not vanish, but their relative slice of the pie will continue to shrink as much of the work they used to do migrates to the marketplace, to be provided more efficiently and at a fraction of the cost. Legal experts wanting to work on the best, most challenging assignments will no longer be bound to law firms and will be able to do this from anywhere in the world using online tools.

Given the sweeping changes that marketplaces have made across finance, medicine and other industries, all this should come as no surprise.

Technology and In-House Counsel

Mike Butler
Tutor, The University of Law

The Law Society estimates that by 2020 around 35% of all solicitors working in the UK will be working as in-house lawyers.[1] The "inside counsel revolution"[2] started in the US in the late 1970s and there is a continuing upward trend globally in the number – and importance – of lawyers employed outside of legal private practice by businesses themselves, be they, for example, corporations or government. How these in-house lawyers address the use of legal technology presents different challenges to those faced by law firms.

The Role of the In-House Lawyer

"Whereas the central task of external counsel is to proffer legal advice and undertake transactions including litigation, in-house counsel are required to deal with compliance, contribute to business decisions, and liaise with external regulatory and investigative bodies from time to time."[3]

The wide-ranging role of in-house lawyers results in a number of key differentiators between in-house and private practice lawyers which influence technology decisions:

- **Scarcity of resource:** The volume of legal work generated by the business will exceed the resources of any in-house legal team. How the in-house team optimizes its resource is therefore critical and the start point is the interface with the business: how can technology facilitate this optimization so that business needs are met but that the in-house lawyers can deliver value where most needed?

- **Risk:** Closely allied to the first point, the role of the in-house lawyer requires in-house counsel to manage risk when providing legal services within the risk parameters set by the organization.

- **Value:** A law firm can demonstrate return on investment through enhanced profitability or client acquisition. In-house teams are perceived as cost centres, so any technology investment needs to be justified in measurable efficiency savings.

- **Scale:** Law firms exist to provide legal services and technology solutions; an in-house legal team is one key function within a much larger, multifaceted organization. What value, if any, can legal technology play across the wider business or, conversely, can the legal function utilize technology from other functions in the business?

Legal Technology as Point Solution

There has been a sharp rise in the last four years of legal technology products. However, as one leading commentator notes,[4] many of these products are "point solutions" – they solve or

---

[1] "The Future of Legal Services", The Law Society, p. 28. Available at: https://www.lawsociety.org.uk/support-services/research-trends/the-future-of-legal-services/.

[2] *The Inside Counsel Revolution* is the title of the book by Ben W. Heineman, Jr (former General Counsel for General Electric), ABA Publishing, American Bar Association, 2016.

[3] S. Hackett, "Corporate Counsel and the Evolution of Ethical Practical Navigation: An Overview of the Changing Dynamics of Professional Responsibility in In-House Practice" (2012) *Georgetown Journal of Legal Ethics*, 25, 317.

---

[4] Professor Daniel Martin Katz speaking at "The Artificial Intelligence in Legal Services Summit", London, 4 June 2019.

aid one specific problem. Moreover, the focus of legal technology vendors has been on solutions for law firms, particularly with respect to due diligence[5] and e-Discovery – functions which are rarely undertaken in-house.[6]

A Blank Sheet of Paper

Richard Susskind urges in-house counsel to start with a "blank sheet of paper" – to start with a legal-needs analysis: what legal needs does the organization have and what legal risks does it face?[7] The starting point is not technology but the wider combination of "people, process and technology", placed within the unique role of in-house lawyers:

- **The business interface:** In-house teams need to consider how they can optimize scarce legal resource while still ensuring the legal needs of the business are met. How does the business communicate with the legal function to maximize efficiency? A good example is Sky's "Legal Front Door" app launched by the Sky in-house legal team.[8]
- **Legal engineers:** Rather than technology vendors, in-house counsel should consider utilizing the experience of the nascent "legal engineer"[9] to assist with issues such as legal triage, process mapping and the design of playbooks.

---

[5] For example, leading technology providers such as Luminance and RAVN (now part of iManage), while having artificial intelligence (AI) technology with wide potential application, have focused at this stage on corporate transactional work.

[6] Although some tools are aimed at in-house teams – e.g. Avvoka ("Google Docs for contracts") and TLT LegalSifter.

[7] Richard Susskind talk. Available at: https://www.youtube.com/watch?v=D_NeuNjCRm8.

[8] https://twitter.com/hayleystallard1/status/1065313563882004480?lang=en.

[9] For example, Elevate Services and Wavelength, although note the latter's sale in July 2019 to law firm Simmons & Simmons.

- **Partnering:** In meeting the legal needs of an organization, there will invariably be a blend of insourcing and outsourcing. In-house lawyers must consider how their external firm can deliver technology solutions – in essence, they need to consider how or if the law firm can act as a software as well as a service provider. For example, if an automation or AI solution is available, should this be done in-house or provided by an external partner who can maintain and upgrade the technology?
- **Resource mix:** Larger in-house legal teams may still be able to achieve cost efficiency through the use of offshoring/near-shoring or even the transfer of staff to external providers.[10]
- **A different type of in-house lawyer:** Traditionally, UK corporations have recruited in-house solicitors with experience from international or large UK law firms. However, there is an increasing demand for lawyers who can understand data and operations – the in-house department of the future should contain data scientists and operations specialists from outside the traditional pathway. Even more important has been the need for far more commercially savvy in-house lawyers, who truly understand the businesses they are supporting, and understand and can solve the underlying business problems their (internal) clients need them to – which just happen to contain legal problems within them.

Walking Forwards

In respect of legal technology, as Richard Susskind notes, general counsel should not "walk backwards into the future".[11] Simply utilizing new technology aimed at law firms is not appropriate. The

---

[10] For example, the proposal in July 2019 to transfer 40 lawyers from BT's in-house legal team of nearly 400 staff to listed law firm DWF.

[11] Note 7.

start point is being able to properly document (in process terms) the legal needs of the organization and then implement a mix of resource and technology which provides value for money to the organization.

But in-house counsel are more than legal operations' providers. They are business advisors and, as such, they need to embrace "networks of mutual assistance"[12] and work collaboratively with the wider business. This in turn may involve the legal function using technology used across the organization (at its simplest, collaborative tools such as Salesforce).

The best General Counsel provide additional value by identifying and mitigating strategic risk affecting the business. Managing risk is an area where new legal technology may yet evolve. Technology advances in the areas of natural language processing and pattern recognition have to date been applied in legal fields such as due diligence; the ability to use these technologies for legal risk analysis and risk scoring would be an exciting opportunity for in-house counsel. Technology for the in-house lawyer should free them to add value: to act as trusted advisor and contribute to the wider strategic and ethical issues facing the organization. As Ben Heineman states:[13]

The practical ideal of the modern General Counsel is a lawyer-statesperson who is an outstanding technical expert, a wise counselor and effective leader … For the lawyer-statesperson, the first question is: "Is it legal?" But the ultimate question is: "Is it right?"

---

[12] This is a theme taken from the General Counsel Strategy Summit in Alicante, Spain, May 2019, as reported at: https://www. addleshawgoddard.com/en/insights/insights-briefings/gregs-blog/ reflections-on-the-lawyer-general-counsel-strategy-summit/.

[13] Note 2, p. 3.

Smart Home or Spy Home?

Ekaterina Safonova

Founder, CEO/Board Advisor/Founder, CTO, CS Consulting and Advisory/Cybertonica/FemFinTech

My wife asked me why I'm speaking quietly at home. I've told her that I'm afraid that Mark Zuckerberg is listening. She started laughing. I started laughing too. And Siri started laughing, Alisa (Russian Alexa) started laughing and Alexa started laughing as well…

We have entered a new reality, an era where simple appliances that we have been using in our day-to-day lives have become "smart". Our phones, watches, TVs, cars, fridges and vacuums, if not a computer yet, will no doubt get there. Are you sure that your smart lightbulb is not secretly waging a cyberwar against you? The Internet of Things (IoT) is changing the way we communicate, pay, play, work and live more generally.

A 2017 Gartner[1] report gives us an idea how the IoT market is developing and how it is going to explode in upcoming years. In 2017 there were 8.4 billion IoT devices in use. They predict this will have risen to 20.4 billion by 2020 and 60 billion by 2022.

"Smart" Lifestyle:

- smart video monitoring and smart locks, connected to your phones and laptops, providing your home with 24/7 security;
- smart thermometer, learning your preferences, in order to adjust the heating to suit you across all four seasons;

- smart pillows designed to stop a snoring partner;
- pacemakers keeping the owner's heart rhythm stable;
- toys singing and talking to our babies to calm or entertain them;
- smart pet feeders that look after your cats and dogs;
- audio systems that know their owners and play their favourite music;
- fridges topping themselves up with food to meet owner preferences, diaries and lifestyle;
- smart lighting providing personal light settings when you work, read, eat or have a family party;
- smart watches monitoring our pulse and the way we sleep, work, walk or exercise; and even
- smart diapers alerting parents when babies need changing, and this list could be continued.

All these gadgets have IP addresses and no need of human-to-human or human-to-computer intercommunication to transfer data.

Smart Challenges

The quid pro quo of the smart world around us is a set of equally smart challenges. Questions are rightly being asked about how an increasing army of gadgets is going to affect our lives? How smart and safe are our homes in reality? Is there any balance between convenience and danger of our personal lives being exposed to fraud? *And where, as some might say does the "worm" hide?* The reality is – our smart homes are not as safe as we used to think…

Our phones, TVs, video cameras for monitoring, kitchen appliances, baby monitors, smart watches and other big and small gadgets hold all data about us and our ambience. This data is then fed back to the technology developers – they would argue – to analyse and improve the products, to make them better at meeting our needs. Although this seems harmless to some, this data has become a sinecure for hackers who extract information from

---

[1] Rob van der Meulen, "Gartner Says 8.4 Billion Connected 'Things' Will Be in Use in 2017, Up 31 Percent From 2016', Gartner, 2017. Available from: https://www.gartner.com/en/newsroom/press-releases/2017-02-07-gartner-says-8-billion-connected-things-will-be-in-use-in-2017-up-31-percent-from-2016 (accessed from 13.09.2019).

connected devices almost without any effort. IoT has built a bridge between digital and physical worlds and our task is to learn how to use it whilst protecting and considering privacy and security.

Recent research from Ben-Gurion University[2] warns us about dangerous flaws detected in fourteen of sixteen sampled smart home devices. But why such a high proportion?

Consumer education: Lack of consumer education is one of the biggest problems. If we don't practice safe internet usage, we make hacking more financially viable and give criminals an ability to co-ordinate large-scale attacks on their targets.

Poor design: Many IoT devices that are flooding the smart market don't consider privacy and security at all – why, on the face of it, would a kettle need cybersecurity protection? In many cheap internet-connected devices, encryption is simply not high enough up the priority list to be adequately implemented.

Insecure passwords: Most IoT devices come with default passwords, which are easily available or simple to crack.

Interoperability: Many home internet-connected devices come from different producers, running on completely different software systems and hardware platforms. Updating and patching them is not always an easy and straightforward task for a customer, who usually has little experience in doing so. In fact, many cheaper devices might not provide any software updates.

To orchestrate the diversity of applications, to make them function properly and to interact with each other and homeowners in a secure and smooth way is a difficult task, but it presents an exciting chance for malicious actors to monetize this raw unprotected data.

This is not a hypothetical concern – there are daily reports of attacks. In 2016, there was a well-orchestrated DDoS attack.[3] Hundreds of thousands of smart devices were dragged into the botnet to perform an advanced attack against many well-known sites such as AirBnb, Twitter, Netflix and many others.

Mirai attacks – a dangerous malware that turns Linux devices into bots, which is translated into "the future" from Japanese – is becoming a serious problem, targeting wireless routers, connected cameras and 32-bit processors used in many IoT devices. If hackers deploy ransomware, users are often forced into having to pay to unlock their devices. Apart of your smart lightbulb joining bot's army, are there any other threats our smart home is facing? With our lives connected to the internet, hackers can remotely scan networks for vulnerabilities, find loopholes to steal, intercept and even modify data. They can use our personal data to commit different types of fraud,[4] including account takeover[5] and synthetic identity creation.

[2] American Associates, Ben-Gurion University of the Negev, ScienceDaily, 2018. Available from: https://www.sciencedaily.com/releases/2018/03/180313084200.htm. (accessed from 13.09.2019).

[3] Chris Williams, "Today the Web was Broken by Countless Hacked Devices – Your 60-Second Summary", *The Register*, 2016. Available from: https://www.theregister.co.uk/2016/10/21/dyn_dns_ddos_explained/ (accessed from 13.09.2019).

[4] Roxanna "Evan" Ramzipoor, "How the IoT is Changing Fraud", Sift Blog, 2017. Available from: https://blog.sift.com/2017/how-the-iot-is-changing-fraud/. (accessed from 20.09.2019).

[5] Def Con security conference hosted an IoT hacking challenge to exploit smart devices for vulnerabilities. Pen Test Partners have hacked a popular model of a Samsung smart refrigerator that leaked gmail login credentials and led to an account takeover attack. Another security concern raised by MedSec Holdings found a loophole in St. Jude Medical pacemakers – while correcting cardio rhythms – which were designed to transmit biometric data of patients to their GPs. This could lead to noticeably serious attacks, such as synthetic identity creation, or could even be life threatening. Colin Neagle, "Smart Refrigerator Hack Exposes Gmail Login Credentials", *NetworkWorld*. Available from: https://www.networkworld.com/article/2976270/smart-refrigerator-hack-exposes-gmail-login-credentials.html. (accessed from 13.09.2019).

While we are at home using our smart devices, fraudsters might learn our behaviours, our habits, disturb our privacy and use obtained personal, often sensitive, data to blackmail victims.[6] In one version of the future, there is a terrible scenario of the smart home becoming a perfect prison, with hackers being able to take total control of the home's network, door and window locks, alarm system, heating, ventilation, water and light supply, audio system and so on. What do we have to do to fight back and keep our homes smart, secure and comfortable?

Basic Defence Measures

To become a difficult target for hackers, there are some basic steps that can be taken at home.

- Wi-Fi should be set to WPA2 encryption that provides protection from interception. Many routers often don't enable WPA2 encryption by default.

- Change default passwords, choosing complicated ones which are changed at regular intervals.

- Update software regularly on all devices, ensuring these devices allow and cater for this.

- Use router-connected new devices that are designed to alert the owner about "strangers" or just block them by scanning the network and devices.

- Use smart multifactor authentication.

- Our homes are likely to continue to be at the forefront of smart technology; key to balancing the benefits with the risks is to maintain strong cybersecurity knowledge and vigilance.

Lot's of challenges lie ahead until our homes truly become smart. To adapt to the upcoming smart reality, start from yourself –be smart.

[6] Jeff Parsons, "Phishing Scam Known as 'Sextortion' is Using People's Real Passwords to Blackmail Them for Supposedly Watching Porn", *Mirror*, 2018. Available from: https://www.mirror.co.uk/tech/phishing-scam-known-sextortion-using-12928730 (accessed from 13.09.2019).

Cybersecurity: Myths and the Hero's Journey

Graham Thomson
Chief Information Security Officer (and interim Head of Data and Analytics), Irwin Mitchell LLP

and Daryna Plysak
Trainee Solicitor, Irwin Mitchell LLP

Introduction

Cybersecurity may seem like a mysterious subject, a black art or a never-ending cost without any return on investment. There are plenty of myths and scare stories and it is not surprising that firms, large and small, are at a loss of what to do, how far to go or how to even start the journey. Why bother? What's the benefit gained from all the upfront ex ante costs of prevention? Is it worth it? Is it really relevant?

It only takes a quick glance at the media to realize there is indeed a problem, one which affects companies and firms of all sizes across all sectors. To tackle this risk, firms, like any other business, need their own cybersecurity battle plan and someone to lead both the charge and the ongoing war. Some might even consider this person to be a warrior. Whether a Joan of Arc or a Boudicca, a Perseus or an Achilles, they will need a hero to fight the ongoing daily barrage, which is becoming ever more sophisticated.

Joseph Campbell, Professor of Literature at Sarah Lawrence College, defines the stages that symbolize the traditional tale of the archetypal hero's journey, and having set up and delivered effective cybersecurity for firms, it turns out that the journey to good cybersecurity has its very own hero's journey.

Problem, What Problem?

The hero in this story knows that beyond any doubt there is a crisis in cyberspace. The world has become highly interconnected – a global network of digital systems that we rely upon for business and in our personal lives. Over half of the world population is online[1] and this will only increase. With the myriad benefits technology offers, there are also many potential risks and harms.

The internet, email and many other IT systems, which sit at the heart of most companies' and law firms' digital infrastructure, were never originally designed with security in mind, and are as a result inherently weak in relation to security. And it is this that has been taken advantage of.

Firms are increasingly targeted by cybercriminals, whether lone wolves or organized crime, competitors or nation states engaged in corporate espionage and war. Motivations include money, revenge and competitive advantage. Furthermore, the insider threat, whether malicious or accidental, is a massive risk. The biggest data loss root cause reported to the UK's legal and data protection regulators by law firms is that of sending client data to the wrong email recipient, accounting for 25% of all personal data breach reports in Q4 2018/19, compared to 5% due to phishing, according to the UK's Information Commissioner Office[2] (the ICO, the UK's data protection regulator). In 2019, security researcher Troy Hunt reported that there was a single "mega data leak" that contained a list of over two billion unique email address-password combinations[3] – cybercriminals routinely use such lists to access online accounts.

---

[1] https://wearesocial.com/global-digital-report-2019.

[2] https://ico.org.uk/action-weve-taken/data-security-incident-trends.

[3] https://www.troyhunt.com/the-race-to-the-bottom-of-credential-stuffing-lists-and-collections-2-through-5-and-more.

The threats are varied, and impacts to firms include direct monetary losses, increasingly large regulatory fines, reputational damage and IT system downtime. Fines reported by the UK's ICO have dramatically increased since the adoption of the General Data Protection Regulation – from fining Facebook the then maximum of £500,000 in 2018[4] to proposing to fine British Airways £183 million in 2019.[5]

Could Your Firm Survive Such an Event?

A 2018 report by the UK's National Cyber Security Centre[6] (NCSC) in conjunction with the Law Society of England and Wales highlighted the four most significant cyber-threats to law firms:

- phishing (the digital equivalent of the confidence trick); data breaches (such as the Mossack Fonseca data heist[7]);

- ransomware (where malware – malicious software – locks away your data until you pay);

- supply chain compromise (where a supplier fails to secure your data); and

- software provider compromise (and used to spread malware).

Additionally, the regulator for solicitors in England and Wales (the Solicitors Regulation Authority) reports that millions of client money is stolen each year; the vast majority due to money transfer frauds with phishing by email as the favoured attack method[8] (known as "Friday afternoon frauds").

No longer can a firm just lock its front doors to protect its client data, nor can anyone dismiss the cyber-threats and resist taking action.

A Call to Action

The first step to addressing the cybersecurity risk is to accept there is a problem, and then to assemble the tools with which to fight it:

1. skilled security professionals who will toil valiantly against the relentless threats;

2. vendors who can provide products acting as a shield to these attacks;

3. white-hat (good) cyber-hackers who will find your weakest links; and

4. (sometimes forgotten) co-workers, all of whom share a responsibility for maintaining good security and looking after clients' information.

Finding the key staff with the skills and expertise to build the security infrastructure and systems is a key risk for many. There has long been a skills gap, and one which does not look to be due to be closed in the coming years – in 2017 it was predicted that there would be 3.5 million unfilled information security roles by 2021.[9] Furthermore, to compound this, cybersecurity roles are dominated by men, with only around 14% filled by females in

[4] https://ico.org.uk/facebook-fine-20181025.

[5] https://ico.org.uk/about-the-ico/news-and-events/news-and-blogs/2019/07/ico-announces-intention-to-fine-british-airways.

[6] https://www.ncsc.gov.uk/report/-the-cyber-threat-to-uk-legal-sector–2018-report.

[7] https://www.theguardian.com/world/2018/mar/14/mossack-fonseca-shut-down-panama-papers.

[8] https://www.sra.org.uk/risk/risk-resources/information-security-report.

[9] https://cybersecurityventures.com/jobs.

the US, 18% in the UK, and 25% in Australia; although the gap is closing year on year.[10]

Finding your "hero" and giving them the support needed to succeed are crucial. Taking action is not optional any longer if a firm or company wants to survive in a highly digitized world. But how?

Create Your Cybersecurity Strategy

At this stage in your cybersecurity journey, your firm may be lost, far from home in uncertain and unfamiliar territory. But there is a well-trodden path, when you know where to look.

Step 1

The first part of even the simplest of cybersecurity strategies is to pick a framework. The framework is the blueprint for effective cybersecurity. It will help identify current risks and weaknesses, and help in designing a roadmap for improvement.

There's no need to invent one, however; there are plenty to choose from and many are free. The examples below are an illustration of what is available. Some are simple, ideal for smaller organizations; others are more complex and may suit larger, well-funded organizations.

A cybersecurity framework is a set of policies, risk-based controls and procedures that treat cyber-risk. They are created and kept up to date by professional cybersecurity organizations and government agencies, and are specifically designed to enhance cybersecurity wherever implemented. They contain the theory, specialist subject knowledge and practical guides. While no framework promises to eliminate all cybersecurity risk, they significantly reduce risk by making incidents less likely and impacts less damaging. It is not uncommon to select more than one framework to apply best of breed of practical controls.

Commonly used international frameworks include:

The US National Institute of Standards and Technology (NIST) framework:[11] These free and detailed documents are aimed at US government agencies, but are just as applicable to law firms. NIST also has a cut-down, easy-to-follow framework called the NIST Cybersecurity Framework. This describes the five main processes that should be covered by controls in any good cybersecurity framework:

1. Identify: understand your environment and assets; know what you need to protect.

2. Protect: develop and implement controls to prevent, limit or contain the impact from cyber-threats.

3. Detect: implement controls to quickly identify cybersecurity events and breaches.

4. Respond: should an incident occur, have the ability to contain the impact.

5. Recover: implement activities to restore data and services impaired by an incident.

The Center for Internet Security's (CIS) critical security controls:[12] A free, detailed and pragmatic list of around 200 security controls in

[10] https://www.isc2.org/-/media/ISC2/Research/ISC2-Women-in-Cybersecurity-Report.ashx, https://cybersecurityventures.com/women-in-cybersecurity, https://www.forbes.com/sites/laurencebradford/2018/10/18/cybersecurity-needs-women-heres-why/#53974b1647e8, https://thefintechtimes.com/study-shows-women-make-up-18-of-cybersecurity-industry.

[11] https://www.nist.gov.

[12] https://www.cisecurity.org.

twenty categories. It highlights controls that are basic and easy to implement, those that are harder but foundational, and those that are more complex. It comes with an implementation guide.

International Standards Organization (ISO) 27001 series:[13] A key benefit of this framework is that it can be independently audited and certified against, allowing your firm to certify its good status to clients.

The UK's NCSC 10 Steps to Cybersecurity:[14] A shortened framework focusing on the key risk areas, which is ideal for smaller firms.

Step 2

The second step is to use the framework to identify the risks specific to the firm. For example, exposure to supplier risk? Reliance on digital records or certain IT systems or websites?

Generally, cyber-risk will be the same for most businesses and these frameworks will mitigate most if not all of those risks. In fact, the CIS states that if just the top five controls are implemented it reduces 85% of the cyber-risk; implementing the rest gets you to 94% risk reduction.[15]

It is neither pragmatic nor necessary to implement all controls from a framework; instead focus should be on those which provide the greatest cost benefit. A risk appetite – set at the level which enables the firm to operate whilst balancing the threat – will feed into this.

[13] https://www.iso.org/isoiec-27001-information-security.html.

[14] https://www.ncsc.gov.uk/collection/10-steps-to-cyber-security.

[15] https://www.cisecurity.org, https://blog.rapid7.com/2016/11/09/using-cis-controls-to-stop-your-network-from-falling-in-with-the-wrong-crowd.

Importantly businesses should not expect a return on investment for cybersecurity. Instead the business case is for risk reduction and the avoidance of costs via fewer incidents, smaller fines and ultimately protection of brand.

Step 3

The third and final step is to implement the controls, and maintain and audit them for continual improvement. This requires appropriate focus and funding. Implementing the controls may mean creating new business processes and ensuring that the right colleagues know what to do. It may mean identifying, purchasing and installing new software or hardware, which will require IT project management. It may require hiring staff or third parties to manage new tasks and responsibilities.

There may be a lot to do, so risk-based prioritization is the key.

Cybersecurity Myths and the Trials: Threats from Within and Without

It takes time to implement cybersecurity controls and it is important to remember that it is not possible to completely eliminate all risk. There will inevitably be cyberattacks, data breaches and incidents, and in these incidents it is about ensuring that the damage is mitigated, limited, that the route to recovery is fast and efficient and that damage to the business as a whole has been contained. There will always be hurdles and roadblocks along the way, and there will be misinformation, fear, uncertainty and doom.

There is no way around this; your heroes must endure these trials and see through the myths. Common myths are as follows:

Cyberattacks are targeted; it won't happen to you, you are too small, too insignificant. Think again. While big data breaches and cyberattacks make the news headlines, 58% of data breach victims are small businesses.[16] Attacks are often indiscriminate and may be automated by bots who know nothing about you or your business. In 2018, it was reported that the average small business website was attacked forty-four times per day.[17] Everyone online is at risk of cyberattacks and breaches.

A good complex password that changes often is good enough. Wrong. Human nature is such that most people just cannot choose or remember strong and unique passwords. Forcing to change them too often makes this even harder. This leaves open the risk of password reuse (using the same password on many sites – remember those billion-odd email address-password combinations leaked), and weak passwords that may look strong but are in fact used by many people can be guessed or socially engineered. (You can see this problem simply by checking your own credentials with the "Have I been pwned" website.[18]) Using two-factor authentication for online accounts has never been more important for businesses.

It's an IT problem and I've got antivirus, that's good enough. If only it was that easy. Whether you call it cybersecurity, IT security or information security, it's a business-wide risk and cannot be solved by technology alone. It takes a mix of people (training and awareness, tests, exercises), process (policies and procedures) and technology to address the risks. People are the first line of defence and all of your colleagues need to know and follow good security practices.

We can eliminate 100% of risk. Dream on. Attacks are relentless, evolving and it is simply not possible to achieve 100% prevention. Therefore, you must assume that you are in a state of continuous potential compromise and be able to detect, respond and recover from cyber incidents as rapidly as possible, as well as prevent them.

Threats are external; our colleagues are saints. They may well be, but accidents and mistakes do happen. The insider threat, whether malicious or accidental, is just as big a risk as the external one; in fact, insider threats can account for up to 75% of data breaches.[19] Your colleagues will need legitimate access to sensitive data and systems, and they need to know how to handle it responsibly.

Cybersecurity is too expensive. It certainly can be pricey, but you can minimize your costs by ensuring that your cybersecurity framework focuses on mitigating the key risks in pragmatic ways. Don't just throw multiple technologies at the problem.

What is certainly not a myth is that you must be prepared for the worst by having an incident management plan – one which has been tested. This is also where technology can assist; there are a number of tools available on the market that can help detect and respond to cyber-incidents automatically.

Help From Unexpected Sources

Cybersecurity is not only an individual company risk; national governments are very concerned about the impact both on public services as well as on the business environment. As a result, there is a swathe of resources to help and support companies – including free online courses[20] (such as Coursera, Cybrary) and free cybersecurity tools,[21] such as the NCSC's Exercise in a Box.[22]

Internally, ensuring that cybersecurity policies are right-sized and a good fit for the company/firm, and don't hinder colleagues

---

[16] https://enterprise.verizon.com/resources/reports/dbir.

[17] https://www.sitelock.com/blog/website-security-insider-q4-2017.

[18] https://haveibeenpwned.com.

[19] https://www.varonis.com/blog/insider-security-threats.

[20] www.coursera.org, www.cybrary.it.

[21] https://www.troyhunt.com/troys-ultimate-list-of-security-links, https://github.com/gchq.

[22] https://www.ncsc.gov.uk/information/exercise-in-a-box.

unduly, is equally important. An effective way of getting this insight and feedback is to ask colleagues to become cybersecurity champions, or other techniques which seek to engage the staff across a company/firm. Tools and approaches which are user friendly, swift and which limit the disruption to normal fee-earning activities will assist in the effectiveness of the security measures put in place. Encouraging reporting of issues, developing a one-stop shop for security issues and using engaging methods such as test phishing emails are a few of the techniques known to be successful.

Now more than ever it is paramount that solicitors have the appreciation of cybersecurity concerning client and company data. Clients, whether an individual or a small business, may well be struggling with cyber-risk themselves. Being able to talk to your clients about cybersecurity solutions with good knowledge and confidence will not just help build the relationship, but may save them from a disaster and will better serve their overall needs.

In amongst the rise of the use of technology in the day-to-day work of a law firm, it is vital that at both the point of purchase and use the security considerations are taken into account. Technology can hugely assist in the speed and accuracy of legal work, but it must not compromise the security of data. Ultimately, the relationship between law firms and clients is based on a contractual agreement and trust; every effort must be taken to maintain this.

Conclusion

Firms are increasingly targets of cybercrime; the enemy is well armed, well resourced and determined. There are threats from within too; the insider threat is equally as big as the risk. The impacts from cyberattacks and breaches can be devastating, and with increasingly large regulatory fines. Firms can no longer ignore the threat. It is time to act.

The voyage to effective cybersecurity may seem like pushing a rock up Sisyphus' never-ending mountain, but the heroes who rise to this opportunity will find that there is much help at hand. Furthermore, there is significant and demonstrable business benefit.

There is no such thing as perfect cybersecurity; it is not a destination, but a journey of risk-based continuous improvement.

Like any good adventure, the journey will have monsters to defeat, wise sages to heed and trials to endure. But the reward of success is a gift to your firm.

Legal Talent Platform Economy – The Beginning of the End?

Dana Denis-Smith
CEO, Obelisk Support

Is the future of the legal professional a freelance one or will they still aspire to climb the greasy pole of partnership to see themselves as "successful" in the profession? Will most lawyers use technology advances to embrace working as self-employed practitioners, much like barristers have done for centuries? Technology platforms for lawyers are on the rise – with the number of lawyers working as freelancers increasing every year (to the tune of 30% or so year on year). This formula to practise law, primarily from the comfort of one's home, is proving a winning recipe for those who love their work but want more control over where and when they deliver legal services to customers and are not as keen to advance through the partnership ranks.

There is also good news on available capital to fuel the growth of the legal talent platform market. Private equity has also taken an interest in the past five years or so, with increased volumes of investments into the virtual lawyer space – from the £3.15 million investment into virtual law firm Keystone Law by Root Capital in 2014 (and their subsequent flotation on the AIM markets on the London Stock Exchange in 2018) to the 2019 investment of Permira into Axiom Law to help them build their on-demand legal talent proposition. Finally, the investment needed to build technology seems to be flowing into the legal sector and the vertical that is on-demand legal talent appears to be a sweet spot which should encourage all those who are looking for more work through this channel. This coupled with recent regulatory changes announced by the Solicitors Regulatory Authority (SRA) to allow freelance lawyers to give legal advice with less monitoring and regulatory oversight is bound to lead to higher numbers of lawyers working for themselves.

The above paints a rosy picture of an expanded and more inclusive profession – there are now 146,625 practising solicitors on the SRA roll in England and Wales, with a further 45,000 or so on the roll but not practising. It is very feasible that the SRA regulatory changes will increase the number of those who aren't currently practising who return to the profession and thus, in theory at least, open access to lawyers to many more individuals but also SMEs – both groups severely underserved by the profession to date mainly due to prohibitive costs. Some estimates place the number of lawyers embracing this new way of working at around 30% of the profession by 2030.

Whereas it is relatively easy to quantify the number of lawyers working via platform businesses (Obelisk Support, a business I set up in 2010, alone counts over 1,500 of such lawyers as active on our platform), the technology that underpins the experience of both lawyers and customers is opaque and not enough of it is visible to the users. The platform businesses often compare themselves to large players in the consumer world – be it Uber or Airbnb – but the investments in their technology are far behind.

Take Uber as an example: Uber became dominant across the world by introducing a simple idea – use a mobile phone app to connect freelance taxi drivers with customers. Easy to order and easy to pay for, Uber quickly established itself as a huge player in the transport industry in the capital. At the other extreme, many black cabs remained non-digital – accepting cash only or being accessible by flagging down on the streets or at taxi ranks. Fast forward nearly five years, and black cab drivers are onboarded onto their own apps and can be ordered and paid for through these; accepting card payments is now compulsory. I've not heard complaints from black cab drivers that because they are freelance drivers they are not empowered to control the time they work or, in more recent years, their income is being reduced from digitization specifically. However, complaints abound still against Uber and any other app that keeps taxi usage at an affordable level, mainly on the basis of reduced safety for passengers or the unfair lower (or non-existent) regulatory requirements.

Many new entrants to the platform economy suggested they could compare the dynamic in the legal sector to the change being seen in the taxi world. Change can appear particularly threatening to a market in transition and it always ruffles a few feathers. Taxis and law are one of my favourite analogies – not least because the billing methods in the two sectors are too similar for comfort (black cabs, like lawyers, also charge in six-minute units), and because in both cases technology has brought down the barriers to entry.

As with black cabs, the world of legal services has changed fundamentally even though that change has yet to trickle down to the consumer market; the further deregulation of individual lawyers by the SRA can bring about that wider access to justice change so many hope for. With taxis, the impact is more direct, but nonetheless in both cases the transition to lighter regulation reminds me of how countries undergoing economic transition manage change to ensure structural reforms embed. In the legal sector, they are the new entrants (alternative business structures or not) that started with a blank sheet of paper and identified and exploited the gaps in the existing landscape – be it human capital, pricing or access.

For an industry that prides itself on being a "people's business", the legal sector has engaged remarkably little in discussing how technology will transform how lawyers will relate to their workplace. We have had the usual calls urging lawyers to "adapt or die"; the veiled threat of the robots will have it all unless lawyers smarten up. But how are law firms transforming their infrastructure to incorporate technology that makes work allocation and productivity a priority?

Over the last decade, there has been an influx of fresh ideas and models of working to the legal sector, with this journey beginning just as the effect of deregulation of the legal services market started to kick in. There have been new propositions focused on a simple idea to empower lawyers to work differently: pay for lawyers as and when you need but also keep the lawyers that cannot work traditional hours for a variety of personal reasons firmly connected to the profession. For example, on the Obelisk Support platform, 20% of the lawyers are returners to the profession, having taken a career gap of more than one year. The waste of good talent was – and remains – one of the biggest challenges of the legal profession, one which is built around people. New entrants have stepped into this space and have created, using smart technology that allows one to map the availability and skills of a lawyer against a client's requirements at great speed, many work opportunities for these self-employed lawyers that were sitting unutilized before.

To facilitate lawyer-to-client matching needs, firms leading in this area have developed a proprietary solicitor pairing software that starts by mining a database of lawyers for the best talent to meet the specific exigencies of clients' needs. This then brings the team together through a transparent process of carefully designed steps and collaboration points. Essentially, it connects and then guides the entire team seamlessly through each project from start to finish. However, the technology is never designed to completely replace humans. Whether it be approving a solicitor search shortlist, creating a client project wish list, or writing up feedback after a job is completed, the platform ensures that a team member can always input his or her expertise.

"The beginning of the end", said one of the black cab drivers at the time they were engaged in widespread protests against Uber gaining a licence. He couldn't have been further from being right – the demand for taxi services has seen a spike, and black cabs, not just Uber self-employed drivers, have benefited from it. Similarly, the legal industry is no exception from being disrupted by technology and professionals that currently use "apps" to manage a lot of aspects of their life outside work will increasingly grow frustrated if technology will not be incorporated more into their working day.

Can Intelligence Be Appropriated: Ownership Over AI

Kate Lebedeva

Junior Research Fellow, University College London and PhD candidate, University of Southampton

In the modern world, artificial intelligence (AI) has become an overarching phenomenon, the "new electricity" that will transform each and every area of our life.

As with every new technology, the question arises as to who is entitled to own it and reap the profit generated by technological advance. This chapter aims to provide an overview of existing, imperfect approaches to ownership over AI and suggests the possible solutions.

What Is AI?

AI is a complex phenomenon. It includes several components – such as algorithms, training data sets and trained models.

A machine learning algorithm defines how a computer learns to link an input (e.g. a picture of an animal) to a specific output (e.g. whether it is a "cat" or a "dog"). Some jurisdictions (like the US) allow patent protection of algorithms, but the criteria of patentability are currently in a state of flux.[1] Therefore, many companies opt for protecting their machine learning algorithms as trade secrets.[2,3]

---

[1] See, for example, "Protecting Artificial Intelligence IP: Patents, Trade Secrets, or Copyrights?": https://www.jonesday.com/en/insights/2018/01/protecting-artificial-intelligence-ip-patents-trad.

[2] The courts could, of course, still force disclosure in certain circumstances.

[3] Prajwal Nirwan, "Trade Secrets: the Hidden IP Right", WIPO Magazine, December 2017: https://www.wipo.int/wipo_magazine/en/2017/06/article_0006.html.

Such trade secrets might be worth billions, as in the case of the Google search algorithm.

Training data sets of the most sophisticated AI systems consist of millions of data inputs (e.g. photos of cats or videos of street traffic). Much of this content could be in theory copyright protected (e.g. Google emails). But often tech companies use it for AI training without any compensation and even awareness of the data subjects of its use (and effective monetization).[4]

Trained models are the statistical data generated through learning. They are best described as "black boxes" that can predict an output based on the input. Because AI tends to improve with every human interaction, the models evolve over time and can struggle to be adequately captured by existing intellectual property (IP) regimes. Moreover, being a result of collaborative efforts of developers and users (who provide and often label the data), they pose this very question of, "Who are the owners of the resulting AI system?"

From Inventor to Owner – The AI Dilemma

It is a staple approach that the IP created through the efforts of several parties (co-inventors) becomes their joint property. Co-inventors have common ownership and control over the IP they have invented.[5]

Yet, the joint ownership regime is ill-suited to deal with the situation when many individuals contribute, often unintentionally,

---

[4] See Benjamin L.W. Sobel, "Artificial Intelligence's Fair Use Crisis", 41 Colum. J.L. & Arts 45, 2017.

[5] "Avoid Jointly Owned Intellectual Property": https://www.ipeg.com/avoid-jointly-owned-intellectual-property/.

to improvement of an invention. For example, the US and China require common decisions from all co-owners at all stages of the IP life cycle. However, each co-owner can license the rights to the invention independently, which can cause havoc in the case of a complex invention such as AI. It might be more appropriate for contributors to claim ownership over the models trained on their data rather than the initial AI algorithm. But in practice, it is very difficult to draw the line between various components of AI and evaluate contributions of algorithm creators and the data owners to these models.

Another approach is to establish who should be incentivized for the development and commercialization of AI. The party who bears the risk for the whole project is assigned the formal "owner" status. This is the direction in which the AI legal regime is currently developing. Large corporations and research centres that fund and lead AI research projects are considered legal owners of the resulting AI systems, including the trained models. Users contributing their data or participating in labelling get nothing in return. In the best scenario, they agree to license their data for free when they accept the terms of use of the platform. In the worst scenario, they do not even know that they help train the algorithms that power commercial products.[6] For example, Google's software called reCAPTCHA uses human answers to simple riddles (like checking all the boxes that contain street signs) to train its machine vision algorithms without explicitly informing users.[7] The benefits of accurate driverless cars will be achieved due to collective efforts of the community, and yet the main economic winner will be Google.

The hands-off approach of policymakers does not improve the situation. It allows the mesh of contractual agreements, trade secrets and stacks of patents to shield the clarity and transparency needed for one purpose: everyone should benefit from AI. This includes the most vulnerable to the rise of AI, like ordinary internet users whose daily jobs might be displaced by these very algorithms they inadvertently help train.

More Questions Than Answers

It is clear that we cannot treat AI like another run-of-the-mill invention. The current AI ownership regime suffers from an imbalance in favour of large companies and relies on their goodwill in keeping AI open. Once this is not in their interest, they could leverage their ownership to rent out AI capacity to governments and businesses without regard to their customers' interests.[8] Society needs a conceptually new approach.

One option is to recognize that single "ownership" over AI is a convenient legal fiction. In fact, most AI systems are the result of collaborative efforts. The law should give users the fair share in advancement of AI,[9] because providing data for AI training is "repackaging of human labour"[10] and should be compensated. Some experts suggest that AI companies should pay levies to public funds that allocate the money among individual AI

---

[6] See Olivia Solon and Cyrus Farivar, "Millions of People Uploaded Photos to the Ever App. Then the Company Used Them to Develop Facial Recognition Tools": https://www.nbcnews.com/tech/security/millions-people-uploaded-photos-ever-app-then-company-used-them-n1003371.

[7] James O'Malley, "Captcha if You Can: How You've Been Training AI for Years Without Realizing It", TechRadar, 12 January 2018: https://www.techradar.com/news/captcha-if-you-can-how-youve-been-training-ai-for-years-without-realising-it.

[8] See Evgeny Morozov, "Will Tech Giants Move on from the Internet, Now We've All Been Harvested?", The Guardian, January 2018: https://www.theguardian.com/technology/2018/jan/28/morozov-artificial-intelligence-data-technology-online.

[9] "Come Harvest Time, Who Owns the Fruits of Machine Learning?", 13 March 2018: https://www.sourcingspeak.com/come-harvest-time-who-owns-the-fruits-of-machine-learning/ or WIPO "Technology Trends 2019: Artificial Intelligence". See also Jaron Lanier, Who Owns the Future?, Penguin 2014.

[10] See Benjamin L. W. Sobel, "Artificial Intelligence's Fair Use Crisis", 93.

contributors.[11] Jaron Lanier proposes a system that would track and value each individual contribution to machine learning.[12] Such contribution should be engraved into the AI model as a "micro-ownership" stamp. Every time the model is applied, the respective "nanopayment" is disbursed.[13] For example, if you have found a partner via a dating site, your data contributes to improvement of the matching algorithm. So, every time a similar couple is matched, you will receive a "nanopayment" for this contribution.[14]

124

At the other end of the spectrum is the "common good" approach, AI becoming a public asset. It might be trickier to implement in the countries where AI is advanced mostly through the private sector

(e.g. the US). That said, the switch to such a "common good approach" regime is still possible, with the owners of AI algorithms becoming trusted managers and bearing the relevant social responsibilities. History is littered with examples of innovations (such as railways or telecom) that have been nationalized or subject to public oversight, as a result of serious market failure in their commercialization.[15]

In both cases the new social contract on AI is necessary to preserve the delicate balance of interests in this powerful and transformative technology. The new forms of ownership should invite people to contribute to the AI economy in more meaningful ways.

---

[11] Ibid 91 and 92.

[12] Jaron Lanier, *Who Owns the Future?*, Penguin 2014, digital version accessible via the British Library.

[13] Ibid 515.

[14] Ibid.

---

[15] See the list of the assets nationalized by country in Wikipedia: https://en.wikipedia.org/wiki/List_of_nationalizations_by_country.

The Electronic Creation Right (ECR)

Israel Cedillo Lazcano
Lecturer in Law/Researcher, Universidad de las Américas Puebla

On 25 October 2018, Christie's sold a rather interesting and mysterious portrait for US$432,500, nearly forty-five times its high estimate.[1] At first sight, one would think that *Portrait of Edmond Belamy* does not offer something extraordinary. It looks like an unfinished work similar to those that one can find in the workshops of plastic artists around the world. However, this piece is unveiled as having been created by an artificial intelligence (AI).

This and other creations generated by AIs have been addressed by different analyses, focused on developing a single unified theory of AI and intellectual property rights (IPRs). Consequently, most of this analysis is superficial in detail, with content that jumps from one right to another, among different industries and is not grounded in practical use.

Rather than a generic attempt to resolve the issues raised, it may be more useful to look at specific use cases and industry sectors. Take for instance the potential risks that could emerge from the introduction of works created by AIs in the plastic arts market. To ease our understanding, we have selected the *Droit de Suite* (DDS) as our leitmotif by which the need for regulation regarding the introduction of works created by AIs in this market will be highlighted.

Artificial Originality and Creativity

Lord Hodge[2] defined AIs as those "computer systems able to perform tasks, which traditionally have required human intelligence or tasks whose completion is beyond human intelligence". From this and other definitions, paired with the emergent market for works created by AIs, one could be tempted to ask if the creation of an artificial creative mind is possible, and if the answer is yes, should we recognize its moral and economic rights for its gradual insertion in the global art market?

The answer to this question is not an easy one. When we talk about IPRs and plastic arts, the first thing that is evident is that most of the regulations on this matter are directed towards the protection of the fruits of the **human mind**. Consequently, following the spirit found in cases such as *Pompeii Estates, Inc. v Consolidated Edison Co.*,[3] the legal ownership of computer-generated works is rather clear in countries like the United Kingdom as we can verify through section 9(3) of the Copyright, Designs and Patents Act 1988, which states that:

> *"In the case of a literary, dramatic, musical or artistic work which is computer-generated, the author shall be taken to be the person by whom the arrangements necessary for the creation of the work are undertaken."*

In a similar way, most of the jurisdictions that follow the European continental tradition conclude that an author is "the natural person who has created a literary and artistic work", as one can verify

---

[1] Christie's, "Is Artificial Intelligence Set to Become Art's Next Medium?", 2018. Available at: https://www.christies.com/features/A-collaboration-between-two-artists-one-human-one-a-machine-9332-1.aspx, Christie's (accessed on 29 December 2018).

[2] P. Hodge, "The Potential and Perils of Financial Technology: Can the Law Adapt to Cope?", 2019. Available at: https://www.supremecourt.uk/docs/speech-190314.pdf, Supreme Court of the United Kingdom (accessed on 14 March 2019).

[3] In this case, Judge Posner argued that "computers can only issue mandatory instructions – they are not programmed to exercise discretion". See [1977] 91 Misc.2d 233 (US), at 237.

through the analysis of Article 12 of the Federal Copyright Law in force in Mexico.

However, the interpretation of these instruments on this line is not universal. For instance, during the discussions related to the enactment of the referred Copyright, Designs and Patents Act, Lord Beaverbrook[4] argued that works generated by a computer do not have an identifiable human creator given that this latter does not make any personal creative effort.

Moral Rights and the Rationale for the ECR

Building on the words of Lord Beaverbrook, it is possible to argue that the moral rights that could derive from a work developed using an AI designed around a neural architecture like a generative adversarial network[5] cannot be assigned to an individual based on the lack of the creative intention that defines these rights. However, can we say that an AI by itself can have and/or exercise these rights? For now, our answer has to be negative. However, in light of the DDS, which is a hybrid right designed to address the failures that characterize our plastic arts markets, it is possible to find a need for an alternative solution.

The DDS is referred to here as a hybrid right because, following the content of regulations, such as the Resale Rights Directive (2001/84/EC), on the one hand, it entitles artists to receive economic compensations when their works are resold through professional art merchants, such as auction houses, galleries and art dealers. On the other hand, just as in the case of moral rights, it is inalienable and unassignable. Based on this latter, how can these rights be assigned? To answer this question, it is reasonable to argue for the creation of an ECR.

The cornerstone of the ECR is based on the framework set by the DDS; thus, it would be exercised only when a professional art merchant is involved in the transaction. Here, the main question emerges: Who would be the beneficiary of the economic rights related to these works? The answer would be the individual or company under whose control the AI developed the work; however, the referred natural/legal persons would not be considered as the authors following the argument set by Lord Beaverbrook. For this purpose, the ECR would be designed as a label aimed to recognize the "moral rights" of the AI entity, which in turn would help us to tackle potential failures relating to information asymmetries that could emerge from mass production of the works or form practices designed to corner the market.

Consequently, under such an ECR, if one wants to sell a painting or a sculpture created by an AI, the intermediary involved in the transaction would have to ask about the characteristics of the computer, which would be labelled as the author of the work. To be subject to this label, the AI would have to comply with a set of minimum requirements, such as the level of complexity of its algorithm and the proportion of human intervention following the example set by cases like *Diamond v Chakrabarty*.[6]

With this element in mind, the ECR would be structured around a definition of "artwork generated by an AI", which would be included in the section of definitions of the IP laws of those jurisdictions that desire to adopt this figure. This definition would contain the basic elements found in existing definitions with the

---

[4] [1988] HL Deb. Vol. 493 col. 1305, 25 February 1988 (UK).

[5] This concept developed by Ian Goodfellow et al. is structured around a pair of neural networks trained on the same data set: one which provides an outcome and a "discriminator" that determines the outcome based on a qualitative and quantitative analysis. See I. Goodfellow et al., "Generative Adversarial Networks", 2014. Available at: https://arxiv.org/abs/1406.2661, Cornell University (accessed on 17 March 2019).

---

[6] In this case, the Supreme Court highlighted the differences between discoveries and creations with human intervention related to microorganisms [1980] 447 US 303 (US).

addition of the element of human intervention and a restriction in the number of copies that can be generated on the same work, and even on the same database, following the spirit of cases like *Grogan-Beall v Ferdinand Roten Galleries, Inc.*,[7] with the aim of restricting market abuses.

Considering the potential material immortality of these artificial entities, the ECR would expire at the end of the period set for ordinary economic rights in the applicable jurisdiction. The main difference would be that the starting point for this framework would be the date of their public release, not the end of the calendar year in which the human beneficiary dies.[8] So, after this period, even if the electronic creator has extended its own existence beyond the terms set by the law for the execution of this right, the creation would be traded in this market in the same way as old masters are traded today.

Although the model set out is not a perfect solution applicable to all the markets for AI creations, it does, however, offer a transitional solution to problems that could emerge in this attractive market. Furthermore, a measure like this will be very difficult to implement in art markets like China and the US;[9] however, other jurisdictions like France, where the very DDS was conceived, can lead to the optimal diffusion and consolidation of this new market through the adoption of the ECR.

Whether there is widespread adoption of the ECR – or something like it – any exploration of the possible approaches will help in developing new ways to address the market power and the asymmetries of information that characterize the art market, and the role that new technologies play if bringing into sharp relief the limitations of the current frameworks.

[7] [1982] 133 Cal. App. 3D 969 (US).

[8] In copyright, the economic rights related to a work end after a period of time determined by each jurisdiction taking as its starting point the death of the author. This condition has been adopted internationally based on the content of Article 6bis (2) of the Berne Convention.

[9] These jurisdictions do not recognize the DDS, *ergo* it would be difficult – if not impossible – to implement a similar figure.

Cryptocurrencies, Distributed Ledger Technology and the Law

4

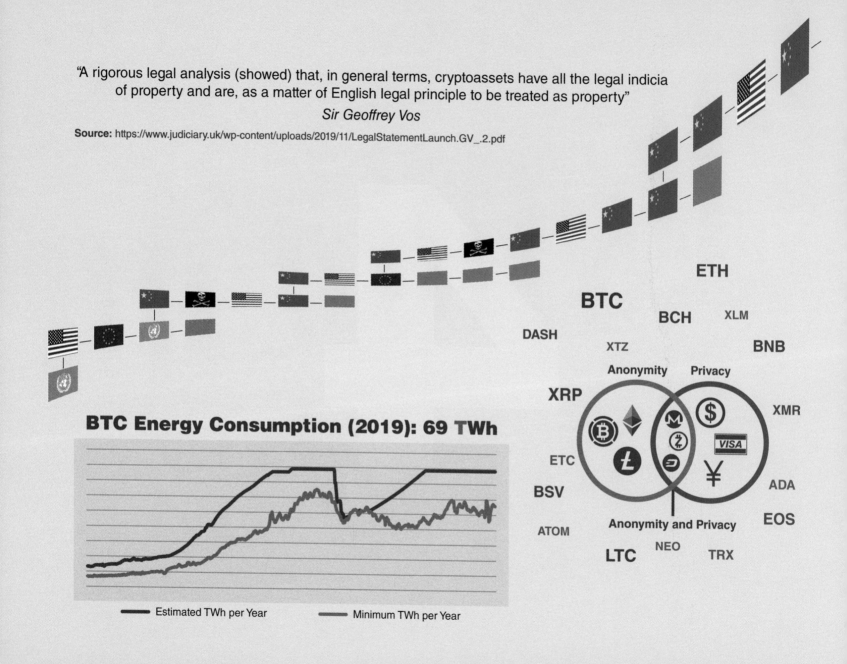

> "A rigorous legal analysis (showed) that, in general terms, cryptoassets have all the legal indicia of property and are, as a matter of English legal principle to be treated as property"
>
> *Sir Geoffrey Vos*

Source: https://www.judiciary.uk/wp-content/uploads/2019/11/LegalStatementLaunch.GV_.2.pdf

BTC Energy Consumption (2019): 69 TWh

Estimated TWh per Year   Minimum TWh per Year

ETH

BTC

BCH   XLM

DASH

XTZ

BNB

Anonymity   Privacy

XRP

XMR

ETC

BSV

ADA

EOS

ATOM

Anonymity and Privacy

LTC   NEO   TRX

Executive Summary

Nita Sanger introduces the key features of distributed ledger technology – widely known as "blockchain" technology – and describes leading application domains, outlining multiple challenges from a legal perspective as well as potential future benefits.

Blockchain technology can support various types, meanings and features of *computational* governance protocols giving rise to a wide spectrum of possible value and utility propositions, both "on-chain" and "off-chain", pursued most often by highly creative and iterative blockchain engineering.

Anna Elmirzayeva addresses the legal status and regulation of cryptoassets from a UK perspective, focusing on cryptocurrencies and stressing that crypto "tokens" will be assessed by a regulator on a case-by-case basis.

Our contributors are not only debating contentious issues, including Libra and Etherium "moneyness", decentralization of cryptomining and trading, since the regulation of cryptocurrencies, utility and security tokens is evolving as fast as the underlying blockchain technologies and protocols.

Due to the global extent of internet-based blockchains and innovation, comparisons of different jurisdictions are relevant and Eleftherios Jerry Floros contrasts Swiss and US regulations of security "initial offerings", while Enrique Agudo Fernandez addresses a fundamentally important concept of cryptoasset market manipulation from a EU and US regulatory perspective.

In the spirit of the foundational principles of company law, Marc Van de Looverbosch and Pierre Berger focus on share registers and share transfer mechanisms, applying a proposed cryptosecurity classification scheme to case studies encompassing several jurisdictions.

In the final chapter, Emanuele Pedilarco illustrates the potential of cryptotokens in supply chain finance, venturing beyond proposals and current exploratory blockchains in supply chains.

Distributed Ledger Technology and the Legal Profession

Nita Sanger
CEO, Idea Innovate Consulting

In the past few years there has been a lot of talk about how blockchain, which is underpinned by Distributed Ledger Technology (DLT),[1] is going to provide digital trust between untrusting parties[2] without the need for an intermediary, and will therefore disintermediate the legal professional. The reality is that whilst DLT will be extremely transformative in the near future, and will impact not just legal services but many other industries, the need for legal professionals is not going away any time soon.

Distributed Ledger Technology: Factors for Adoption and Use Cases

DLT is a network of digital data that is consistent, replicated, shared and synchronized across multiple sites, countries or institutions. It is a peer-to-peer database that replicates and saves an identical copy of the ledger on each node in the network and updates itself independently, without the need of a central authority. Distributed ledgers may be private or public and permissioned or permissionless. Each transaction is essentially unalterable and can only be changed if 51% of all nodes agree. To understand the impact of DLT, there is a need to assess the factors that will drive adoption of the technology, the industries that will be on the forefront of adoption, potential use cases and finally the issues and challenges that still need to be addressed.

There are a number of factors that will assist with the successful adoption of DLT,[3] such as:

- digital assets that can be stored and transferred in a virtual world;
- a market with multiple players and high transaction volumes;
- significant market pain points that need to be addressed;
- low trust in the existing market infrastructure; and
- the benefits of adoption outweighing the costs of implementation.

Finally, the most important aspect of DLT, and also its biggest challenge, is the need for a network of players in the ecosystem that will work together to solve a common problem for the "greater good", adhering to common industry, regulatory, security and privacy standards, without a central authority to monitor the network. As a result, initial DLTs are likely to be industry focused and will solve for industry-specific pain points.

The main DLT use cases can be divided into three broad categories: maintaining records, conducting transactions and a combination of the two, which are further divided into six areas of focus, as shown in Figure 1.

---

[1] https://en.wikipedia.org/wiki/Distributed_ledger.

[2] Satoshi Nakamoto, "Bitcoin: A Peer-to-Peer Electronic Cash System", 2008.

[3] https://www.mckinsey.com/business-functions/digital-mckinsey/our-insights/blockchain-beyond-the-hype-what-is-the-strategic-business-value.

For maintaining records			For conducting transactions		Combination
Information registry	**Identity management**	**Smart contracts**	**Transaction registry**	**Payments network**	**Other**
Description Distributed database to store information	Distributed database storing identity-related information. Often referred to as self-sovereign identify (SSI), where information is controlled by the individual	Conditions recorded on the blockchain to digitally facilitate, verify, or enforce the negotiation or performance of a contract	Distributed database to record exchange or flow of assets on a digital platform	Distributed database to record and execute on payment transactions between participants, underpinned by either cash or crypto-currencies initially will be driven by financial services	Use cases will combine the capabilities from the other groups or specific use cases that do not fit into the earlier categories
Use cases • Land titles • Patents • Intellectual property • Music rights • Food safety and origin	• Drivers licences • Passports and other identity cards • Know-Your-Client (KYC) • DNA and other healthcare information • Voting	• Vendor payments • Professional services (legal, financial, temporary, contract) • Insurance claim payouts • Music downloads	• Fractional investing in real estate, other precious metals and minerals, etc. • Supply-chain and traceability of food, drugs, mining, etc.	• Cross-border peer-to-peer payments or transfers (money or cryptocurrencies) • Cryptocurrency trading	• Financial inclusion for un- or underbanked, combining identity and payments • For better healthcare services for patients, leveraging identity • For supporting the settlement of refugees, including identity, registries and payments

Figure 1: DLT areas of focus and use cases

The industries that have been on the frontline of experimentation with DLT are **public sector, financial services and healthcare**. Many other industries are continuing to experiment with the use of DLT, with modest success to date, e.g. real estate for title registry, music industry for digital rights management and the food and beverage industry for food safety and origin. In the near term, many of the countries in the developing world will lead the way in the adoption and implementation of DLT to solve some of the significant challenges facing their citizens, and potentially use it to leapfrog ahead of many of the other developing nations with inefficient and crumbling systems. In the future, DLT will likely enable the creation of new business models and revenue streams.

To date, the most successful use of DLT has been in cryptocurrencies,[4] of which bitcoin is the most well known. The

[4] https://en.wikipedia.org/wiki/Cryptocurrency. A cryptocurrency (or crypto currency) is a digital asset designed to work as a medium of exchange that uses strong cryptography to secure financial transactions, control the creation of additional units and verify the transfer of assets. Cryptocurrencies use decentralized control as opposed to centralized digital currency and central banking systems. The decentralized control of each cryptocurrency works through distributed ledger technology, typically a blockchain, that serves as a public financial transaction database. Bitcoin, first released as open-source software in 2009, is generally considered the first decentralized cryptocurrency. Since the release of bitcoin, over 4,000 altcoins (alternative variants of bitcoin or other cryptocurrencies) have been created.

introduction of cryptocurrencies was an attempt to disintermediate the $1.9 trillion payments industry that is expected to grow to $3 trillion within the next five years.[5] In mid-2019, the daily trading volume of cryptocurrencies was $52.5 billion.[6] While there are many advantages to using cryptocurrencies, such as ease of use, low cost, transparency and anonymity[7] there are also many disadvantages, such as lack of scalability, cybersecurity, volatility and lack of intrinsic value, which have made many financial experts such as Jamie Dimon and Warren Buffett wary of them.[8] In addition, many "bad actors" in this space have given cryptocurrencies a negative reputation. Most business leaders across the board agree that DLT has significant potential to transform commerce.

Despite the hype, the widespread adoption of DLT for commercial use will take an additional three to five years, as the technology is at a nascent stage and several issues still need to be resolved, including:

- having a clear value proposition for its use;

- getting traditional industry players that historically compete with each other to work together to solve their common industry challenges;

- creating a network that targets to disintermediate traditional players in the industry, whilst needing their financial support, industry expertise and customer network; and

- establishing common industry standards to which all participants in the ecosystem will adhere.

[5] "Global Payments 2018: A Dynamic Industry Continues to Break New Ground", McKinsey, October 2018.

[6] https://coincheckup.com/global.

[7] https://ccoingossip.com/advantages-and-disadvantages-of-cryptocurrency/ (7 August 2019).

[8] https://www.prescouter.com/2017/11/disadvantages-of-cryptocurrencies/ (November 2017).

Impact of Distributed Ledger Technology on Legal Services

To understand the impact of DLT on the legal profession we need to look at the "practice of law" and the "business of law".[9] For the successful adoption of DLT for commercial use, the following legal issues need to be addressed:

Distributed ledger technology legal issues to be addressed

The successful commercial use of DLT will require the network to be very secure, and be resistant to hacking, while protecting the privacy and anonymity of the nodes and their transactions.

For the "practice of law" the legal industry[10] will play a vital role in the adoption of the technology by:

- training the participants in the ecosystem on the use and legal implications of the technology;

- guiding corporate clients as they run DLT use cases, then implement the technology to run their business;

[9] *Practice of law definition*: The giving of legal advice or of representation of another as an agent in a court of law or through rules of court, or in the preparation of legal documents or in dispute or contractual negotiation. The exercise of the profession of barrister, solicitor, attorney or lawyer. *Business of law definition*: The providing of a combination of legal, business and tech capabilities to augment customer (both corporate and law firm) expertise and improve their efficiency and effectiveness, including services such as legal project management and business analysis.

[10] https://blocksdecoded.com/blockchain-issues-security-privacy-legal-regulatory-ethical/ (3 October 2018).

- working with regulators to establish legal and regulatory standards and frameworks for the use of the technology;

- being a critical part of relevant industry and legal consortiums to develop common industry-specific standards; and

- collaborating with other legal service providers to leverage DLT to serve existing clients.

For the "business of law", the legal industry will be a "follower" in the adoption of DLT and move to it after its clients have adopted the technology. Once the use of DLT becomes ubiquitous for its customers, the legal industry can use the technology for improving its efficiency and effectiveness in serving its customers in the following areas:[11],[12]

- execution of legal services, such as dispute resolution and arbitration, development and execution of smart contracts and filing corporate returns;

- verification and authentication of legal business operations for customers, e.g. document management, billing and expense management;

- performing legal tasks such as maintaining a chain of documents during custody cases, merger and acquisition transactions, recording and maintaining historical case-related information and notarizing documents;

- providing "access to justice" to those currently living outside the protection of the law leveraging digital platforms, providing legal advice at lower costs.

Conclusion

The legal industry will play a key role in the adoption of DLT, educating relevant players in the legal ecosystem, helping corporates understand the legal and regulatory implications as they adopt it for their business and working with the regulators to establish standards. They will also be critical in establishing common industry standards for the legal profession and collaborating with other legal service providers to serve clients more efficiently and effectively. However, the legal industry will not be an early adopter in the use of DLT for its own use and will only adopt it after its customers have started using it to run their business.

---

[11] https://www.techradar.com/news/7-ways-blockchain-will-change-the-legal-industry-forever.

[12] https://www.disruptordaily.com/blockchain-use-cases-legal/.

Cryptoasset Regulation: Clarification and Guidance

Dr Anna Elmirzayeva
PD National Lead in Legal Technology and Innovation,
The University of Law

As jurisdictions all over the world race to build the most advanced and innovative systems of regulation for cryptoassets, which come in various shapes and forms,[1] the UK government is equally ambitious to maintain the status of London as the world's leading financial centre. Being the second largest legal services market in the world, a home to over 200 large international law firms,[2] clarity on the status of cryptoassets is key to establishing confidence in industries that choose UK jurisdiction for business and dispute resolution.

Several governmental initiatives have been working to create a state-of-the-art legislative framework. Following a public consultation on Wednesday 31 July 2019 the Financial Conduct Authority (FCA) has issued a finalized guidance on cryptoassets.[3]

---

[1] Some of the examples include the creation of the European Blockchain Partnership in April 2018: https://ec.europa.eu/digital-single-market/en/news/european-countries-join-blockchain-partnership; the European Blockchain Observatory and Forum was established in February 2018: https://ec.europa.eu/digital-single-market/en/news/european-countries-join-blockchain-partnership: Malta has declared itself "The Blockchain Island", passing a series of Regulatory Acts in July of 2018: http://www.justiceservices.gov.mt/LegalServicesSearch.aspx?type=lom&pageid=29.

[2] The Lawyer's top UK 200 law firms revealed: https://www.thelawyer.com/top-200-uk-law-firms/.

[3] Guidance on Cryptoassets, Financial Conduct Authority. Available at: https://www.fca.org.uk/publication/policy/ps19-22.pdf; the FCA is also working together with HM Treasury and the Bank of England as part of the Cryptoasset Taskforce final report, which can be found here: https://assets.publishing.service.gov.uk/government/uploads/system/uploads/attachment_data/file/752070/cryptoassets_taskforce_final_report_final_web.pdf.

To identify key aspects of legal uncertainty surrounding the status of cryptoassets in private law of England and Wales, the LawTech Delivery Panel's Jurisdictional Task Force[4] also held a public consultation with key market stakeholders.[5]

Classification of distributed ledger technology (DLT) cryptoassets can be confusing, particularly because traditional financial concepts are mixed with new legal parameters relevant to crypto realities. We are so used to associating the term "cryptoasset" with Bitcoin or Etherium that we effectively equate it to the concept of cryptocurrency. In fact, cryptoassets are not limited to monetary value. Use of DLT and blockchain in particular has opened up the possibility for the creation of a wide variety of cryptoassets all possessing different characteristics and functions.

The FCA has branded what we know as cryptocurrencies as "exchange tokens". Since the term "token" is used frequently in blockchain, it would be useful to distinguish between various types of tokens used in DLT applications.

The starting point is to clearly define what cryptocurrencies or "exchange tokens" are. These are intended to be independent means of exchanging and potentially storing value in the crypto world. They are meant to mimic the properties of real-world fiat currencies[6] in that they could be exchanged for value of some kind. Tokens not used as a means of exchange are divided into two categories: utility tokens and security tokens. What separates these "non-exchange tokens" from cryptocurrencies is that they

---

[4] The LawTech Delivery Panel is a government-backed, industry-led body. It has a number of task forces, one of which focuses on jurisdictional issues, led by Sir Geoffrey Vos.

[5] Public consultation took part in June 2019: https://www.lawsociety.org.uk/news/stories/cryptoassets-dlt-and-smart-contracts-ukjt-consultation/.

[6] The term "fiat currencies" is used to refer to real-world currencies issued by state governments and central banks, like pound sterling, dollar, yen, etc.

are always dependent on the environment within which they are first created and can only be used within such an environment.

The starting point for categorization of exchange tokens could be the degree of their decentralization. Two broad categories emerge from this assessment. These are *fiat cryptocurrencies* (or state-backed cryptocurrencies) and completely *decentralized cryptocurrencies*. The most vivid example of the latter is Bitcoin, a completely decentralized and disintermediated unit of exchange, not controlled by any government or authority.

Decentralized currencies, on the other hand, are created by DLT platforms themselves and are a result of functioning consensus protocols that effectively govern the platform and help keep records of platform interactions up to date. In their guidance of 31 July 2019, the FCA confirmed that these decentralized "exchange tokens" are not regulated though anti-money laundering rules may apply.[7]

State-backed or fiat cryptocurrencies are state-controlled implementations of DLT protocols. These currencies exist in cryptographic form but are issued and governed by state central banks.[8] Centralized crypto solutions are explored by many countries.[9] In some jurisdictions they are seen as a means of combatting financial instability or financial sanctions. Some, like Sweden for instance, are contemplating it as a solution allowing asylum seekers to have access to a verifiable and secure means of value transfer.[10]

Utility tokens are probably the most popular choice of cryptoasset for blockchain startups. These tokens represent functions within a predefined ecosystem and are often referred to as "platform tokens". They are issued by the DLT platform, often using processes very similar to those used for the creation of decentralized cryptocurrencies. One of the main features of utility tokens is that they create a closed and sustainable economy within platforms. Think of an eBay type of environment, where all users, buyers and sellers are transacting and using a means of exchange native to the environment.

Utility tokens could be used to pay for services within a platform.[11] For instance, projects built on the principles of distributed computing, where underutilized hardware space on participants' machines is used to store data. Hosts are paid for storing the data in native tokens exchangeable for cryptocurrencies or fiat.

The FCA have confirmed that utility tokens remain largely unregulated. The true challenge in trying to create a legislative framework for these is in the decentralized nature of the platforms they belong to. Unlike the internet, where jurisdiction of the service provider may limit some of their functions, blockchain and DLT have no comparable central authority. Decentralized platforms, in

---

[7] Guidance on Cryptoassets, Financial Conduct Authority. Available at: https://www.fca.org.uk/publication/policy/ps19-22.pdf.

[8] Some state-backed cryptocurrencies could also be "stable coins" – exchange tokens backed by fiat currency or commodity to minimize their volatility. For instance, Venezuelan perto or "pertomoneda" is a central bank-issued cryptocurrency backed by the country's oil and mineral reserves.

[9] Examples include Venezuelan petro, Swiss e-franc initiative and Swedish e-krona. China, Russia, Iran, Thailand, Estonia and Turkey are amongst the many who are contemplating state-backed cryptocurrencies.

[10] More information on e-krona is available from the Sveriges Riksbank website: https://www.riksbank.se/en-gb/payments--cash/e-krona/.

[11] As Ether is the second most popular investment on the market when it comes to cryptoassets; it is often associated with cryptocurrencies. In fact, it was initially created as an Etherium platform native token to be used to pay for services, such as running smart contracts. Ether has come to be perceived as cryptocurrency over time. Various operations on Etherium are prices in Ether's smaller units, known as gas. More information is available on the Etherium website: https://www.ethereum.org/.

their extreme representation, are virtually impossible to tie to any particular jurisdiction.

Another regulatory challenge that needs to be dealt with are the rules for DLT projects for fundraising, known as initial coin offerings (ICOs). As projects do not need to have proof of concept at the stage of the ICO a lot of these pose major risks for consumers and investors.

Finally, security tokens, which regulators pay particular attention to, in essence represent crypto versions of traditional investment mechanisms. Unlike securities in financial industry, these tokens could represent ownership of any physical asset such as real estate, commodities, intellectual property rights or financial instruments (bonds, stocks or shares in a business). Security tokens entitle their holder to a repayment of a sum of money or a share of future profits, and their value is directly linked to the rising or falling value of the asset they represent. These tokens as well as e-money tokens are likely to fall under the Food Safety Modernization Act regulations. As assets to which these tokens are linked are regulated and are based in specific jurisdictions, they are easier to regulate.

The FCA has reiterated that the underlying characteristics of each token will remain key to whether it is likely to be subject to regulation and require authorization.

The Legal Implications of Digital Security Offerings

Eleftherios Jerry Floros
CEO, MoneyDrome X

> "Digital securities offer many opportunities to streamline, modernize and digitize the entire investment process."
>
> *Source: STOcheck on Medium*

ICOs – initial coin offerings that burst onto the crypto scene with fever pitch – created an entirely new industry for startups to raise "crazy" amounts within a very short time period. During the 2018 peak of the hype, many platforms raised incredible amounts in the tens and even hundreds of millions within a few days, and some within record-shattering minutes. But like any hype, many of the shooting stars of the ICO universe crashed and burned, leaving investors out of pocket. Enter the STO – security token offering – which is considered by many the new "ICO 2.0", the only difference being that this time around, investors receive some form of equity participation or profit sharing on revenues. Sounds good in theory but in reality it's a whole different ballgame.

Why? Because at the time of this writing, there's no official definition for security tokens, let alone applying applicable law in the appropriate jurisdictions.

In trying to define a "digital security" or "security token", we first must define the purpose a token will serve. There are a variety of purposes of which the three most common are:

1. Financial asset token – representing assets of a financial type

2. Payment token – a medium of exchange

3. Consumer token – commonly known as a "utility token" serving a functional purpose on a particular platform

Digital securities or security tokens are commonly referred to as "cryptoassets" that have intrinsic features of an underlying asset (including "tokenized" assets such as art, copyrights, fractional ownership of property, etc.) or financial instruments that may include equity participations in companies, assets or revenue sharing/earning streams. In terms of economic and financial markets' function, these security tokens are analogous to equities, bonds or derivatives (i.e. listed market securities).

In short, a digital security is an "investment contract" that needs to be registered with the relevant financial authorities where the security is issued, as well as every single investor must receive an investment prospectus when intending to buy.

FINMA Leads but SEC Rules

Switzerland has taken the lead in crypto, issuing guidelines on the definitions of coins and tokens. Although these guidelines have not yet become law, it is, however, expected soon. On a global scale, everyone still looks at America's mighty Securities and Exchange Commission (SEC) to set the standards for global regulation but this has been everything but impressive so far and confusing at best.

The SEC is considered the "beacon" of securities regulation and the primary government institution whose authority is respected globally. Any bank, brokerage or financial institution will take any SEC advice, regulation or recommendation into account, regardless of where these entities may be based because the securities industry is vastly dollar denominated. Even for other currency denominations, rules set forth by the SEC must be complied with and adhered to if a security is to be effectively traded on the global financial markets. The fragmented global regulation of crypto securities has given financial authorities such as Switzerland's Financial Market Supervisory Authority (FINMA) the impetus to issue guidelines in relation to the issuance of tokens.

Whilst FINMA may currently lead the crypto regulation race, it's only a matter of time before the SEC will be in the driving seat and take pole position again.

The US Supreme Court and Considerations of the "Howey Test"

The Securities Act of 1933 prohibits the offer or sale of a security, except certain exempt securities or in certain exempt transactions, unless the security has been registered with the SEC. The litmus test for defining a security token was established by the US Supreme Court back in 1933 but is it still relevant and applicable in today's digital age?

Exasperating the validity and effectiveness of the Howey Test is the Securities Act of 1934, which regulates the secondary trading of securities between persons and entities that are often unrelated to the issuer, namely brokers and dealers.

ICOs for all intents and purposes are unregulated securities with the primary objective of gaining value (the element of profit as defined by the Howey Test) on the secondary markets, in particular on unregulated crypto exchanges sprinkled around the world.

Under the guise of being "utility tokens", almost every ICO in the peaks of 2017 and 2018 issued tokens that were destined to be traded on crypto exchanges with only a very few actually serving a purpose of "utility", that is, a token to be used within a viable ecosystem.

As a result of ICOs issuing "utility tokens" instead of shares, the entire ICO market collapsed at the end of 2018 along with the crypto crash and ensuing "crypto winter", leaving many disgruntled investors with vast amounts of useless and/or worthless tokens.

Whilst the after-effects of the ICO market collapse will linger on for many years to come, the ICO industry has evolved and reincarnated itself into the issuance of initial exchange offering and STO formats.

These "Band-Aid" reincarnations of ICOs have offered little comfort in relation to the legal implications of offering unregulated securities on – for the most part – unregulated crypto exchanges.

The bleeding might have stopped but the cure is still far away.

The Life cycle of a Security Token

Most issuers of security tokens underestimate or even completely disregard the "life cycle" management of any security, and that can become a very big and expensive problem in the near future. The complexity involved is very challenging and can be difficult to implement, as tracking and keeping records of issued securities on a global scale can easily result in breach of regulatory compliance.

The life cycle of an issued security is of crucial importance in order to ensure regulatory compliance and oversight. While blockchain offers all the benefits of immutable/tamper-proof transparency and tracking, the problem arises with the issuance of digital securities via unregulated exchanges and brokers.

For example, in the US, "Reg D." compliant securities can only be sold to accredited investors and this means that any securities sold must be registered in a "private placement memorandum"; these investors must then be onboarded manually after thorough anti-money laundering/know your customer checks, and finally the "transfer agent" must record all holders of these securities in their proprietary database.

Once these securities reach the secondary markets – the crypto exchanges scattered around the world – this record-keeping and regulatory oversight evaporates, the securities issuer and retail investor are usually unknown to each other and there's no longer the regulatory compliance as required by SEC or any other financial authority. At this stage, any security effectively has become unregulated and from that point on a "regulatory nightmare" for financial authorities when these things go wrong.

Global Regulation

Digital securities are an entirely new asset class within the financial markets but global regulation will inevitably be required sooner rather than later.

With the advent of tokenization of real-world assets, these digital securities will usher in the fast-paced global regulation of digital securities because at that stage, tokenized securities will largely be held by retail investors as opposed to the established financial institutions, and therefore regulation will become of paramount importance to safeguard investors at the retail level.

Until the major financial regulators around the world establish the appropriate legal framework for the issuance of digital securities, it will be the duty and responsibility of the security token issuer to appoint the necessary legal and compliance teams in order to ensure that issued security tokens are compliant with the applicable laws of the jurisdiction in which the pertinent securities are issued.

Through effective global regulation, digital securities will become the new norm in financial trading and that will positively impact the financial markets around the world.

Cryptoassets and Market Abuse

Enrique Agudo Fernandez
Magistrate

When talking about cryptoassets, market manipulation is a common topic. This might have something to do with the lack of a clear regulatory framework, but that does not mean regulations do not exist and that uncertainty should play in favour of those pretending to get unfair benefits from the current situation. If cryptoassets qualify as financial instruments and if we focus our attention on the integrity of financial markets, then we should be aware of the fact that current regulations on market abuse will apply.

Definition and Classification of Cryptoassets

One of the clearest examples of the difficulties currently presented to regulators by the relatively recent emergence of distributed ledger technology (DLT) has to do with the emergence of a new type of asset, whose nature, concept and classification have no consensus yet, otherwise referred to as cryptoassets.

While recognizing there is currently no legal definition of cryptoassets in EU laws, the European Securities and Markets Authority (ESMA) defines them as "a type of private asset that depends primarily on cryptography and DLT" and distinguishes the following varieties: (1) payment type; (2) investment type; (3) utility type; and (4) hybrid type.

In the US, the Securities and Exchange Commission (SEC) uses the expression "digital asset" to refer to "an asset that is issued and transferred using distributed ledger or blockchain technology, including, but not limited to, so-called virtual currencies, coins, and tokens".

In December 2018 there were more than 2,050 different cryptoassets representing a total market capitalization of around 110 billion euros, down from a peak of over 700 billion euros in January 2018.

Cryptoassets as Financial Instruments

Although cryptoassets do not represent a threat to financial stability, they raise specific challenges for regulators as there may be a lack of clarity as to how the regulatory framework applies to such instruments. One of the main challenges has to do with the legal status of cryptoassets, because it determines whether financial regulations apply.

A survey of National Competent Authorities (NCAs) conducted by the ESMA in 2018 highlighted a majority view that some cryptoassets may qualify as financial instruments. Although the Markets in Financial Instruments Directive (MiFID II) defines financial instruments, the classification of cryptoassets as financial instruments depends on the NCA and on the specific local implementation of EU law. In the EU, where cryptoassets qualify as financial instruments, a full set of rules apply (Prospectus Directive, Transparency Directive, MiFID II, Market Abuse Directive, etc.).

In the US the term "security" includes "investment contracts" and other instruments such as stocks, bonds, etc. The SEC has said that anyone considering an initial coin offering or otherwise engaging in the offer, sale or distribution of a digital asset needs to consider whether the US federal securities laws apply. Considering that in the US whether a contract, scheme or transaction is an "investment contract" is a matter of federal law, a threshold issue is whether a digital asset is a "security" under those laws.

Recently, the SEC has published a framework for analysing whether a digital asset has the characteristics of a "security", with particular reference to the "Howey" case. In this case the US

Supreme Court developed a flexible test for determining whether an "investment contract" qualifies as a "security". This test applies to any contract, scheme or transaction regardless of whether it has any of the characteristics of typical securities, and focuses the analysis not only on the form and terms of the instrument itself but also on the circumstances surrounding it and the manner in which it is offered, sold or resold. Following this, an "investment contract" for the purposes of the Securities Act means "a contract, transaction or scheme whereby a person invests his money in a common enterprise and is led to expect profits solely from the efforts of the promoter or a third party".

Considering the above, digital assets should therefore be analysed to determine if they have the characteristics of a "security" under the federal laws. If they do qualify as securities, then these laws will apply, including – inter alia – the Securities Act of 1933, the Securities Exchange Act of 1934 and the Commodity Exchange Act of 1936.

Market Abuse

Cryptoassets may be traded or exchanged for fiat currencies or other cryptoassets on specialized trading platforms. The ESMA estimates there are more than 200 trading platforms operating globally with a daily trading volume in the range of US$10–15 billion, down from a peak of around US$70 billion in January of 2018.

Generally speaking, the issues pertaining to platforms trading cryptoassets are no different from the ones that exist on trading venues for traditional securities, including whether the platform has adequate measures to deter potential market abuse.

It is commonly accepted that an integrated, efficient and transparent financial market requires market integrity, and that market abuse harms that integrity.

The concept of market abuse encompasses unlawful behaviour in the financial markets. More precisely in Europe, Regulation (EU)

596/2014 on Market Abuse (MAR) prohibits: (1) insider dealing; (2) unlawful disclosure of inside information; and (3) market manipulation.

Market manipulation comprises in this EU Regulation a number of activities, for example: placing orders to give false or misleading signals about the supply, demand or price of a financial instrument; disseminating information (including rumours) through the media with the same purpose of giving misleading signals; securing a dominant position over a financial instrument to fix prices; etc.

The MAR includes measures to prevent and detect market abuse, indicates the competent administrative authorities and establishes a catalogue of administrative pecuniary sanctions and other administrative measures. As a complement, Directive 2014/57 (EU) on Criminal Sanctions for Market Abuse (MAD) requires Member States to provide at least for serious cases of insider dealing, market manipulation and unlawful disclosure of inside information to constitute criminal offences when committed with intent. So, in the EU context, where cryptoassets qualify as financial instruments, and provided they are traded or admitted to trading on a trading venue, both MAR and MAD would become applicable.

Shifting locations, in the US the SEC defines market manipulation as an "intentional conduct designed to deceive investors by controlling or artificially affecting the market for a security". Although market manipulation regulation in the US might be found on different statutes and rules, it should be highlighted here: Section 9 ("Prohibition Against Manipulation of Security Prices") and Section 10 ("Regulation of the Use of Manipulative and Deceptive Devices") both of the Securities and Exchange Act, and also Sections 9(a)(2) and 4c(a)(2) of the Commodity Exchange Act.

Market manipulation can result in government investigations and disciplinary actions, as well as criminal charges and civil lawsuits by investors and others who were harmed. Some examples of manipulation referred by the SEC are: (1) spreading false or misleading information about a company; (2) engaging in transactions to make a security appear more actively traded; and (3) rigging quotes, prices or trades to make it look like there is more or less demand for a security than is the case.

In a more global context, and not linked with any particular regulatory framework, the following expressions are commonly used to describe abusive/manipulative practices: "insider dealing", "pump and dump", "wash trading", "matched orders", "painting the tape", "marking the close", "front running", "spoofing", etc.

Conclusions

There may be a false perception that cryptoassets are outside the scope of current regulations and thereof manipulative behaviours must simply be accepted. Nothing is further from reality. Where cryptoassets qualify as financial instruments, existing regulations will apply. This means that participants in these markets have to comply with regulations, that the supervisory authorities have the duty to ensure compliance and that unlawful behaviour that threatens the integrity of the market can be sanctioned not only administratively but also as criminal offences in the most serious cases.

Cryptosecurities: Traditional Financial Instruments on a Distributed Ledger

Pierre Berger
Partner, DLA Piper UK LLP

and Marc Van de Looverbosch
Lawyer, DLA Piper UK LLP

Distributed Ledger Technology and Share Registers

Distributed ledger technology (DLT), also known as "blockchain", has been developed to answer a specific question: how do you create digital money that can be transferred between parties who do not necessarily know or trust each other, without having to rely on a central party to create money and verify or settle transactions?[1]

Yet the technology offers a wider range of applications than just acting as a payment platform. DLT can serve as a source of inspiration particularly in situations where (1) one wishes to mitigate the dependence on a central party, and/or (2) parties who do not necessarily know or trust each other have to efficiently and repeatedly reach an agreement about a certain set of facts.[2]

Some similarities can be observed between the issues that the inventors of digital money experienced as problematic, and the problems which an ordinary register of shares in a company faces. A share register is usually controlled and kept by the management of the company, i.e. a central party. It may occur, however, that certain shareholders do not necessarily trust the management. One could, for instance, imagine a situation in which the minority shareholders have a difference of opinion with the reference shareholders. Given that the management usually consists of representatives of these reference shareholders, minority shareholders may wish to mitigate the management's power over the share register.

In this case, the decentralized design and cryptographic security of a DLT system could provide all shareholders with the necessary guarantees that the share register cannot be tampered with. Moreover, the distributed nature of a DLT system ensures that all shareholders always have access to the share register without having to physically travel to the company's headquarters. Also, there is no reason to fear the loss of the sole original copy of the share register, given that, in a DLT context, different parties have an identical original copy of the share register.[3]

It is worth noting that DLT networks can be tailored to the goals they are designed to achieve. One can, for instance, limit the circle of people who are authorized to view the blockchain, or to register information on the blockchain. As with an ordinary database, it is also possible to hide certain parts of the blockchain from certain participants or, conversely, to grant special access rights to certain participants (such as a regulatory authority). The consensus protocol can also be adapted to the specific context. For example, the validation of a transaction can be left to the parties to the transaction, so that other participants in the network do not need insight into the transaction.

[1] A. Antonopoulos, *Mastering Bitcoin. Programming the Open Blockchain*, Second Edition, O'Reilly Media, Inc., 2017, 4.

[2] K. Werbach, "Trust, But Verify: Why the Blockchain Needs the Law", *Berkeley Technology Law Journal*, 2018, 1, 18.

[3] M. Van de Looverbosch, "Crypto-effecten: tussen droom en daad", *Tijdschrift voor Rechtspersoon en Vennootschap-Revue Pratique des Sociétés*, 2018, 193, 198, para. 20.

Cryptosecurities

One can also go beyond merely keeping the share register on a blockchain. DLT could also be used to issue and transfer title to shares and other securities, similar to how cryptocurrencies such as Bitcoin are issued and transferred (hence the term "cryptosecurities"). This could offer a number of additional advantages. The integrity and consistency of shareholding data could potentially significantly improve if all shares in a company were cryptoshares. Thanks to the cryptographic algorithms inherent in a DLT system, the company's capitalization table would always be correct and up to date.[4]

Classification Matrix

Different types of cryptosecurities exist, depending on the degree of legal recognition and technological support they enjoy.[5] A distinction can be made between (1) recording (i.e. keeping the securities ledger up to date), (2) title transfer, and (3) issuance of cryptosecurities. The matrix below proposes a descriptive classification of cryptosecurities based on these three elements.[6]

Examples

Example of a cryptosecurity of category A1

A category A1 cryptosecurity makes minimum use of DLT and enjoys no explicit legal recognition. Borsa Italiana launched an initiative to allow non-listed small and medium-sized enterprises to keep track of their stock ledger by using a DLT platform.[7] This platform is only designed to keep track of the cap table, not to transfer title to shares. This implies a low level of technological reliance on DLT ("category A"). The project takes place within the limits of existing legislation, such that there is no explicit legal support for DLT ("category 1").

Example of a cryptosecurity of category B1

In December 2016, Overstock.com, Inc., a North American online retailer listed on Nasdaq, completed the first-ever issuance of cryptoshares.[8] The cryptoshares were issued in the form of book entry shares (for which no share certificates were issued), registered in the stock ledger of the issuer in the name of the

---

[4] For a recent legal analysis of a DLT-based securities settlement system, please refer to B. Garré and S. Van de Velde, "Can Securities Be Issued, Traded and Settled on DLT? Legal Considerations from a CSD's Perspective", *Financieel forum/Bank- en financieel recht*, 2019, 130–148.

[5] For a classification of cryptosecurities by legal recognition, see Direction Générale du Trésor (France), "Consultation publique sur le projet de reformes législative et réglementaire", 24 March 2017, 4–5: https://www.tresor.economie.gouv.fr/Ressources/File/434688. For a discussion of degrees of integration of DLT with the existing interrelated structure of listed securities, see P. Paech, "Securities, Intermediation and the Blockchain: An Inevitable Choice between Liquidity and Legal Certainty", LSE Law, Society and Economy Working Paper 20/2015, 26–28. For a reflection on degrees of technological support, see K. Werbach, "Trust, But Verify: Why the Blockchain Needs the Law", *Berkeley Technology Law Journal*, 2018, 1, 43–48.

[6] See also M. Van de Looverbosch, "Classifying Cryptosecurities", Distributed Ledger Law, 17 May 2018: https://distributedledgerlaw.org/2018/05/17/classifying-cryptosecurities/, and M. Van de Looverbosch, "Crypto-effecten: tussen droom en daad", Tijdschrift voor Rechtspersoon en Vennootschap-Revue Pratique des Sociétés, 2018, 193–207.

[7] See https://www.reuters.com/article/us-lse-blockchain/london-stock-exchange-group-tests-blockchain-for-private-company-shares-idUSKBN1A40ME.

[8] See http://investors.overstock.com/phoenix.zhtml?c=131091&p=irol-newsArticle&ID=2230245.

		Technological support ("Tech")		
		A | Weak	**B | Moderate**	**C | Strong**
Legal recognition ("Law")	**1 Weak**	Tech: DLT is used to support the securities register. DLT is not used for the transfer or issuance of securities.	Tech: DLT is used to maintain the securities register. DLT is used to support transfers. DLT is not used for the issuance of securities.	Tech: Registration, transfer and issuance are done via DLT.
		Law: No explicit legal recognition of registration, transfer or issuance via DLT.	Law: No explicit legal recognition of registration, transfer or issuance via DLT.	Law: No explicit legal recognition of registration, transfer or issuance via DLT.
	2 Moderate	Tech: DLT is used to support the securities register. DLT is not used for the transfer or issuance of securities.	Tech: DLT is used to maintain the securities register. DLT is used to support transfers. DLT is not used for the issuance of securities.	Tech: Registration, transfer and issuance are done via DLT.
		Law: Express legal recognition of the evidentiary value of DLT in case of registration and/or transfer. No explicit legal basis for issuance via DLT.	Law: Express legal recognition of the evidentiary value of DLT in case of registration and/or transfer. No explicit legal basis for issuance via DLT.	Law: Express legal recognition of the evidentiary value of DLT in case of registration and/or transfer. No explicit legal basis for issuance via DLT.
	3 Strong	Tech: DLT is used to support the securities register. DLT is not used for the transfer or issuance of securities.	Tech: DLT is used to maintain the securities register. DLT is used to support transfers. DLT is not used for the issuance of securities.	Tech: Registration, transfer and issuance are done via DLT.
		Law: Express legal recognition of the possibility to register, transfer and issue via DLT. Registration provides at least a rebuttable presumption that one is a securities holder. Transfer via DLT is binding on the issuer and third parties. Issuance via DLT is based on an explicit legal basis.	Law: Express legal recognition of the possibility to register, transfer and issue via DLT. Registration provides at least a rebuttable presumption that one is a securities holder. Transfer via DLT is binding on the issuer and third parties. Issuance via DLT is based on an explicit legal basis.	Law: Express legal recognition of the possibility to register, transfer and issue via DLT. Registration provides at least a rebuttable presumption that one is a securities holder. Transfer via DLT is binding on the issuer and third parties. Issuance via DLT is based on an explicit legal basis.

shareholders.[9] The shares are exclusively traded on a multilateral trade facility that is operated by a subsidiary of Overstock.com, Inc. Transactions in the cryptoshares are settled almost immediately ($t + 0$). The platform comes with some quite radical built-in transfer restrictions: the cryptoshares cannot be sold short or pledged.

In summary, a transaction would unfold as follows.[10] First, the transaction is recorded in the internal ledger of the multilateral trade facility. The updated ledger is then automatically published on the internet (on an anonymized basis). Finally, a cryptographic hash of the updated ledger is registered on the Bitcoin blockchain. This cryptographic hash serves as a digital fingerprint that can be used to verify the accuracy of the internal ledger.

Considering this setup, the Overstock cryptoshares can be classified as category B1: there is a moderate reliance on DLT (category B), but no explicit legal recognition (category 1).

Category C3 Cryptosecurities

A category C3 cryptosecurity heavily relies on DLT for its registration, transfer and issuance, and enjoys explicit legal recognition in terms of its validity, enforceability and probative value. This category includes securities issued directly on a DLT platform pursuant to a statutory possibility to do so.[11] The securities can be transferred via the DLT platform from the moment they are issued. Such transfers are binding on the issuer and third parties. Registration as a security holder in the DLT system provides at least a rebuttable presumption that the registered person is a security holder. Thus, there is a high degree of technological reliance on DLT ("category C") and a high degree of legal recognition ("category 3").

The first category C3 cryptosecurities have yet to be issued. Several jurisdictions, such as Delaware, France, Luxembourg and Wyoming, have enacted legislation to enable the issuance of cryptosecurities.[12] This makes them eligible as the first "category 3 jurisdictions".

Conclusion

The degree of technological reliance on DLT and legal recognition are essential characteristics of a cryptosecurity. It can therefore be useful to describe cryptosecurities initiatives on the basis of these characteristics. This helps in quickly getting to the essence of an initiative and facilitates communication. The classification matrix proposed in this chapter provides a framework for this.

---

[9] This is remarkable because in the US almost all shares of listed companies are registered in the stock ledger of the issuer in the name of Cede & Co., a nominee of Depository Trust Company.

[10] See the prospectus dated 9 December 2015, pp. 34–36, in particular p. 36, and the prospectus supplement dated 14 November 2016, pp. S-52–S-57, both available via the EDGAR database of the US Securities and Exchange Commission at: https://www.sec.gov/edgar.

---

[11] In a civil law jurisdiction, this process could be entrusted to a notary. The notary could ensure that the correct number of shares of the correct type is registered in the name of the correct persons on the platform.

[12] See M. Van de Looverbosch, "DEEP Securities", Distributed Ledger Law, 16 January 2018: https://distributedledgerlaw.org/2018/01/16/deepsecurities/, and M. Van de Looverbosch, "Luxembourg Joins Cryptosecurities Club", Distributed Ledger Law, 26 March 2019: https://distributedledgerlaw.org/2019/03/26/luxembourg-joins-cryptosecurities-club/.

The Use of Digital Tokens for the Boost of Supply Chain Finance

Emanuele Pedilarco
Lawyer and PhD, Grimaldi Studio Legale

Introduction

In the aftermath of the recent financial crisis, businesses have tried to find new ways of financing. Looking for new alternatives to traditional bank lending is, in fact, key to supporting the real economy in the future. One way in which this can be done is through supply chain finance (SCF).

SCF is generally considered as a set of technology-based business and financing processes that link the various parties in a transaction – buyer, seller and financing institution – to lower financing costs and improve business efficiency. SCF provides credit that optimizes working capital for each involved party. For instance, under SCF, suppliers sell their invoices or receivables at a discount to banks or other financial service providers, often called factors. In return, the suppliers enjoy faster access to the money they are owed, enabling them to use it for working capital, whilst buyers generally have more time to pay. Instead of relying on the creditworthiness of the supplier, the bank deals with the buyer.

SCF is one of the many sectors whereby technology can be of great assistance, especially where the parties require financing guarantees – very relevant in cases where there are concerns regarding the borrower's ability to meet its obligations.

The Use of Digital Tokens in SCF

Even as an alternative way of lending, SCF, as well as any traditional lending, needs *a set of valid, secure and enforceable guarantees*. So, although nowadays the financing process can be dealt with by all relevant entities with technology and procedures which are much more speedy (thanks to, for example, the use of electronic invoices), the required recourse to "traditional" forms of guarantee can slow the financing process or even discourage the relevant parties to proceed with SCF.

As a matter of fact, instead of using "traditional" guarantees (e.g. pledge on shares, pledge on bank accounts, mortgage or pledge on a supplier's products/goods), lenders and borrowers, in the context of the SCF, may make use of so-called "digital tokens" as a form of legal guarantee.

From a general perspective, according to guidance from the European Security and Markets Authority, a "digital token" is "any digital representation of an interest, which may be of value, a right to receive a benefit or perform specified functions". Digital tokens are considered part of "cryptoassets", likewise cryptocurrencies. Cryptoassets are types of private asset that depend primarily on cryptography and "distributed ledger technology" (DLT), which is a means of saving information through a distributed ledger, a repeated digital copy of data available at multiple locations. DLT is built upon public-key cryptography, a cryptographic system that uses pairs of keys: public keys, which are publicly known and essential for identification, and private keys, which are kept secret and are used for authentication and encryption.

From a practical perspective, digital tokens can represent the given value of the supplier's goods and, in turn, be used as guarantees of a financing transaction. This could lead lenders and borrowers to exchange, in an easy, speedy and efficient way, "digital tokens" which, as indicated above, may represent goods or values of the supplier in the context of financing.

An Example of How Digital Tokens Can Be Used in the Context of SCF

Many businesses require the use of warehouses, whereby stocks of goods are kept for a number of different reasons (e.g. for features of the product, like ham, wine and cheese, or for efficiency reasons in case of market requests/demands). Those goods represent the inner value of the business but are also illiquid by their very nature and therefore difficult to trade. The SCF aims, inter alia, to facilitate the financing of companies whose business, sometimes, requires the use of deposits and warehouses.

As such, the borrower would aim to make available the goods piled up in the warehouse in a way that would facilitate financing. In such cases, instead of guaranteeing financing with traditional means (e.g. a pledge on shares, a pledge on a bank account, a mortgage or a pledge on the supplier's products), the parties make use of digital tokens which incorporate, as indicated by the definition above, *a digital representation of an interest, which may be of value, or a right to receive a benefit or perform specified functions*. In particular, a digital token will incorporate and represent the ownership of a predefined set of goods of the supplier, which will pass, as guarantee to the lender, by exchanging the digital token.

Let's consider a practical example. On one side is a company that has, for its own business purpose, a huge warehouse with valuable and/or illiquid goods and a need to finance its activities. On the other side is a typical lender that might be ready to finance such a company if and to the extent that (1) it believes that the company is able to achieve its business purpose in a reasonable and sound way, and (2) it receives sufficient financial guarantees.

In such a context, digital tokens might be helpful. By executing relevant agreements, (1) the lender could finance the supplier's business; (2) the supplier could sell the goods to the lender as a guarantee by providing a digital token which incorporates the transfer of the goods' ownership; (3) the lender would, in turn, grant the supplier the use of the goods for its business purpose (i.e. for the sale of the goods); and (4) the supplier would repay the lender (also for the interests' part) with the proceeds of the various sales of goods.

In this way:

1. the borrower would efficiently make use of its warehouse, using it as a guarantee, without losing the opportunity to sell the goods and repay the debt; and

2. the lender would have ownership of the goods as well as the control, monitoring and supervision of the warehouse by means of the digital token (which would, on the one hand, represent and incorporate the transfer of the goods and, on the other hand, track the entry/exit of the goods from the warehouse).

Conclusion: Tokenization as a Boost for the Supply Chain Finance Sector

Although at a nascent stage, the development of "*tokenization*", i.e. the representation of traditional assets on DLT, could bring benefits also to the SCF business. In fact, it has the potential to create beneficial outcomes for lenders and borrowers. As *tokenization* is a method that converts rights to an asset into a digital token, it is effectively a means to represent ownership of assets on DLT. As such, virtually anything can be tokenized, ranging from physical goods (from wines to metal products) to traditional financial instruments (like shares). The use of digital tokens has therefore the potential to make alternative financing more efficient and secure by making transfer of ownership easier and faster, and also reducing the need for intermediaries. In addition, the use of digital tokens may reduce risks and costs associated with "traditional forms of guarantee", providing positive results for lenders, borrowers and, more generally, market participants.

Smart Contracts and Applications

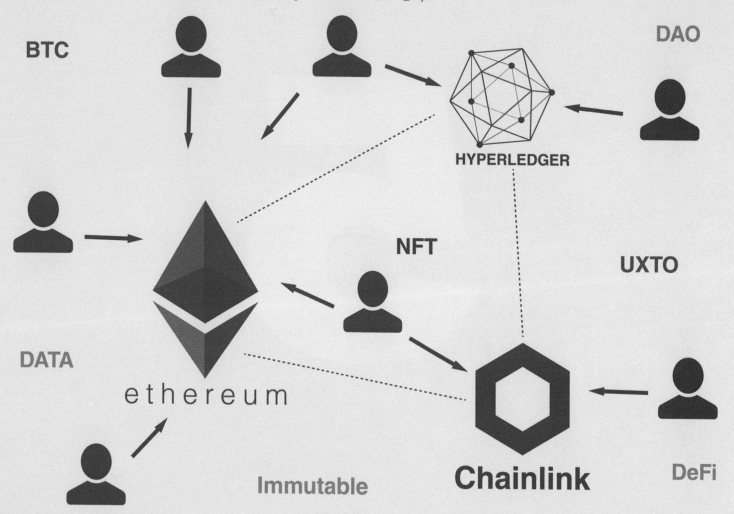

"The terms of the **smart contract** must be recorded in computer-readable code (…) the legal statement concludes that a smart contract can be identified, interpreted and enforced using ordinary and well-established legal principles."

Sir Geoffrey Vos

Source: https://www.judiciary.uk/wp-content/uploads/2019/11/LegalStatementLaunch.GV_.2.pdf

BTC

DAO

HYPERLEDGER

NFT

UXTO

DATA

ethereum

Immutable

Chainlink

DeFi

Executive Summary

"Smart (legal) contracts" have the potential to fundamentally change automated (computational) contract law. Robert Peat describes the principles illustrated by the ISDA framework, providing the foundation for derivative trading across global investment banking. The ISDA is developing its own digital law platform proposition and intriguingly it is not unique and the impact of introducing any of them can be significant.

Martin Davidson et al. discuss how contracting will be changed by introducing standard digital forms and representations of contract clauses, leading to potentially *self-executing* agreements. Self-executing agreements are foundations of future decentralized autonomous organization's legal *persona* and are discussed by Željka Motika, focusing on links between traditional and smart legal contracts.

Anne Rose describes the blockchain-driven foundations of smart contracts and illustrates several potential applications. Her review includes current regulatory, interoperability and standardization efforts as well as a number of potential risks.

Luigi Telesca provides a detailed technical description of a smart contract execution platform proposal based on codifying a legal contract in prose and assembling collections of contract templates.

The future Internet of Things is calling for new, highly scalable economic mechanisms and Christian Spindler describes an innovative pay-per-use solution framework, close in spirit to previous chapters.

LegalTech's Impact on the Role and Job of a Lawyer

Robert Peat
Director, Robert Peat Consultancy Limited

Whether in literature, or in reality, lawyers have been known to be curious; they can, as Charles Dickens wrote, "always [be] picking up odds and ends for [their] patchwork minds" with the knowledge that this could prove invaluable.[1] However, with the development and introduction of legal technology (LegalTech), traditional tasks conducted by lawyers such as drafting of agreements, due diligence, negotiation of contracts, litigation and structuring of transactions may be taken away from them and placed in the hands of technology. Yet, it is foreseeable that these "curious" and "inquisitive" lawyers will not disappear at the hands of LegalTech. Arguably, LegalTech will provide a prodigious opportunity for lawyers to extend client interaction and stimulate business. Understandably, the legal issues and potential reach of these developments are too extensive to discuss at length in this chapter. Instead, the chapter will attempt to frame what it considers to be potentially major areas of change and access their conceivable impact on the forthcoming role of lawyers.

There is the possibility for "smart legal contracts" (SLCs) to displace the legal system's core ability to enforce agreements.[2] Where lawyers used to fulfil the task of producing contracts, so-called "legal engineers" may now take their place.[3] There is discussion around a definition for SLCs; for our purpose to better understand the issue, we will take Stark's definition that SLCs refer to legally enforceable contracts, or elements of legal contracts where use of code verifies, articulates and enforces the agreements between the parties.[4] It is conceivable to imagine a derivatives trade document, such as an International Swaps and Derivatives Association (ISDA) Master Agreement, being translated in large sections into automatically executing code or merely expressing the duties of each parties in uniform contractual code. Therefore, as code cannot have a semantic detail like natural language, and lawyers are trained in words not code, the requirement for legal drafting is consequently minimized, or at worst removed. Nonetheless, the issue still stands, code must present something *legally* enforceable. At this moment, law is not written in code. Lawyers are skilled in understanding the complexities of the written law in a way which non-lawyers (for example, coders), let alone computers and artificial intelligence (AI), are not. Undoubtedly, SLCs will increasingly be written in code but this will mandate cooperation between lawyers and technologists to reach a middle ground. This middle ground is a Ricardian contract, whereby natural language sits alongside code to place the defining elements of a legal agreement in a format that can be expressed and actioned in software.[5]

While we shouldn't expect all lawyers to learn to code, they will have to become curious as to how code *works*.[6] Indeed, they will have to grapple with the probable presentation of new normalcies in the world of contract, just as they did when technology such as facsimile challenged the postal acceptance rule.[7]

---

[1] Charles Dickens, *The Works of Charles Dickens: Little Dorrit*, vols 1 and 2, Books Incorporated, 1867, 537.

[2] Kevin Werbach and Nicolas Cornell, "Contracts Ex Machina", *Duke Law Journal*, 2017, 101, 103.

[3] Ibid, 163.

[4] Joshua Stark, "Making Sense of Blockchain Smart Contracts – Coindesk", CoinDesk, 2019: https://www.coindesk.com/making-sense-smart-contracts (accessed 24 August 2019).

[5] Ian Grigg, "Financial Cryptography in 7 Layers", Iang.org, 2000. https://iang.org/papers/fc7.html (accessed 6 October 2019).

[6] Such issues were discussed at length during a two-day conference at the University of Oxford in preparation for their AI in Law research project: https://www.law.ox.ac.uk/unlocking-potential-artificial-intelligence-english-law/work-package.

[7] *Entores Ltd v Miles Far East Corporation* [1955] EWCA Civ. 3.

Furthermore, while code may become the new presentational norm, lawyers will be required to have significant input to ensure that legal norms are presented correctly by this code; for example, an intention to create legal relations between the parties can have nuanced detail of the objective observer's view point.[8] Arguably, without a legal interpretation of these objective standpoints, the final code may by incorrect. There is ample evidence to suggest that lawyers are engaging with this developing world. For example, the Accord Project, which has aimed to introduce a common format for SLC while maintaining a focus on commercial contracts, has garnered commitment from a range of law firms to the project, including Allen & Overy and Baker McKenzie, and suggests collaboration will offer lawyers new opportunities to impact the expanding use of LegalTech.[9] Such expanding horizons are exemplified by the British Standards Institute commissioning a steering group to examine developing a Publicly Available Specification for Smart Legal Contracts. Undoubtably, there will be input from technologists; however, many lawyers were appointed. For example, Dr Anna Donovan (Lecturer in Law and Vice Dean (Innovation) UCL) has commented on her ability to add valued input as an appointed member.[10] It will be interesting to see the finalized specification from the British Standards Institute; nonetheless, such projects represent the immense impact of lawyers on developing LegalTech.

In the securitization and derivatives space, ISDA published its updated 2018 Credit Support Deed (and Annex) for Initial Margin (IM CSA).[11] Traditionally, these documents, alongside Master Agreements, were negotiated by humans, alterations in language were drafted by lawyers and the most technology was used would be to send blacklines of relevant documents via email. IM CSA, however, introduced "ISDA Create" to the scene. ISDA Create is an online platform which will allow users to produce, deliver, negotiate and execute documents.[12] A role which many lawyers use to fill in negotiating could foreseeably be replaced by less skilled workers using this platform. ISDA Create is not alone in this sphere. Other companies such as "Clause" and "Exari" (acquired by "Coupa" in May 2019) have attempted to develop platforms where agreements are designed, negotiated and stored.

Furthermore, ISDA, working with legal data consulting firm D2 Legal Technology, has created a Clause Taxonomy and Library for its Master Agreements – the project's high-level aim is to harmonize and standardize the way derivatives agreement language is presented and represented. A new legal agreement data standard is being created by which the over-the-counter derivatives industry will create a taxonomy of clauses that exist in these documents, and enumerate and classify the various business outcomes that might be achieved from variants of those clauses, then allowing business outcomes (according to the classification) to be mapped to wording – and model wording that can be used for this purpose. Hence, both of these advances in LegalTech risk alienating lawyers who will no longer need to "creatively" draft agreements, nor will they have the

---

[8] *Carlill v Carbolic Smoke Ball Company* [1892] EWCA Civ. 1.

[9] "About the Accord Project", Accordproject.org, 2019: https://www.accordproject.org/about (accessed 6 October 2019).

[10] "Dr Anna Donovan Appointed to BSI Smart Legal Contracts Steering Group", UCL, 2019: https://www.ucl.ac.uk/laws/news/2019/feb/dr-anna-donovan-appointed-bsi-smart-legal-contracts-steering-group (accessed 8 October 2019).

[11] "Initial Margin Implementation Under EMIR and the ISDA 2018 Credit Support Deed (for IM)", Ashurst.com, 2018: https://www.ashurst.com/en/news-and-insights/legal-updates/initial-margin-implementation-under-emir-and-the-isda-2018/ (accessed 26 August 2019).

[12] "What Is ISDA Create – IM? | International Swaps and Derivatives Association", International Swaps and Derivatives Association, 2018: https://www.isda.org/2018/05/24/isda-create-im/ (accessed 26 August 2019).

same level of freedom as they may be increasingly constrained to the view which is presented by projects such as ISDA Clause Taxonomy and Library.

Nevertheless, it is lawyers, law firms and legal technology consulting firms who have played a large part in creating and driving these projects. It's unlikely that lawyers would have worked tirelessly in researching language variation in ISDA Master Agreements for ISDA Clause Library in order to destroy their own profession. It is more accurate to suggest that these lawyers will be ever more important in playing a part in making sure these platforms produce suitable documents, and the language is correct. A primary example of where the input for lawyers was essential was for ISDA Create. Global law firm Linklaters, along with its flagship LegalTech and AI platform *nakhoda*, were mandated by ISDA to act as counsel for the project and provided the expertise in consulting and drafting the next generation of these collateral documents.[13] Such projects complement the role of lawyers, making them more productive by reducing the time it takes for negotiations, digitally capturing information and processing contract data to drive enhanced business outcomes.

Additionally, such developments do not remove the need for lawyers further down the line – for example, if there is a contentious litigation issue. It is arguable that litigation and arbitration will be relatively impossible to replicate entirely with a machine due to the need for reasoning, professional empathy and logic engaged by skilled litigators and arbitrators.

The words "due diligence" or "DD" likely fill any junior lawyer or trainee with dread, having provided them with many sleepless nights and lost weekend plans. However, if LegalTech continues to rise at the current rate, we may see this task consigned to the past. Yet this may not be cause for celebration for junior lawyers, or law firms. As the removal of more menial tasks such as DD becomes greater, it may necessitate a reduction in the number of junior lawyers, followed by a reduction in associates. The traditional law firm model will have to be challenged and reformed. If we imagine a pyramid with the base being juniors and narrowing to partners at the top, this will alter to take account of technologists being embedded with lawyers. Such an issue was discussed at the Bucerius Law School conference.[14] This general consensus that while the number of employees per law firm would remain the same but the ratio of skilled lawyers will decline is likely true.[15]

Moreover, this reduction of lawyers may lead to less profitable law firms, in turn meaning less available work for trainees, which adds to the vicious cycle of the supposed end of lawyers. There is, however, cause to be optimistic – junior lawyers and trainees are well versed in picking up technology; the proposed alteration in business models may see a tightening of recruitment and a reassessment of requisite skills looked for by recruiters, but ultimately those affected are well equipped to reskill. Law firms' increasing use of AI is also not too worrisome – as a partner at global law firm TLT discussed regarding their partnership with US technology firm LegalSifter, the increasing use of technology will allow lawyers to become more valuable.[16] There is logic in suggesting that by removing the menial tasks and streamlining the process, a law firm can allow its lawyers to generate more revenue, interact with clients more and produce a higher quality of work.

SMART CONTRACTS AND APPLICATIONS

13 "About the Accord Project", Accordproject.org, 2018: https://www. accordproject.org/about (accessed 6 October 2019).

14 Christian Veith, Michael Bandlow, Michael Harnisch, Hariolf Wenzler, Markus Hartung and Dirk Hartung, "How Legal Technology Will Change the Business of Law", Boston Consulting Group & Bucerius Law School, Hamburg, January 2016, 10.

15 Ibid, 11.

16 Alex Taylor, "TLT's Legal Tech Kit That Can Advise Not Just Triage", The Lawyer | Legal insight, benchmarking data and jobs, 2018: https://www. thelawyer.com/tlt-legalsifter-legal-tech-kit/ (accessed 27 August 2019).

To suggest this would spell the end of lawyers is incorrect; rather, lawyers will find a new beginning in which they can expand their horizons and practice the skills they have spent years developing without the shackles of menial tasks.

In summary, there is a new horizon for lawyers and law firms to contend with. There is no doubt that currently, and in the future, there will be major shifts in the practice and structure of the legal industry due to LegalTech. But this should not be cause for concern. Rather, these shifts represent opportunities and possibilities for lawyers to expand their patchwork quilt of knowledge, to engage with new professionals and ultimately utilize the enabler which LegalTech will be. We could go as far to say that this isn't even a juncture for lawyers and law firms – it is a new beginning.

Smart(er) Contracts – Digitizing Contracts for a New Age

Martin Davidson
Chief Legal Intelligence Officer, ThoughtRiver Limited

Lachlan Harrison-Smith
Head of Lexible, ThoughtRiver Limited

and Emanuela Denaro
Legal Engineer, ThoughtRiver Limited

Introduction

The contract, critical to the global economy, is broken. The prose drafting on which commercial lawyers rely is not fit for purpose. A major cause of this dysfunction is a lack of standardization. True digitization is required for a new digital age where goods and services are demanded instantly, and people require the right information at their fingertips. Contracts should make it easier for us to transact successfully, seamlessly deliver on our promises and know our rights and obligations. Here we imagine such a future and suggest how it could happen.

Costly Contracting and the Need for a Digital Contract Standard

Every contract ever agreed performs the same basic task: it asserts the rights and duties of the parties in a way that can be enforceable should the need arise. However, there is no one way to draft a contract.

Some lawyers may disagree, but a great share of the variation in clause drafting is purely cosmetic.[1] Our own analysis across 1.5 million contracts found 330,000 distinct formulations for governing law clauses,[2] though it is hard to imagine that all these differences could be substantive. Even within individual firms, lawyers prefer to evolve old precedents rather than rely on specialist standard wording, only leading to more drafting and redrafting.[3] The draftsman's craft is presented as a professional differentiator, yet this creates opaque contracts and "leaks" value from transactions.[4]

Looking outside the world of commerce, the lack of standardization in prose drafting makes it hard for non-lawyer individuals to assess their risk. It is no wonder that time-pressured consumers skip over the pages of fine print at point of sale.[5] Regulatory regimes may differ between jurisdictions but the contracts they govern

---

[1] Robert Anderson and Jeffrey Mans, "The Inefficient Evolution of Merger Agreements", George Washington University Law School Faculty Publication, 2016: https://scholarship.law.gwu.edu/cgi/viewcontent.cgi?referer=&httpsredir=1&article=2467&context=faculty_publications.

[2] Minor changes in text (e.g. the governing law in question and use of synonyms "agreement"/ "document"/"contract") do not count as a new template.

[3] See Anderson and Mans above, note 1, 2016.

[4] Beverly Rich, "How AI Is Changing Contracts", *Harvard Business Review*, 12 February 2008: https://hbr.org/2018/02/how-ai-is-changing-contracts and sources cited therein giving estimates of lost value in transactions.

[5] UK Department for Business, "Energy & Industrial Strategy, Statutory Report on the Implementation of the Consumer Contracts (Information, Cancellation and Additional Charges) Regulations 2013", July 2019: https://assets.publishing.service.gov.uk/government/uploads/system/uploads/attachment_data/file/814448/Statutory_Report_on_the_Implementation_of_the_Consumer_Contracts.pdf.

do fundamentally similar things (e.g. mobile phone contracts[6]). Why then do they look different? Clearly, the "cost" of contracting resonates far beyond the realm of big business and commercial transactions.

Digitization, not just standardization

So, is standardization the answer? Standard form contracting is widely used but it is not a panacea and does not realize the potential offered by a truly digital, information-rich contracting standard.[7] Projects already exist to establish data definition standards for legal practice.[8] Such measures are useful steps forward, but what if we could digitize contract meaning and therefore measure, and trace and analyse *all* our contractual obligations in an instant?

Commercial technology available today already reviews and analyses contractual language through advanced machine-learning and natural language processing (NLP) techniques. ThoughtRiver, for example, uses a scalable ontology called Lexible™ (Figure 1), at the heart of its machine-learning application. This is a digitization method to standardize contractual meaning in the form of digital units. Such technologies allow digital contracting standards to become an achievable goal.

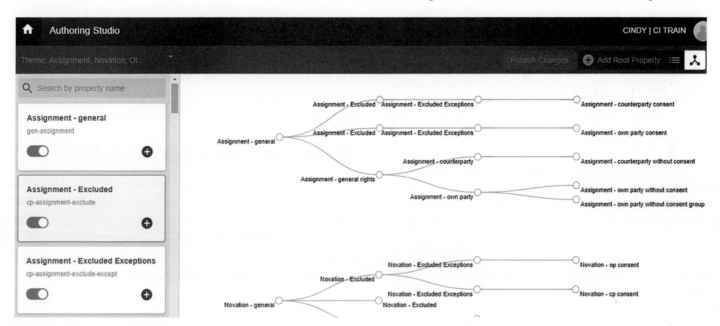

Figure 1: Lexible screenshot

[6] C. Bisping and T.J. Dodsworth, "Consumer Protection and the Regulation of Mobile Phone Contracts: A Study of Automatically Renewable Long-Term Contracts Across Jurisdictions", *Journal of Consumer Policy*, 2019, 42, 349–375.

[7] Kristen B. Cornelius, "Standard Form Contracts and a Smart Contract Future", *Internet Policy Review Journal on Internet Regulation*, 7, 2, 15 May 2018.

[8] https://www.sali.org/.

Imagine a World of Smart Contracting

With standardization of contractual meaning alongside standards for the digital form and construction of contracts, business and consumers alike can reap huge benefits. All stakeholders stand to benefit from the use of a "smart(er) contract". A digital source of truth represents rights and obligations of the parties with transparency, clarity and speed. In doing so it removes the inherent frailty of human-drafted contracts that have the tendency to introduce rule-based ambiguity.[9]

The concept of smart(er) contracts will therefore likely work best in industries built on a clear system of rules, for example insurance, banking and real estate, as the coded terms can express the full range of contractual commitments. Smart(er) contracts will also need to be linked to real-world events and so a true machine-executable "smart(er) contract" also needs to move beyond the realm of so-called "smart contracts" in blockchain to realize its full potential.[10]

So, taking an example, research has shown that eight out of ten people cannot understand their insurance policies.[11] The tendency by insurers to use uncommon language with layers of protective qualifications to foresee each eventuality leads to complexity and an unnavigable policy despite consumer regulation requiring terms to be in plain English.

Imagine a world where these terms are represented digitally: a consumer could easily obtain a basic summary of their terms but could also interact with a chat robot to interrogate them to explore coverage of a potential or given claim. Better still, with a self-executing policy interoperating with your car, a crash could trigger a claims process, sending information to relevant parties automatically. Consumers could benefit further from the ability for insurers to personalize price-optimized policies offered on demand and in response to a specific consumer.

For the insurer, the use of digital terms would provide the opportunity to manage risk across their entire insured portfolio and, using data analytics, better able to stress test scenarios in different market conditions. For an industry required to capitalize appropriately against risk exposure it would allow the insurer to do this precisely rather than by extrapolating from inherently imperfect sampling. The ability to apply changes to terms dynamically at scale would also have the benefit of being able to react to regulatory or market conditions quickly.

It is easy to see how these benefits could translate to the banking world for mortgage contracts or other industries where regulation and consumer imperatives require transparency.

Building Smart(er) Contracts

The above scenarios may soon become reality. Even brief research reveals a wide array of very different digital contracting projects.[12] Our view of a smart(er) contract envisages a truly digitized legal agreement easily readable by both machines and human eyes.

Lexible as a key piece of a future digital contracting standard

True standardization of legal interpretation is a real challenge for any digital contract project. Software platforms can assist by capturing different parties' rights and obligations at a granular level, across all different types of agreements, forming a key part of a "big-data"

---

[9] LSP Working Group, "Developing a Legal Specification Protocol: Technological Considerations and Requirements", 14 February 2019.

[10] We broadly agree with the view of the LSP Working Group, see above note 9.

[11] https://www.ft.com/content/086b9740-6808-11e8-8cf3-0c230fa67aec.

---

[12] See https://legalese.github.io/legalscape.html;LSP Working Group, above.

approach to contract description,[13] but also beginning the move towards purely digital contracting, with each "node" being a verifiable digital building block in its own right. Is this a complete answer for our smart(er) contracting goal? No, but it could be a part of the solution.

We accept that contracts are sets of rules and that there should be a code-based building engine allowing the creation of self-executing agreements.[14] Blockchain may have its limitations[15] but it could provide a secure backbone for automated transactions in smart(er) contracts.[16]

We envisage a user interface in which users will use standard nodes of meaning to describe and constitute the contract (Figure 2). The "nodes" could stand on their own or operate within programmable logic structures (e.g. to execute automatically if certain conditions are met).

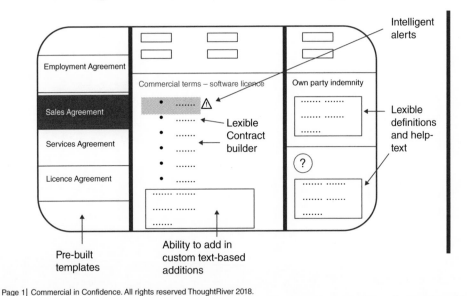

What might a future Lexible builder app look like?

- Intelligent alerts
- Employment Agreement
- Commercial terms – software licence
- Own party indemnity
- Sales Agreement
- Lexible Contract builder
- Services Agreement
- Lexible definitions and help-text
- Licence Agreement
- Pre-built templates
- Ability to add in custom text-based additions

- Easy to create new contracts from templates or from scratch
- Flexible inputs e.g. easy to insert custom text if Lexible does not have a relevant property
- Forces a logical structure to minimize conceptual errors
- Automatic error and issue checking

Figure 2: Future contract builder

[13] And we acknowledge the limitations of text-based approaches – see LSP Working Group, pp. 26–27, above.

[14] Numerous examples are presented in the LSP white paper, above note 9: see, e.g. RuleML: http://ruleml.org/index.html, Stanford Computable Contracts Initiative https://legisway.wolterskluwer.de/en/the-stanford-computable-contracts-initiative.

[15] Kelvin Low and Eliza Mik, "Pause the Blockchain Legal Revolution", forthcoming, *International & Comparative Law Quarterly*: https://papers.ssrn.com/sol3/papers.cfm?abstract_id=3439918.

[16] The work of the Accord Project Forum seems very useful in this regard: https://www.accordproject.org/.

Taking from each of these approaches, our vision of a smart(er) contract would have several advantages:

- clear understanding of the terms agreed amongst the parties using standardized, digital meaning units;

- better risk management of the contractual terms;

- secure transactions and automated execution of the contract;

- high flexibility across different types of contractual clause and agreements; and

- easy translation in different languages (not relying on specific NLP).

Conclusion

We therefore see recent breakthroughs in contract *description* as an important move towards a future of fully digital smart(er) contract *creation*. Smart(er) contracting will unlock transactions for the digital age, allowing individuals and corporates alike to satiate their need for speed and data-driven insight. To make this possible, we are calling for those who share our vision to join us on our journey to develop Lexible as a contract description framework and a tool for building the smart(er) contracts of the future.

Smart Contract and Traditional Contract

Željka Motika
Lawyer, Motika Law Office

Rapid technological progress creates the urge needed for the equal development of regulatory framework and design of new legal instruments to be used in various transactions, which have hitherto been legally unrecognized and non-regulated. With the emergence of blockchain technology followed by smart contracts, the question has been raised whether a smart contract is a contract or a program code.

Traditional Contracts Compared to Smart Contracts

The simplest and widespread legal definition of a traditional contract is that it is the agreement between the contracting parties regarding the essential elements of the contract. The law considers that the contract is created when the parties agree on the essential terms of the contract. Accordingly, the agreement is reached through communication in any human language spoken by people, as well as through acts of acceptance by humans, that represent expression of free will of the parties to be bound by such a contract.

If a smart contract is analysed from this traditional point of view, i.e. as the process of reaching an agreement between the parties, a smart contract would not pass the test and would not be qualified as a contract in a traditional way. Namely, when reaching an agreement on the essential terms of a matter that is stipulated through a smart contract, the contracting parties, humans, first agree on essential terms in human communication that is afterwards translated into programming code. Therefore, the contract is created in a traditional way, between humans, by reaching an agreement through natural language; therefore, a smart contract is an instrument that enables a more automated execution of the traditional contract, not its replacement.

In conclusion, until humans accept programming code as a natural means of communication between themselves, as is the case with any natural language, a smart contract should not be seen as a contract, but only as a technical instrument that allows a traditional contract to be executed automatically – via software code.

It is easy to expect that the further development of technology will increase the presence and use of smart contracts in legal transactions. Therefore, it becomes increasingly important for lawyers to find a place and define the role of smart contracts in legal systems.

The Interface with Blockchain

We should not lose sight of the fact that the law has recognized the legal capacity to legal entities – companies and organizations – which are fictional characters represented and managed by humans. If we go a step further, we can ask ourselves why we should not recognize the legal capacity to another fictional character – the decentralized autonomous organization (DAO), which functions independently and is based on the algorithm.

Both legal entities and the DAO are intangible, without its will and operates on the basis of the will of the people who defined its operations. But unlike legal entities wherein people still execute the decisions, the DAO can operate based on predefined rules contained in a smart contract without further human involvement.

Based on the said characteristics of the DAO and its similarity to legal entities, we can start thinking of the creation of the legal framework that would recognize the legal capacity to the DAO.

A potential approach that legislators could apply could be to recognize the legal capacity to the DAO through the DAO's registration in official registers and under the conditions prescribed by law. The DAO, like a legal entity, could have a founding act, but it could be in the form of a smart contract containing a set of predefined rules that the DAO should pursue its purpose autonomously. Like legal entities, the DAO should acquire a legal capacity in the moment of registration and be qualified as a subject of rights and a holder of rights and obligations.

A possible example of introducing a DAO into legal life and granting a DAO right to be a legal subject could be existing forms of trusts, foundations and legacies as legal instruments through which a person could manage and dispose of its assets, during life or after death, to meet the goals of the foundation. In the existing order, trusts, foundations and legacies are people-governed entities and their work depends on the decisions of the humans involved in its management. In order to fulfil the goals for which these legal entities are founded, they have certain assets. For the purpose of this study we will consider intellectual property rights as their potential assets. Namely, the holder of certain intellectual property rights may bequeath such rights to the foundation for it to be commercially exploited by the foundation in order to fulfil the goals of the foundation.

This is where blockchain technology comes into play. Intellectual property rights are by their very nature such rights that can be fully transmitted and exploited using blockchain technology without human involvement. Namely, the author of a certain copyright (book, music) could transfer and exploit such rights through blockchain and smart contracts.

The potential of blockchain technology to transfer the rights and assets and to exploit them raises the question: can such technology be recognized as the entity which has the legal capacity and consequently the responsibility for its activities? Namely, if it were legally possible for an author to form his or her trust, foundation or legacy as a legal entity of a DAO, the author could ensure the fate of his or her decisions without the possibility of someone changing them. If the DAO were legally regulated as a legal entity, an author would be able to transfer intellectual property rights to the DAO. In that case, the DAO, as a legal entity and as the intellectual property right's holder, could enter into smart contracts with both users of intellectual property rights and users of funds earned by the DAO by exploiting the transferred intellectual property rights. In this case, smart contracts that the DAO concludes for the purpose of exploiting intellectual property rights (e.g. contracts with publishers) could be considered as legally binding agreements, since the agreement was reached by the DAO entity in the form of programming language, which is for the DAO its "natural language".

The above-described structure provides excessive legal grounds for establishing the DAO in a form of sui generis legally regulated entity with its property and as an independent holder of legal rights and obligations. A more detailed development of the described structure would address various outstanding issues like the jurisdiction issue of the DAO, property issues and third-party liability issues, and would also eliminate or limit common blockchain-related issues that have risen when applying existing anti-money laundering rules. The line of issues and possible solutions and opportunities is much bigger and leaves a lot of room for legal wit and further regulatory development.

Getting Smart: Blockchain and Smart Contracts

Anne Rose
Associate and Co-Lead Blockchain Group, Mishcon de Reya

"Smart contracts" are gaining momentum with the development of distributed ledger technologies. What makes these legal agreements innovative is that their execution is made automatic through the use of computers (although some part may require human input and control), and they are enforceable either via tamper-proof execution of computer code or by legal enforcement of rights and obligations. Non-blockchain-based smart contracts have been around for a while (e.g. vending machines and digital rights management systems). As at the date of writing this chapter commercially viable blockchain smart contract solutions are starting to emerge, which are confined to relatively narrow sets of operations that are well suited to the model of self-executing electronic contracts.

This chapter briefly examines the origins of blockchain smart contracts and how they work, and the potential uses of this new technology as well as technical limitations or barriers associated with greater adoption of smart contracts. The chapter concludes that international standards are needed to provide guidance by promoting harmonization across disciplines. However, this requires thoughtful consideration and development of new legal frameworks.

Origins of Blockchain Smart Contracts and How Blockchain Smart Contracts Work

Smart contracts have been around for years. Nick Szabo first coined the term "smart contracts" defining them as a "set of promises, specified in digital form, including protocols within which the parties perform on these promises".[1] In essence, they are pieces of codes that generate transactions if the conditions encoded in them are met.

However, the name is a slight misnomer, as "smart contracts" are neither "smart" nor "contracts" in the traditional sense in which these terms are understood. The word "smart" refers to the automation process and the fact that the computer code has a degree of autonomy without recourse to human control. The word "contract" may be interpreted to mean either: (1) a legal contract enforceable in the courts of law, or (2) an agreed chain of actions that, although not enforceable in law, cannot be tampered with once started.

To illustrate the concept of a basic smart contract using blockchain, consider this simple scenario: Kate wishes to stay in Bob's holiday home on the beach for £500 at the weekend if no rain is forecast for that weekend. Kate and Bob both agree that, if rain is predicted on the preceding Thursday, Kate will not come and will therefore not make any payment to Bob. If, on the other hand, no rain is predicted, Kate will need to ensure she has sufficient funds in her wallet for the transaction to go through. Once validated, Bob will: (1) send Kate a door code to the holiday home, and (2) receive £500 in return.

In order for these actions and decisions to be "translated" into a smart contract, all these conditions will first need to be placed on a blockchain in computer code after having been validated in the consensus process.[2] If the underlying blockchain is public,

---

[1] Nick Szabo, "Smart Contracts: Building Contracts: Building Blocks for Digital Markets", 1996. Available at: http://www.fon.hum.uva.nl/rob/Courses/InformationInSpeech/CDROM/Literature/LOTwinterschool2006/szabo.best.vwh.net/smart_contracts_2.html (accessed on 6 August 2019).

[2] In short, consensus mechanisms are protocols that make sure all nodes (devices on the blockchain) are aligned with each other and agree on which transactions are legitimate and are added to the chain. There are many different ways of reaching consensus.

all users on the platform are able to see and testify the computer code underlying this agreement.

Second, the smart contract will connect with an oracle. An oracle can be one or multiple persons, groups or program that feed the software relevant information about the state of the outside world. In this particular example, it may be an app with weather forecasts on the Thursday preceding the holiday weekend. If the weather forecast does not predict rain, the contract next needs to consider the amount of funds Kate holds. If Kate holds sufficient funds in her wallet, the contract will be executed: Kate will receive a door code to the property for the weekend and Bob will receive £500.

Potential Use Cases

With the growing adoption of distributed ledger infrastructures based on blockchain technologies, smart contracts have gained prominence. In different industries, smart contracts on permissioned blockchains (e.g. those platforms where users are not freely able to join the network) have been used to propose specific solutions to different problems. For example, in the banking sector, smart contracts are being used to eliminate intermediaries (e.g. central banks, clearing houses, etc.) to speed up, and reduce the cost of, clearing and settlements.[3] In supply chains, smart contract systems have also become popular to create an immutable record of goods along supply chains to solve problems such as evaluation of provenance, loss of goods, insurance fraud and authenticity of high-value goods.[4]

---

[3] See, for example, R3 Corda. Available at: https://www.r3.com/ (accessed on 6 August 2019).

[4] See, for example, Everledger. Available at: https://www.everledger.io/ (accessed on 6 August 2019).

Technical Limitations or Barriers and Regulatory Issues

However, there are a number of technical limitations or barriers as well as regulatory issues. Due to word limit constraints, this chapter focuses on three issues: reliance on computer software, semantics and identity.

Reliance on computer software

Smart contracts will need constant testing and monitoring to ensure that the code does not contain any bugs or errors and that the code is not susceptible to hackers. For any smart contracts running on a blockchain network, failure to carry out such monitoring could have undesirable consequences especially considering the nature of a blockchain network (i.e. it is very difficult to reverse what has already been done).

Semantics issues

The content of a smart contract may have no equivalent terms in a natural language contract, since their automation is not necessary or possible (e.g. potentially indeterminate standards such as "reasonable"). Whilst smart contracts remove the ambiguity inherent in natural language, in some circumstances the parties to an agreement may prefer the flexibility provided by such ambiguity.

Furthermore, the same word may have a different meaning to a lawyer than to a computer scientist. For example, the word "execution" for a lawyer refers to the signing of an agreement, whereas for a computer scientist it will refer to the running of a computer code. "Termination" to a lawyer will refer to the end of the performance of a contract. A computer scientist, however, will take "termination" to mean the end of the running of a computer program. These two events may not be coterminous. Lawyers and computer scientists will need to work together to ensure there is no confusion.

Identity

On public, permissionless blockchains (e.g. those platforms where users are freely able to join the network), there are potential issues regarding identifiability as the use of pseudonyms and other methods render the contracting parties anonymous to one another, making it hard to ascertain who is being contracted with. This could give rise to cases involving mistaken identity or misrepresentation, or issues of a party lacking legal capacity to enter into a contractual relationship. In order to solve these issues, a number of solutions is being explored. One example is multiple signature verification, where parties all need to agree to the execution of a smart contract before it is executed.[5]

On private, permissioned blockchains, this will be less of an issue as each party's identity is verified before allowing use of the blockchain network.

Conclusion

Compliance with existing legal and regulatory systems is imperative if blockchain, and blockchain-based applications, are to have a real-world impact. In the smart contract space, there are numerous examples of attempts to create interoperability and a seamless interaction between the on-chain and off-chain spheres. One example is the Blockchain Arbitration Forum project, which seeks to provide for arbitration processes to resolve disputes.[6]

In light of increased automation, international standards are necessary to provide guidance by promoting harmonization across disciplines. For example, the Australian standards organization is in the process of developing international standards to support blockchain technology and in 2016 it created ISO/TC 307 on the standardization of blockchain technologies and distributed ledger technologies.[7] Creating new standards requires careful consideration of the development of new legal frameworks and greater collaboration between computer scientists and lawyers.

---

[5] Conde de Leon, "Blockchain: Properties and Misconceptions", 2017, 11/3 *Asia Pacific Journal of Innovation and Entrepreneurship*, p. 296. Available at: www.emeraldinsight.com/doi/full/10.1108/APJIE-12-2017-034 (accessed on 11 August 2019).

---

[6] Available at: http://blockchainarbitrationforum.org/ (accessed on 6 August 2019).

[7] Available at: https://www.iso.org/committee/6266604.html (accessed on 6 August 2019).

Legal Prose to Code: Restructuring Contract Templates for Blockchain Automation

Luigi Telesca
CEO, Trakti

and James Hazard
Founder, CommonAccord

In a world increasingly run by digital platforms and machine-to-machine communication, the ability to perform legal and compliance processes in real time is a necessity, not a nice-to-have. The speed and velocity of economic activity, secured and regulated by legal systems, suffers from the use of outdated legal infrastructure. Technology runs faster than the law; the original warning of Professor Lawrence Lessig's "Code is Law" (Lessig, 1999, 2006).[1] This gap is now a pervasive reality. Challenges to legal compliance and governance are growing as economic systems become more connected, global and automated, empowered by IT infrastructures, executing in clouds and ignoring national boundaries. Although legal professionals, administrators and regulators are awash in digital information, they create, manage and represent contracts in a way that is sharply limited by legacy technologies (Darmstadter, 2010).

Conventional handling of contract agreements requires extensive human support and involvement, despite the fact that the great majority of contract prose restates similar ideas. As estimated by the IACCM on average spending for finalizing a contract (from draft, negotiation, to signature) can vary between $6,900 for simple contracts and $21,300 for mid-complexity contracts, while the optimized cost for top performing companies is still $3,800 and $14,000 (Cummings, 2017).[2] This means that globally, between 30 and 40% of costs during contractualization phases are lost annually for unnecessary activities.

More importantly, inefficiencies of current document practices create bottlenecks to transacting and compliance processes, hide systemic risks (De Bandt and Hartmann, 2000; Kavassalis et al. 2018) and reinforce a trend toward massive data aggregations that are now recognized to be burdensome and dangerous.[3] With the current wave of digitalization and the reduction of companies' back-office infrastructure, new alternative approaches are required to compete in such dynamic markets.

Some advocates hope to entirely replace words with "code", with smart contracts and similar algorithms as paradigms. We argue that even as "code" comes to implement most contract interactions, legal "prose" remains a critical part of a transacting system and can be made nearly as efficient as code. Prose sets expectations, establishes legitimacy and provides guidance for edge cases and disputes (Hart, 2017, Hart and Bengt 2010). Many of the major drawbacks of prose, repetition, ambiguity and opacity can be greatly reduced by a simple expedient: collaborating on prose with the same tools as coders use to collaborate on code. Building on the experience of CommonAccord and Trakti, we propose an "Open Trust Fabric" (OTF) initiative to accelerate this transition and assure the public benefit.

We fully acknowledge the capabilities of "code", mathematical and procedural expressions that handle transacting. Computer-mediated transactions enable new forms of contracts and the records created by computers can allow the implementation of

---

[1] https://www.harvardmagazine.com/2000/01/code-is-law-html.

[2] https://blog.iaccm.com/commitment-matters-tim-cummins-blog/the-cost-of-a-contract.

[3] For awareness of problems in cyberspace, see, e.g., "The Paris Call for Trust and Security in Cyberspace": https://www.diplomatie.gouv.fr/IMG/pdf/paris_call_text_-_en_cle06f918.pdf.

conditional logic that can be automatically monitored and verified, enabling more efficient transacting (Varian, 2010). The benefits of computational contracts are very clear from both economic and operational perspectives.

But prose is a useful complement to code. At the end of the 1980s,[4] a group of computer scientists and cryptographers started analysing how to streamline financial transactions in a secure and compliant framework. In 1995, Ian Grigg and Gary Howland, with their Ricardo project, proposed an innovative method to "identify and describe issues of financial instruments as contract".[5] The method offered a way to represent provisions in human and machine-readable format, and provided a cryptographic approach to uniquely identify the contract. This approach enhanced the smart contract concept (Szabo, 1994),[6] since in the "real" world, algorithmic transacting always has a complement of legal text. They coined the term "Ricardian" for this hybrid of code and prose.[7]

Ricardian contracts remain the exception. In most transacting, contract agreements are still a static element in a dynamic framework. They are Word or PDF documents interpreted by humans and "translated" into performance requirements, enterprise and payment management systems. Interpretation is error prone and the cost of coordination of activities is enormous. Furthermore, the reconciliation of contracts and transactions requires an additional level of analytical tools that keeps the operation complex, approximate and expensive.

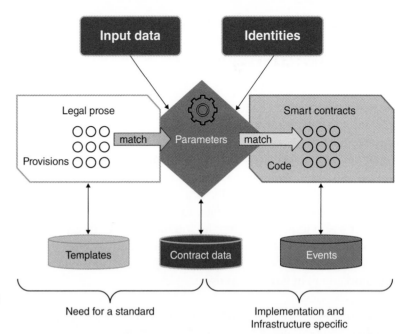

Figure 1: Connecting Legal Prose to Smart Contracts

Templates are a more effective way to handle legal prose. Templating is being accelerated by numerous Ricardian approaches, including projects like OpenLaw,[8] Trakti,[9] Clause,[10] Monax[11] and others. For example, Trakti offers an end-to-end unified platform for smart, executable and compliance contracts. Lawyers using Trakti can codify a legal contract in prose, define parameters and connect and trigger trusted smart contracts and

---

[4] https://www.activism.net/cypherpunk/crypto-anarchy.html.

[5] Originally introduced in Ian Grigg, "Financial Cryptography in 7 Layers", 4th Conference on Financial Cryptography, Anguilla, 2000, Springer-Verlag LNCS 1962. All papers are at http://iang.org/papers/.

[6] http://szabo.best.vwh.net/smart.contracts.html.

[7] See also Christopher D. Clack, Vikram A. Bakshi and Lee Braine, "Smart Contract Templates: Foundations, Design Landscape and Research Directions": https://arxiv.org/abs/1608.00771.

[8] http://www.openlaw.io.

[9] https://www.trakti.com.

[10] https://clause.io/.

[11] https://monax.io/.

verify and approve pieces of code that could run on different blockchain infrastructures to automate contract patterns and enable the automated performance of the contract on the selected blockchain infrastructure.

But each platform has its idiosyncrasies. To overcome those barriers and offer a common playing field for lawyers and regulators to codify prose, we propose an initiative focusing purely on templating, creating an open library of models that can be used in all systems. A common corpus of contract templates. All kinds of templates can be integrated, from "my" forms of businesses and agencies to model documents, industry standards and legislation. Despite the existence of many islands of template standards – a vast dispersed archipelago – we believe this to be the first comprehensive process of standardization of legal documents.

This leads to the need for public-interest curation of the templates and their components, a new form of legal codification,[12] To facilitate such codification and enable convergence, we propose an OTF alliance, a collaboration to encourage creation and management of legal document templates that can be used across all transacting platforms. Based on the experience and demonstrations of the CommonAccord[13] project, we propose to model contracts as objects in a graph. In computing and mathematics, a "graph" is a structure of "nodes and edges" (circles and connecting lines). Graphs are used in data science and sometimes in law, but there has not been a common graph format[14] for legal prose. A graph approach can express all transactions and relationships as references to reusable, machine-verifiable elements. Trends in IT, business and law reinforce this kind of approach and it should accelerate convergence of the various platforms towards full interoperability. Agreement on semantics can come from legal templating.

The OTF methodology and open platform will facilitate the design and definition of contract templates, offering unique identifiers that can be consumed by Ricardian contract platforms or copied into conventional documents. Templates can be adapted ("forked") and integrated ("merged") in an open process. A common format for templates can formalize the way contracts are designed and implemented, and introduce contracts as dynamic organisms that can proactively manage relationships and assets, track obligations, reduce risk in transacting and enable new business models. For instance, a graph can express (1) the parties to the contract and other related entities,[15] (2) the deal points (parameters), (3) the legal prose,[16] (4) the infrastructure and the code logic to automate the transaction,[17] (5) the properties and assets that can be the subject of contracts, and (6) the data sources for events.

---

[12] A collection of contract templates that can be referenced by unique identifiers generalizes projects such as CreativeCommons.org or the proposed "Contract Wiki" of George Triantis: https://law.stanford.edu/stanford-lawyer/articles/disruption-and-%E2%80%A8innovation-in-transactional-law-practice/.

[13] http://www.commonaccord.org/.

---

[14] Court cases have a well-developed system of cross-referencing in which each case is a node and the citations to precedents and legislation are edges.

[15] See, for instance, the comprehensive global taxonomy of "legal persons" at: https://www.gleif.org/en/about-lei/introducing-the-legal-entity-identifier-lei.

[16] Legal prose is subject to many standards efforts. Among them are construction contracts (e.g., Federation Internationale des Ingenieurs-Conseil, American Institute of Architects), energy contracts (aipn.com) and genetics (ga4gh.org).

[17] Contract logic is also subject to standards efforts, notably financial contracts: https://www.actusfrf.org/.

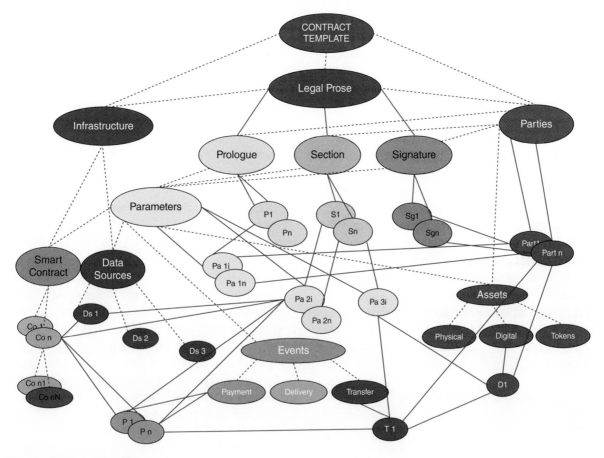

Figure 2: The Prose Object Model

If we represent contracts this way, then companies can be seen as an ecosystem of contracts where each event statement is a mere list of transaction points with references to the appropriate nodes in the graph. Each new event statement also adds to the knowledge of the graph. Contracts become "computable" in the Ricardian sense. These can be linked and consumed by contract management systems, distributed ledger technologies, enterprise resource planning systems and accounting and reporting systems of companies. Without this unified contract modelling approach,

which envisions bringing contract taxonomies under a common roof, the increasing digitization of the economy will further increase systemic risks, and pose impossible challenges for regulation and forecasting. Smart contract and blockchain implementations will never go mainstream.

Graph expression of contracts can also radically increase transparency and overall performance of an economy. In this connection, we are initiating the OTF as part of a study for the

European Commission on "Modelling the EU Economy as an Ecosystem of Contracts".[18] Among the goals is to demonstrate reporting and prediction advantages of a graph approach to contracts. Having clear contract modelling structures connected with distributed transacting platforms would make it easier to interpolate production data generated by the implementation of those contracts and the impact on the European and National Accounting Systems. This would offer more accurate measures for policymaking, streamline the implementation of a digital European Single Market, facilitate regulatory supervision and improve risk monitoring. Nearly all of the inefficiency, costs and opacity of forming and managing legal relationships can be eliminated by adopting template-handling practices that are already well established in the open source software community. Software engineers have perfected these methods for their own use; businesses, lawyers and regulators can directly adopt them. Current trends in transacting such as blockchains will accelerate the transition. The transition can be further accelerated and guided in the public interest by a formal collaboration among stakeholders that we propose as an "OTF".

References

Cummings, T. (2017). The Cost of Contracts, *IACCM*.

Darmstadter, H. (2010). Precision's Counterfeit: The Failures of Complex Documents, and Some Suggested Remedies, *The Business Lawyer*, 66, 1, 61–83. Retrieved from: http://www.jstor.org/stable/25758526.

De Bandt, O. and Hartmann, P. (2000). Systemic Risk: A Survey, ECB Working Paper No. 35.

Grigg, I. (2000). *Financial Cryptography in 7 Layers, 4th Conference on Financial Cryptography*, Anguilla, 2000, Springer-Verlag LNCS 1962. All papers are at: http://iang.org/papers/.

Hart, O. (2017). Incomplete Contracts and Control, *American Economic Review*, 107, 7, 1731–1752: https://doi.org/10.1257/aer.107.7.1731.

Hart, O. and Bengt H. (2010). A Theory of Firm Scope, *Quarterly Journal of Economics*, 125, 2, 483–513.

Kavassalis, P., Stieber, H.A., Breymann, W., Saxton, K.E., Gross, F.J., Brammertz, W., Bertolo, S. and Dragiotis, A. (2016). DTD Powered by ACTUS: An Innovative RegTech Approach to Financial Risk Reporting.

Lessig, L. (1999). Code and Other Laws of Cyberspace.

Lessig, L. (2006). Code: Version 2.0.

Szabo N. (1994), Smart contracts in Essays on Smart Contracts, Commercial Controls and Security: http://szabo.best.vwh.net/smart.contracts.html.

Varian, H.R. (2010). *Intermediate microeconomics: a modern approach*. New York: W.W. Norton & Company.

---

[18] Our research is partially funded by the EU DG JUST contract ref. JUST/2018/RCON/PR/JU03/0118: https://ec.europa.eu/newsroom/just/item-detail.cfm?item_id=638348.

The Legal Framework of Pay-Per-Use Financing

Christian Spindler
CEO, DATA AHEAD ANALYTICS GmbH

What Is Pay-Per-Use Financing?

Digital transformation enables business opportunities that make use of the broad availability of data. Pay-Per-Use, or Infrastructure-as-a-Service, describes a set of business models that transfer traditional, product-centric transactions towards IT-based services. One segment with high potential for Pay-Per-Use is the machine industry, which will be our case in the following. We talk about Industry 4.0, or the Industrial Internet of Things (IIoT), when referring to digital transformation in the machine industry.

To Buy, to Lease or to Pay-Per-Use?

The machine industry is coined by a product-centric business model: a manufacturer sells machines to a customer. A bank may finance the transaction with a corporate loan. Whereas this business model is simple and easy to apply, it comes with pain points for all involved parties. First, the transaction price is usually paid in a single or very few instants. This transaction binds capital which easily ends up in the seven-digit range for complex machines. Second, the purchase contracts typically offer no flexibility for the customer to match outgoing cash flows (i.e. payments) with incoming cash flows (i.e. production sales), with negative impact on liquidity. Third, asset purchases are not scalable, but individual deals are closed for each asset or asset upgrade.

Leasing relieves one of these points: stretching payments over the lease period binds less capital in the asset. Still, the other pain

points exist. Leasing contracts typically involve rigid payment schemes and do not provide flexibility in situations of stressed liquidity. Scalability of leasing contracts is poor, as they are designed for leasing individual assets.

Pay-Per-Use financing relieves all three pain points and provides manufacturers with means to upsell further services along with the assets. As amortization payments are coupled to the revenues an asset generates, financing cost can almost scale 1:1 with incoming cash flows. Dependent on the contract design, accounting can be simplified, and asset ownership may reside at the manufacturer – reducing bound equity and debt financing of the customer. Further benefits are the possibility of real-time depreciation of assets, as their remaining lifetime value is known more precisely with continuous monitoring. This results in improved asset valuation for due diligence processes.

Pay-Per-Use Business Models

Pay-Per-Use models are applied in various settings. Most prominently, a customer purchases an asset, financed by a bank, or the customer only purchases usage rights of the asset and ownership stays with the manufacturer.

Bank Pay-Per-Use-Finances Asset

In the first setting where a customer purchases an asset, the bank may offer a loan contract where payments are based on the utilization of the asset. For example, the bank may charge 100% amortization rate if the asset was used 160 hours a month and may charge only 50% amortization rate if the asset was used only or less than 80 hours a month. There are already four "tuning parameters" in this loan model: the monthly amortization rate, the maximum and minimum monthly hours, and the minimum amortization rate. More parameters can be designed into the contract as needed. In the end, the bank offers flexibility to the customer, and thus may charge a premium on the interest rate for financing.

Customer Buys Service Level Agreement

In the second setting, the manufacturer of an asset abstains from the sale of the part or machine. Instead, the manufacturer provides the machine's output as a service against a subscription fee. Manufacturers of power plant turbines may receive payments per operating hour of the turbine. Compressor manufacturers sell pressurized air as a service, instead of compressors. This life cycle-based approach transfers the operative and maintenance risk in scope of the negotiated service level agreement onto the asset manufacturer.

What Are the Prerequisites for Pay-Per-Use?

Industrial Internet of Things

One reason for the growing pay-per-use market is that technological prerequisites have matured. The IIoT makes sufficient data for pay-per-use available. Modern injection moulding machines provide up to 100 sensors for parameters such as plastic process temperature, motor revolution, raw material condition and produced part quality. This data is used to analyse if the machine runs with correct parameter settings and can also be used to bill the machine usage.

Data Logistics

In more complex settings, Pay-Per-Use requires extension of use-based cash flows of individual asset components to the entire supply chain. With Pay-Per-Use, the cash flows between customer, manufacturer and suppliers are split up. The manifold service cost allocations must be mapped in the accounting and actual payment transactions.

Design "Use" of the Asset

The clear definition of "use" is crucial for pay-per-use. "Use" may not only mean on or off, but comes in many shades, depending on the process model. An asset may differentiate between:

- Regular use. Asset produces high-quality products ready for sale.
- Non-use. Asset is used neither for production nor in an intermediary state (e.g. maintenance).
- Commissioning/ramp-up. Asset is producing parts not ready for sale, as parameters are yet to be tuned.
- Maintenance. Asset operates in an irregular manner due to maintenance tests.
- Quality deterioration. Asset produces in a regular process, but output yield decreases below a defined threshold, e.g. through a defect sensor in the production process.
- Hardware or software upgrade. New hardware or software on the asset improves throughput or output yield and thus makes production time more valuable.

Risk Management

New services for the supervision and control of Pay-Per-Use risks must be developed and implemented. Risks must (and can) be detected early and eventually hedged or mitigated.

- Determination, calibration and assessment of cash flow default risks can be performed with established credit risk models to support contract design.
- New risk models assess risks which occur through non-use of the asset. These risk models can then input into price models, e.g. by negotiating prices for periods of not using the asset.
- Services to adapt price components resulting from change usage behaviour must also be developed and implemented to respond to changed market conditions.

Supply Chain Settlement

Pay-Per-Use requires an implementation of services between manufacturers and suppliers in order to enable automated billing along the entire supply chain. Several requirements need to be fulfilled:

- Contributions of individual components for service fulfilment can be determined based on the asset's sensor data.

- Payment goals and payment obligations can be calculated dependent on the service agreements (e.g. based on smart contracts between manufacturer and supplier).

- Payment obligations between manufacturer and supplier can be automatically triggered.

- Processing of transaction and payment information for involved functions at manufacturer and supplier, such as accounting, treasury and account management, must be secured.

Data Governance

Questions around the handling of the manifold of data in the Pay-Per-Use process must be addressed and answered in the contract design:

- Who does the data at individual process steps, especially the IIoT data obtained from the asset itself, belong to?

- What about personal data, such as operator logs at the asset's software interface?

- How do you treat warranty issues?

Given the potential of high claims, there must be and will be an appropriate risk allocation in Pay-Per-Use contracts. Given, on the other side, the strong benefits for all involved parties, we expect that pay-per-use financing and service agreement models will disrupt the still product-centric industries in the upcoming years.

Legal Technology: Increasing or Impeding Access to Justice?

6

- 5.9m adults in the UK have never used the internet
- 27% of disabled adults in the UK have never used the internet

Source: 21st Century Challenges – Informed discussion form The Royal Geographical Society (with IBG)

When faced with legal issues, in 76% of the time, these were ignored or had to be resolved without the assistance of professional legal assistance

Source: Analysis of Potential Effects of Early Legal Advice – The Law Society of England and Wales – 2017

Barriers to improve access to justice through innovation and technology are:
- Widespread confusion, variation and fragmentation

Source: Technology Access to Justice Report, Law Society of England and Wales – 2019

Access to common data and lack of trust

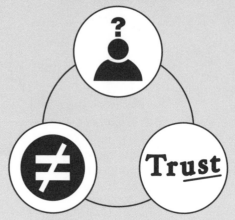

Digital and legal literacy

Inequality of resources available for non-commercial purposes

Funding

Regulatory concerns

Executive Summary

The law can be seen as an arrangement of principles and rules. These are set up through social establishments to oversee conduct and human rights, shape governmental issues and matters of finance and commerce, and create constructs of opportunity for people.

The foundational basis of our legal systems centres on justice and fairness. This suggests that we can all access and assert our rights within the available legal frameworks. However, the rising costs and complexity of attempting to assert one's legal rights has meant that there any many who simply do not obtain the recourse they are entitled to and "give up on justice". In other cases, they might attempt to represent themselves, for example, in court – although this has tended to result in measurably worse outcomes than if they had retained or had available the correct legal resources. It is for this reason that many have regarded access to justice as a hallmark of a civilized society. In England and Wales, the Access to Justice Act 1999 saw the biggest changes to access to justice in the legal system for fifty years, seeking to ensure that while legal aid was available to those who needed it, it was subjected to independent government assessments to ensure that every application met the necessary requirements in terms of the merits of the case. In addition, it ensured that the applicant did not have the financial means to pay for their representation themselves. There is, however, a huge unmet need for legal services affecting the large majority of individuals and small businesses.

Historically, solutions to the access to justice problem have sought to increase the availability of self-help remedies (which lessen the reliance and need for legal professions) and the use of *pro bono publico* (often referred to as *pro bono* work), which is professional (in this case legal) work undertaken voluntarily and without payment for the benefit of those who are unable to afford them.

Many have argued that improving access to justice requires the reduction of the role played by lawyers in the justice process and, for example, courts. This might be through the design of systems of recourse and access to justice that are simplified processes to better allow non-legal professionals to take the lead. Technology has also played an increasing role in helping to reduce the reliance on lawyers, or to drive down the cost of using legal professionals. In the latter case, it is hoped that these efficiency gains will trickle down to those individuals who are most needy of the support to achieve justice and assert their societal rights.

There is also, however, a real concern that technology may in some cases be reducing access to justice. For example, with the rise in the role technology plays in persuasive presentations to the court, will self-represented litigants really be able to compete in court against a large corporate with access to the most high-tech data analysis tools? The technology needed might just come at too high a price for many sections of society to afford, who might also, at a far more basic level, be without the skills or equipment needed to, for example, navigate the internet or other digital tools.

As we have seen in the chapters in the book so far, there has been a huge focus on LegalTech in profitable commercial law sectors. Market forces have to date resulted in a lack of focus on digital technologies that directly support all members of society to support their (often latent) legal needs.

This part seeks to explore these issues, looking at transformation programmes to modernize courts, the emerging tech tools to assist with disputes and the process of going to court, questions of funding and databases to try to ensure that fair and just outcomes can be determined. The part, however, closes by reminding us that there is a real double-edged sword to LegalTech in the context of access to justice – the technology may exacerbate the issues with fairness in how we can obtain justice. Furthermore, technology is rarely of itself a magic bullet. Without a hard look and improvement of the underlying business processes, we may simply spend time and public funding on systems and we will struggle to truly increase access to justice.

Legal Technology: Increasing or Impeding Access to Justice?

John Finnemore
Partner, CMS Cameron McKenna Nabarro Olswang LLP

Introduction

I was appalled to be reminded by a friend recently that we are coming up to twenty years' practice in the law. I trained with him and we have survived another eighteen years after that in separate firms of deals, deeds and de minimis.

This cannot be, I thought to myself. I am young! I still have much to learn! I still want to do lots of different things in my legal career!

Sadly, he is right. We have both seen a very great deal change in that period, and even more so recently. LegalTech has become a growing and developing sector full of interesting companies set to change the way in which we undertake legal practice. From the likes of Orbital Witness, who have a fabulous product that helps real estate lawyers review legal title, to Lexoo, who empower flexible working for clients and solicitors alike.

A brave new world indeed – one we should embrace – but it made me think back to what had changed since I started. Thinking about it, LegalTech is just the latest cycle in the growth and development of technology in the law. There have been many.

Jump back to twenty years ago. Finnemore is sat in a dimly lit, smelly room at his first law firm. The room is smelly because it is next to the smoking room (Google that if you are too young to remember it) and the waft of Marlboro Lights is strong. Finnemore is in this room because it is a data room for a major transaction in which one financial services business will be sold to another. Yes,

the actual room is the data room. No Dropbox; no Merrill Datasite. Physical files line the walls and are in boxes around the room. There is one index, a lengthy document which has been torn and drawn on by lots of people.

Attending this data room are lawyers from a certain law firm whose turn it is to attend. They have that day to review the material they have been sent to look at because, the following day, another law firm will attend representing another bidder. The atmosphere is tense; time is not on their side and there is a lot to go through. Finnemore, resplendent in his cheap suit and tie, is instructed to close the data room at 7 pm. Finnemore does not want to do this. It is now 6.59 pm and the lawyers are huddled around a document looking concerned. Finnemore feels stressed. Gathering all of his trainee muscle, he stands up and says forcefully "Erm…I…errr…I have to shut the data room now."

The look they gave me still haunts me.

Roll forward only two years from there and we had online data rooms, a tech advance which was designed to make my life a lot easier. These were surely the greatest innovation we could conceive of! The law firm could upload the data to an online portal, people can then review at any time of the day or night and I don't have to act like the world's worst bouncer.

Still, problems raged. Uploading the data often meant scanning thousands and thousands of pages in. Whose job? My job. Boxes of documents would arrive from the client's office. I then had to index it all, scan it all in (one scanning machine doing one page at once) and then upload it to the data room. File bigger than 2MB? Upload fail. File in wrong format? Upload fail. File contains pictures? Upload fail.

This process took a very, very long time. Even when it went online, the data room became a source of debate between the lawyers. We had to agree the terms of access, the terms of download and there would invariably be a row about whether or not the documents could be printed. This is all now (largely) standardized but, at the time, caused weeks of delay.

Roll forward to now and data rooms are a smooth operation. I recently acted on a deal where we uploaded heaps of files within 24 hours. It would have taken weeks previously. The client benefits because we can move on with the deal and they don't have to pay for our team to upload these documents – it is essentially automated.

What caused this? Competition and the development of the technology. A number of data room providers now operate in the market, each attempting to make their offering more attractive to the lawyers who buy these products. My firm now has a white labelled offering that we know and understand so that we can deliver the data room quickly and so that it does not become a deal blocker rather than a deal facilitator.

It is this sort of advance in technology that the law is a ripe use case for. Twenty years of technology development has taken me from the risk of emphysema to having a product which will help me deliver client services better and more quickly. That disruption has already occurred and is continuing – there are some very exciting product developments around data room in the offing driven by the new LegalTech sector members. The next step is certainly full data room searches. Some products do this to an extent already; it could shortly save countless chargeable hours when optimized.

Technology has also come to document signing, the bane of many a lawyer's life.

Roll back, again, to twenty years ago. This time, Finnemore needs someone to sign a document. It is Christmas Eve and Finnemore wants to go home to drink sherry and eat mince pies. Finnemore cannot go home until this document is signed because it is needed for use in court in the US on Christmas Day.

Finnemore calls the client who needs to sign this document. The client tells Finnemore that it is Christmas Eve and he is with his family. If Finnemore wants the document signed, Finnemore better fax it.

Finnemore spends a long time fighting with the fax machine. Everyone else has gone home leaving Finnemore to repair the fax machine (more luck than judgment) and send the fax. Finnemore does this eventually. Finnemore receives a notice back though telling him that the fax cannot be received because the fax machine on the other end has no paper in it.

Finnemore fumes and rages. He calls the client who, unsympathetic, trudges upstairs at his no doubt enormous house to load the fax machine with paper. Finnemore sends the fax again. The fax cannot be read because Finnemore, who can sometimes be an idiot, has faxed it upside down. Finnemore sends the fax again, this time received on the other end. Client signs and faxes back. Law firm fax fails. Finnemore begs client to send again. Law firm fax works. Finnemore, exhausted, faxes this to the US. The US ask Finnemore to have the client sign again in a different place. Finnemore considers a career change.

This story was the norm; a ridiculous charade played out in many law firm offices all around the country. Finnemore was not unusual as a lawyer who spent most of an afternoon sorting this out.

Roll forward to now – DocuSign or HelloSign would make this process twenty times easier. A very simple app on a mobile to allow the signing of a document. Finnemore could have had the signing done, from home, and eaten mince pies at the same time!

It is that difference which technology has allowed. The ability to deal with something time critical quickly and efficiently with a digital time stamp which helps in checking the veracity of the person signing. LegalTech will no doubt grasp the opportunity to develop this further – we can do much more with this and the first person to successfully link that to a payment flow at scale will have a truly disruptive piece of technology.

These changes, and the excitement of seeing how many more changes might impact the legal world, are why I am so pleased to be able to introduce this chapter. In here alone we have articles about disruption which would have been unthinkable twenty years ago.

We must also see, though, that development can be difficult. Just as Finnemore's first experience of an online data room was tricky and made something worse, so can LegalTech cause an issue for someone approaching the court system. A process which is unwieldy or, even worse, does not work at all makes the problem far worse.

The LegalTech disruption also needs to focus on the improvement it makes for access to the law. The law is unwieldy, complex and, at times, out of date. The chapters in this part look at access to the law from the perspective of parties litigating, parties seeking justice or people who are fighting the immigration system. Each of these people needs to be remembered when seeking disruption – how can the existing system be turned around to give access to justice?

It is too easy for legal technology to purely address the issues of people like me, in dusty offices of law firms working for large corporate entities, and not instead focus on those who could benefit the most. This may mean encouragement by social enterprise but that should attract no less interest from legal practices and court systems seeking to improve access to justice.

Small businesses, up against mountains of issues when dealing with the court system, could benefit from technology to help that. Moneyclaimonline was one movement towards that many years ago but one driven by the need to make court more efficient rather than a need to provide claimants or defendants with easy process. A claimant would likely embrace the ability to automate the drafting and signature of a contract as well as the enforcement of that; we are a long way from there in any real sense.

Individuals faced with a complex and unwieldy process, such as a divorce claim or when seeking asylum, should benefit from the advances that the corporate and commercial world has seen. How can this learning be applied to court process to give a better outcome? How can it be implemented without making the position worse for those seeking justice?

It is in this thinking that older, fatter, greyer Finnemore hopes that some of the developments within commercial law that he helped (in a very small way) push along might bring someone a better outcome in the justice process and well beyond the confines of the City and corporate law. Or, at the very least, mean they do not need to find fax paper at three in the morning.

The Crucial Role of LegalTech in Access to Justice

The Law Society of England and Wales

Access to justice is a fundamental component of the rule of law, a functioning democracy and a thriving economy. Globally, at least 253 million people are currently facing injustice, 1.5 billion people are unable to resolve their justice problems and 4.5 billion people overall are excluded from the opportunities the law provides.[1] The Hague Institute of Innovation and Law estimates that there are three types of justice problems: lost income, damaged health and the cost of seeking redress. This is costing OECD countries between 0.5 and 3% of their annual GDP. Within the UK this amounts to between £10.5 and £63 billion per annum.[2]

Since the financial recession hit in 2008, UK austerity measures and the scale of cuts to legal aid and local authority funding to the advice sector have resulted in a severe reduction in people's ability to exercise their rights and unlock their economic potential. Across the public, private and third sectors, resource allocation and the need for greater efficiencies have been driving the demand for both better processes and the adoption of technologies. The Law Society conducted extensive research on the use of innovation and technology across the English and Welsh access to justice sector. Key findings included:

- Significant work is being done by firms, advice clinics and in-house teams to meet legal need which is supported by technology. The government has taken positive steps through the Legal Support Advisory Group and its ministerial commitments to support new forms of technology to make justice more accessible. There is, however, much more to be done – in most cases, better data management, information sharing and coordination are needed.

- Technology is not the silver bullet to make the justice system more accessible. It is an important tool as long as it is part of an innovation strategy which is centred on the person with unmet legal needs and framed by the resources and purpose of the organization.

- The consumer-facing market is less mature than the business-to-business market on legal technology adoption. Recently, resource allocation and the need for greater efficiencies have driven demand for technological solutions.

- Online resources are the primary means of providing information to the public. However, face-to-face remains the most popular way for delivering advice, followed by mobile apps, which are often used at the start of the process.

- Barriers to technological adoption include: widespread variation, lack of access to data, inequality of resources, duplication of products, funding and regulatory concerns.

- Innovation is being led and used by the third sector, including law centres and pro bono clinics, often working with firms and universities to provide services. This is more commonly found for disputes in housing, family, employment, debt and social welfare.[3]

To appreciate the complexity of access to justice innovation and technological enablement, there is a clear need to develop an innovation blueprint, which Qiyin Chuah defines as facilitating human-centred justice. This blueprint should be:

- person centred – based on the individual with legal needs;

- rooted in the business – which takes into account the organization's vision;

---

[1] United Nations, Report of the Justice Taskforce, 2019.

[2] Hague Institute of Innovation for the Law, Elephant in the Courtroom, 2019.

[3] The Law Society, Technology, Access to Justice and the Rule of Law, 2019.

186

- planning process, resources and capabilities;

- supported by an infrastructure – with an indication of the teams or individuals who will use it and maintain it, including built in-house capacity for scrutiny, overseeing and steering; and

- operated by practitioners or support staff – to assist legal users to navigate these technological aids or solutions able to evaluate success and identify areas for future improvements.[4]

As illustrated by all contributors to this chapter, innovation and technological adoption for access to justice and court modernization will bring about a wide array of social and organizational benefits. These could include greater access to legal advice through the development of an SMS messaging service, access to the courts through the use of video hearings, meaning that litigants in more remote locations will still be able to participate. Also, internal innovation for access to justice organizations can make operations more efficient and less resource intensive. For example, the implementation of practice management software will not only drive efficiency but also make legal services more affordable to their end user. However, with 11 million adults in the UK still lacking basic digital skills and citizens' levels of trust in government data use being at an all-time low of 27%, the access to justice problem is far more nuanced than just a question of technology alone.[5]

The chapters in this section are an important contribution to the debate and this book will no doubt be used as a reference point for wider reflection on how to make the justice system more accessible.

---

[4] Ibid.

[5] World Economic Forum, IPSOS, 2019.

Digitizing Disputes

Laurence Lieberman
Partner, Disputes and Investigations, Taylor Wessing LLP

Introduction

The digitization of the dispute resolution system is inevitable. This section sets out recent advances in the use of technology by courts and in the conduct of litigation, predicts how things will evolve in the next few years and considers the benefits and downsides.

Court Use of Technology

Video hearings

Online broadcast of court hearings is increasing. Recently, the English judiciary's YouTube channel hosted a live stream from the Court of Appeal. The principle of transparency is crucial to the concept of open justice and public confidence in the legal system. Other developments include remote court hearings by videoconference where each of the parties and the judge are all in separate locations. This increases access to justice for litigants who live far from the relevant courtroom, and will be essential in large countries or those with large rural populations, such as India.

Online court filing

E-filing of court documents has been mandatory since October 2017 for represented parties in the English business and property courts. Litigants and interested parties can search court documents with far greater ease than a paper system. The digital record also brings certainty, important where disputes arise as to whether a claim was filed within a limitation period.

Online dispute resolution

Many courts are investing in digitization and running various pilot schemes for areas such as probate and for uncontested divorces. For smaller value claims, entirely online dispute resolution processes are now available, and are likely to grow into aspects of complex commercial cases in due course. In the UK, the online civil money claims service, which at the time of writing is scheduled to go live in 2020, deals with a high volume of low-value disputes, with participants being able to conduct proceedings without a lawyer, improving access to justice in this large part of the disputes market.

Legal costs technology

Technology will simplify and accelerate outcomes for the costs of litigation. Litigants would benefit from electronic cost budgeting from their lawyers to obtain more accurate and timely predictions of the likely cost of litigation, and therefore make informed decisions on whether to commence or continue it. E-budgeting tools draw on historical data from similar cases to make budget predictions more accurate. The courts are also engaged, introducing electronic bills of costs imported from lawyers' time recording systems into online precedents, containing narratives, chronology, hourly rates and costs claimed compared with the approved/agreed budget.

Summary of Disputes Focused Software

A number of software developments are also impacting the conduct of litigation, and are becoming more and more sophisticated.

Predictive coding. In this data-heavy age, it is no longer realistic to conduct an entirely human review of electronic documentation. Emails in particular have proliferated in volume, so even in mid-sized cases there may be many thousands of documents that need to be reinforced. The creation of predictive coding, also known as technology/computer-assisted review, uses machine learning technology to review and categorize large numbers of documents based on an initial human review of a sample set. That initial review samples a small set of documents randomly selected from a larger data set, identifying documents that are relevant, privileged and so on. The software learns from the human review, using algorithms to build rules to automatically categorize documents to replicate (or "learn from") the human user's method, taking into account factors including file type, common terms, custodians, recipients and other metadata. The program then applies this model to the larger data set to classify documents. The human user reviews the machine's first output and corrects errors, so that within another two or three rounds of human review, the machine then achieves its aim using high levels of accuracy (e.g. 95%+). In English litigation, predictive coding is becoming the norm and was recognized judicially in the landmark case of *Pyrrho Investments v MWB Property & Ors* [2016] EWHC 256 (Ch), not least because of the massive time and cost savings it brings for litigants. It can be used in any large-scale document review exercise, including arbitrations and internal and regulatory investigations – it has been well publicized that it was used as part of the UK's Serious Fraud Office's Rolls Royce investigation.

AI in Disputes

A rapidly evolving area of legal technology is artificial technology (AI) data analytics.

Power and scope of AI

There are an increasing number of AI-backed tools and platforms focused on the dispute resolution field. These can offer sophisticated sifting through large volumes of historical court and case data to try to predict how particular judges in a particular type of case are likely to decide. Other tools can manage and interrogate documents, audio and web-based data using AI to find patterns in behaviour, identify when an individual might be lying and uncover connections between companies and transactions not immediately obvious to a human user. A current hot area is "smart" case management. This enables users to upload pleadings and other key documents, and have the software rapidly analyse the material and propose answers to legal submissions based on case law or civil procedural rules, cutting down the time spent (and therefore costs) on these tasks by a human user.

Limitations

Whilst the potential for AI LitTech is exciting, there are limitations. Statistical accuracy is one. Any AI tool is only as powerful as the size and relevance of the data set it analyses. For example, the huge volume of case law in the US might mean AI tools there are more useful (through their greater development) than in other countries. Also, few cases get to trial and a reported judgment, and many cases go to arbitration, which is confidential, so AI case assessment products are inevitably reaching opinions based on perhaps 10% of all disputes.

Lawyers also have to be careful from a risk and professional reputation perspective not to abdicate responsibility for advice and decision-making to the tool, and there is no adequate regulatory framework in place yet for this.

Security, cybersecurity and manipulation are also a threat as they are for any technology system.

If we start to see AI used by judges in decision-making, the algorithm used may come under increasing scrutiny under data privacy regulation and AI ethics-driven policies, or be the subject of disclosure requests, given the need for transparency of justice.

Predictions for LitTech in the Next Decade

Virtual court hearings

With advances in global high-speed internet and hologram technology, video conferencing could be replaced by holograms, for the added reality of the witness actually being "in the witness box". The physical court room could become obsolete and with virtual reality advances, an entirely virtual reality hearing is likely, retaining all the benefits of a hearing "in person" but affording substantial cost and time savings, particularly for international disputes where parties are spread across the world.

Immediate fact checking

Electronic document bundles and automatic real-time transcription of court proceedings already exist. Cases can turn on the performance of witnesses on the stand. Judges must believe a witness is being honest for their evidence to be credible. At present, the ability to challenge oral evidence relies on the legal team being able to recall facts and the content of documents, which might only have been seen once or twice, often months in the past, when their significance was less. If, however, live transcription was connected to software with access to the court bundles, and all the other documents in the case, it could trawl the document universe for inconsistencies between oral and documentary evidence, and relay it to the advocate in real time.

Social mobility

Technology may also improve access to the legal profession, allowing geographically remote lawyers to participate more easily. Diversity may also improve, both in the profession and the judiciary, by allowing professionals to achieve a greater balance between work and family commitments.

Humanize with LawTech Lawyering

Qiyin Chuah
Founder and Director, QC Immigration

Introduction

Through the development and deployment of legal technology we have the choice and ability to enhance the core human element in the legal industry. This would improve access to justice for all under the current political, legal, social and economic conditions. Whilst we have come a long way on this evolutionary path, the big question remains: where are we going?

Access to Justice: Clients

With the internet as the ever-expanding knowledge bank and network, legal resources are becoming more readily available on the internet, often at a low barrier of entry.

Crowdsourcing

The UK financial crisis of 2007–2008 led to the austerity programme introduced by the Conservative and Liberal Democrat coalition government in 2010.[1] With legal aid cuts and significant reductions in public funding to date, fundraising or petitioning for causes through various online channels (change.org, crowdjustice.com, etc.) and social media campaigning can provide fast and effective support to those with exceptional or compassionate causes. Compelling crowdsourcing can gain traction rapidly beyond borders and time zones, with diverse possibilities in terms of funding, support and influence.

Virtual courtroom

Communication technology continues to transform the legal landscape. Many courts are facing long waiting lists for oral hearings due to the lack of space and resources. With the increased use of virtual court hearings and online dispute resolution, these cost-effective alternatives complement the traditional courtroom. For instance, the HM Courts & Tribunals Service has just announced plans to roll out its "reformed digital asylum service" across all hearing centres to cover asylum appeals by the end of January 2020,[2] with the aim of being more efficient. Whilst it has been reported that the success rate for appellants in court hearings conducted via video link are considerably lower than appellants who attended in person,[3] one may also argue that this would still be more preferable than proceedings in the complete absence of the appellant whose physical attendance is not possible due to being abroad or in detention. Modern technology within the courts and judiciary diversify resources, improve the quality of decision-making and reduce overall litigation costs.

Apps

Following in the footsteps of the private sector, central governments and local authorities are warming up to the idea of paperless procedures. One of the most notable efforts comes from the UK government in coping with preparations to leave the European Union. With the narrow transitional period following Brexit, the Home Office requires all qualifying EU citizens to regularize their statuses via the EU Settlement Scheme, which can be done via the website or the EU Exit: ID Document check app. This is a significant step in the right direction within the public sector.

---

[1] *Metro News*, "What is Austerity and What Does it Mean in UK Politics?", 28 June 2017: https://metro.co.uk/2017/06/28/what-is-austerity-6740771/.

[2] HM Courts & Tribunals Service, "Reform Update", Summer 2019: https://assets.publishing.service.gov.uk/government/uploads/system/uploads/attachment_data/file/806959/HMCTS_Reform_Update_Summer_19.pdf.

[3] Legalfutures, "Video Technology for Courts Still has Long Way to Go", 7 May 2019: https://www.legalfutures.co.uk/latest-news/video-technology-for-courts-still-has-long-way-to-go.

Access to the Justice System: Professionals

When considering innovation, we must put ourselves in the client's shoes – what would the change mean for them? The rise of LegalTech sees new providers entering the market with novel approaches to legal services.

Breaking away from tradition

The legal profession has generally not been swift to embrace the unprecedented technological changes, and it is finding it increasingly hard to avoid the technological tidal wave. Sceptical lawyers perceive technological tools and apps as overhyped and distracting to their intellectual routine. For example, case management systems that are usually built as one-size-fits-all, which are slow, crash often and offer redundant features not tailored to the particular practice area. Lawyers, by nature and nurture, tend to be risk averse. New and disruptive technologies may not be welcomed in the legal sector in the way that disruption is celebrated in other sectors, if they drastically change conventional working habits instead of complementing the status quo.

Nevertheless, progressive-minded lawyers are warming up to the idea of choosing suitable technology that could significantly reduce their administrative paperwork and add value to their practice. It may perhaps be unfair to generalize that lawyers are reluctant to embrace technology, rather, their conscientious nature is inclined to adopt the wait-and-see approach.

Jobs

Despite the ongoing debate about an oversupply of law graduates, there is increased optimism amongst law students and legal professionals with job prospects expanding beyond the traditional legal practitioner, introducing exciting hybrid occupations with unconventional working environments.

Alternative career paths emerge for law graduates or those who would like to combine their legal and technological skill sets. Many startups or solo practitioners utilize apps enabling them to operate as virtual law firms, thus entering the market with low overheads. Technology support teams working seamlessly across jurisdictions and time zones have not only increased prospects for global lawyering, but also introduce greater transparency, mobility and flexibility for those who choose not to commit to full-time office jobs or those who choose to undertake a portfolio career pursuing side hustles simultaneously. Law firms are reinventing their procedures and cultures to serve not only the needs of modern clients, but also to attract and retain tech-savvier Millennial and Generation Z staff. Fresh opportunities await the innovative, creative and entrepreneurial lawyers.

Culture

To meet the needs of demanding clients and modern employees, we would have to rethink how we deliver legal services. Technology at the workplace forces law firms to reinvent their cultures. Being a paperless law firm may have been unheard of a decade ago, but there is increased optimism amongst agile organizations to sustain a minimalist culture with the help of cloud computing and collaboration tools. The benefits include space and cost savings while maximizing data and productivity. Clients tend to feel more assured when they are given greater transparency and accessibility to their cases and caseworkers. On the other hand, employees generally welcome an innovative culture at the workplace, as it tends to reduce bureaucracy and mundane administration. Therefore, organizations who take advantage of the right LegalTech can provide higher-quality legal services at lower cost with a faster, wider reach.

Ethics

One can only imagine the endless possibilities artificial intelligence (AI) and machine learning would bring to ease the workload of lawyers. However, these are expensive to develop and deploy, hence they are very much underutilized in the legal sector. In law, no two cases are ever the same. It is certainly feasible that machines can be constructed to "learn" new rules and ethics over time, overriding less desirable behaviours. Where technology replaces individuals, how do you ensure that consistent ethical and regulatory standards are maintained? The future of LawTech rides heavily on how far we can humanize AI and machine learning in our day-to-day advisory work.

Conclusion

The ultimate aim of legal technology is to empower both clients and legal professionals. Whilst LegalTech can increase accessibility to law and justice, it can also alienate if it does not sufficiently cater to real needs. The human element remains its biggest challenge.

LawTech lawyering means practising law in ways we never did before, with a mission to humanize law more than ever. After all, one person's disruption can be another's salvation.

From Fair Hearing to *FairTech Hearing:* Improving Access to Justice in the UK Asylum and Immigration Process

Dr Imranali Panjwani

Lecturer in Law, Anglia Ruskin University and Head of Diverse Legal Consulting

Home Office decisions on asylum and immigration claims have been described as a "lottery"[1] and the Law Society argues there are "serious flaws in the way visa and asylum applications are being dealt with".[2] The fundamental question is how do we improve access to justice for asylum seekers who are fleeing unimaginable persecution? Should their lives depend on a legal system suffering from "long delays, poor decisions, and a total lack of information?"[3]

Technology can be used to solve two problems arising from Home Office and judges' decisions. A database of key religious and cultural terms pertaining to the asylum seeker's country of origin can be created so that the Home Office has a clear understanding of the background of immigration cases. Delays and lack of information occur because the Home Office uses poor secondary sources which conflict with primary source data. Additionally, a program can be created to accurately determine the risk of harm in the asylum seeker's country of origin. Whilst a judge would have final authority, algorithms pertaining to primary source data (e.g. percentage of internal displaced people, threat of terrorist attacks, availability of food and shelter, etc.) can be utilized to guide the legal process. Often there is an inconsistent understanding of the threat of persecution in a particular country, meaning asylum seekers are not guaranteed procedural and substantive justice in the UK immigration process. LegalTech can change this and give asylum seekers a fair hearing or a "FairTech" hearing.

Creating a Database of Key Terminologies

When writing expert reports for immigration and asylum cases, I have noticed that key cultural, theological and legal terminologies of minority groups are not understood by the Home Office, judges and lawyers. This results in incorrect and poorly informed asylum decisions. In one case, I had to write an expert report for an asylum seeker who claimed he was persecuted on account of his religious beliefs in the country he was fleeing from. The First-Tier Tribunal refused to grant him asylum on the basis of the UK country guidance and information which stated that his religious beliefs were "not physically, linguistically or legally distinguishable" from other religious sects in his country.[4] As a result, the asylum seeker in question would not be distinguished from other religious groups and therefore was not a target of persecution. However, the Tribunal and UK country guidance and information failed to consider the legal and theological differences between various religious groups.

---

[1] K. Brewer, "Asylum Decision-Maker: 'It's a Lottery'", 2018, BBC News: http://www.bbc.co.uk/news/stories-43555766?intlink_from_url=http://www.bbc.co.uk/news/topics/c302m85qe1vt/uk-immigration&link_location=live-reporting-story (accessed 21 May 2019).

[2] Law Society, "Failures in UK Immigration and Asylum Undermine the Rule of Law", 12 April 2018: https://www.lawsociety.org.uk/news/press-releases/failures-in-uk-immigration-and-asylum-undermine-the-rule-of-law/ (accessed 21 May 2019).

[3] Refugee Action, "Waiting in the Dark: How the Asylum System Dehumanizes, Disempowers and Damages", 2018, London: https://www.refugee-action.org.uk/wp-content/uploads/2018/05/Waiting-in-the-Dark-A4-16-May-2018.pdf (accessed 21 May 2019).

[4] UK Country Policy and Information Note Pakistan: Shia Muslims, January 2019, p. 11: https://assets.publishing.service.gov.uk/government/uploads/system/uploads/attachment_data/file/772985/CPIN-Pakistan-Shias-v2.0_Jan_2019_.pdf (accessed 22 August 2019).

An Example Differentiating Sunni and Shi'a Muslims

Religious groups may be jurisprudentially distinguishable from each other, even if physically and linguistically they may not be. Such differences include the way both groups pray and laws pertaining to charity and marriage.

This kind of deeper analysis can also be applied to apostasy (*irtidad*) where the apostate (*murtad*) renounces Islam.[5] This renunciation is a source of great sadness for a Muslim family and something they would not want to expose to their wider community. The Home Office's argument that an apostate's parents would continue to force their son or daughter to go to a mosque and that an asylum seeker should give more evidence of the shame that his/her family would feel is simplistic. In fact, some Muslim families may not want to risk exposing their son's or daughter's renunciation of Islam in their community by forcing them to go to a mosque. Their son's or daughter's lack of performance of rituals or adherence to beliefs could plausibly be observed within their local mosque, putting them at risk and bringing shame on their family. It may, at times, be better to stay at home where local community members are not able to observe their rituals and knowledge of beliefs. Moreover, even if one accepts the Home Office's argument that proof must be given to show his/her family's shame, it is difficult to demonstrate a family's sense of shame with hard evidence – this is an internal psychological and emotional state.[6]

In order for British courts to have a more nuanced understanding of an asylum seeker's background, I propose that a database should be created which defines key cultural, theological, legal and any other terminology relevant to asylum seekers' cases. It is possible that the Home Office has their own database of terms but certainly from the numerous decisions that I have read this database appears to be rudimentary and largely based on secondary sources. The expertise of the database that I am suggesting should organically come from Muslim scholars and communities themselves using primary data. Scraping tools, efficient data extraction and effective governance of the sources utilized should also be used to keep such a database updated at all times. This then becomes a reliable repository for the Home Office and immigration judges to use when analysing a country and the claim of asylum seekers. The database could be replicated for other minority and religious communities in the UK or around the world.

Algorithms to Analyse the Threat of Persecution

The second problem I have noticed when analysing country guidance and information is that it is not updated regularly, and key threats of persecution are not analysed. The result is that the Home Office does not always know what is happening on the ground in countries where persecution exists. A pertinent example is the Home Office's approach to the way in which political parties function in other countries and where geographically violence could exist in villages and towns. For example, in one report that I wrote, I observed that the Home Office took a simplistic view of political parties operating in the Middle East who were striving for justice, equality and peace in their own country. The political party in question had a fluid membership structure from volunteers and protestors to high-profile leaders and decision-makers.

However, the UK country guidance and information began with the presumption that only high-profile members of such political

---

[5] al-ʾAmili, Muhammad b. Makki al-Jizzini, "Al-Lumʾa al-Dimashqīyya fī fiqh al-ʾimāmīyya", Qum: Intisharat Dar al-Fikr, 2013, p. 246, and Al-Tusi, Muhammad ibn Hasan ibn Ali Abu Jaʿfar, *A Concise Description of Islamic Law and Legal Opinions*, translated by A. Ezzati, London: ICAS Press, 2008, ch. 20, p. 492.

[6] UK Home Office decision refusing an asylum claim dated 22 January 2019. Asylum seeker's details kept confidential.

parties would be persecuted. Moreover, such persecution would only occur in certain regions of the country in question, not in specific villages or towns. The problem with this analysis is that it failed to deeply analyse the philosophy and structure of political parties who attract young men to volunteer and protest for their rights but are later arrested by state police. When these young men flee their country because of a lack of fair trial, torture and terrible prison conditions, they are not granted asylum because they are considered to be less important to their political party.

The reality, however, is that in dictatorial regimes, political parties must be flexible and adaptable to achieve their democratic objectives. Their membership tiers may appear to ascend as logical grades (such as party leader, vice-party chairman, secretary, etc.) but on the ground these levels can be skipped or amalgamated into other positions. So, a person may undertake activities such as volunteering and participating in demonstrations but may not be officially designated with a membership title because of a fluid membership structure or because of internal procedural biases that exist in the political party itself.[7]

The problem of a general analysis of asylum seekers' circumstances is compounded by the lack of specific information about their villages, communities and infrastructure. It is entirely possible that a village that is not well known could be a target of persecution but there is hardly any data on it. My suggestion is that algorithms can be created based on primary data that shows the likely level of persecution in a region. Geographical data, statistics of deaths, police records, first-hand observations, regional infrastructure and more can be inputted into the algorithms to identify whether or not persecution exists in a region and towards particular political parties or social groups. Rather than dismissing asylum seekers on the basis of a general analysis of a region, a "tech" approach to such claims may assist judges when deciding whether to grant asylum or not.

In conclusion, my argument is that the creation of a database of key terminologies and algorithms to analyse specific threats of persecution may yield fairer results for asylum seekers. This is because their cultural, religious, theological and regional backgrounds can be understood more deeply by lawyers, the Home Office and the judiciary. Perhaps immigration and asylum tribunals can evolve from a fair hearing to a "FairTech" one, thereby correcting the "serious flaws" in the system as identified by the Law Society.

---

[7] See the Country Policy and Information Note: the Muslim Brotherhood, Home Office, July 2017, and Khalil Al-Anani, *Inside the Muslim Brotherhood – Religion, Identity and Politics*, Oxford: Oxford University Press, 2016.

The Dark Side of Technology in Law: Avoiding the Pitfalls

Sebastian Ko
CEO, A.I. Vermont

"Technology is a double-edged sword", so the adage goes. In law, technology could enable or impede access to justice. Too often nowadays, the media heralds uncritically the development and adoption of technology-enabled solutions to problems arising from legal practice and proceedings (LegalTech). Many legal professionals are still unable to get comfortable with LegalTech adoption, because commonly associated risks have yet to be adequately addressed in the market. The associated costs/return on investment and sufficiency of supporting resources and training have also presented significant hurdles. This chapter examines the pitfalls facing legal innovators, technologists and users today, and how they could be avoided.

The growth of LegalTech solutions has been glacial when compared with other professions, even in the areas where there has been some level of adoption (in-house and Big Law, the pace and scale is somewhat limited).[1] The availability of better technologies in legal services, on the whole, has profound implications on access to justice.[2] The converse is also true. We have experienced frustrations when we called automated telephone services of banks and public utilities to obtain essential customer services. What should take minutes ends up taking hours. In LegalTech, operational as well as legal and regulatory requirements impose non-trivial friction on the efficient delivery of legal solutions.

New Solutions, Old Risks...in New Forms

New legal solutions are blending technology products and legal services. It is plausible to imagine in time that this would enable end-to-end solutions to businesses and individuals. Indeed, increasing technology use in legal services could drive changes in business models, and a move to a more integrated system akin to software-as-a-service solutions. In this environment, one can imagine law firms delivering their services on online platforms that are developed and maintained by in-house teams or technology vendors, where clients would be charged on comprehensive fixed-fee arrangements. Law firms have already started to invest in technology solutions, with products sometimes marketed and sold as co-branded or white-labelled software. Each of these go-to-market configurations has its own set of legal challenges.

LegalTech providers must ensure regulatory compliance in the jurisdictions where they operate and sell their solutions, including the avoidance of providing services that might constitute the unauthorized practice of law, especially important in jurisdictions where this is defined broadly, such as the US, versus a very limited interpretation in England and Wales.[3] In providing legal services, including those on technology platforms, lawyers must observe their professional conduct rules, such as restrictions on fee-sharing arrangements, marketing and

---

[1] See Victoria Hudgins, "The Larger the Legal Department, the More Likely It's Using Tech", LegalTech News, 2019: https://www.law.com/LegalTechnews/2019/07/02/the-larger-the-legal-department-the-more-likely-its-using-tech/?slreturn=20190724104522 (last visited 20 February 2020).

[2] Roger Smith, "Technology and Access to Justice: A Help or Hindrance?", Law, Technology and Access to Justice, 2019: https://law-tech-a2j.org/digital-strategy/technology-and-access-to-justice-a-help-or-hindrance/ (last visited 20 February 2020).

[3] See Alison Hook, "The Use and Regulation of Technology in the Legal Sector Beyond England and Wales", Legal Services Board, 2019: https://www.legalservicesboard.org.uk/wp-content/uploads/2019/07/International-AH-Report-VfP-4-Jul-2019.pdf (last visited 20 February 2020).

referral practices. These issues can get tricky where technology solutions are provided cross-border.

The operational risks are compounded in product–service hybrids. In terms of data protection and security, a multitude of risks arises from how data is collected, stored, processed, transmitted, used and discarded. Legal and compliance issues relating to the failure of control and supervision are routinely complicated where data is transmitted on multiple third-party networks (with different security and communication standards) and across jurisdictional boundaries.[4] Over the past decade, lawyers have been scrutinizing these challenges vigorously when considering adoption of cloud-based technologies. Data breaches, system mismanagement and other cybersecurity incidents could lead to inadvertent disclosures of electronic documentation and messages, and consequently the loss of confidentiality and legal professional privilege (LPP). Law firms have long been targets of cyberattacks, because they are by and large not tech-savvy organizations but they do handle highly sensitive client data.[5] It is unclear if LegalTech providers will similarly be high-risk targets. Moreover, parties with different interests may be sharing strategic resources, exchanging highly sensitive documentation and communication, and otherwise transacting on the same online platforms. In these cases, LegalTech vendors should apply robust know-your-client and conflicts of interest protocols similar to those of law firms, although they are not subject to the same professional regulations and codes of practices. In practice, this might be difficult to implement where technology vendors are not led or advised sufficiently by legal professionals.

"I'm Sorry, Dave…I Can't Do That": AI Complications[6]

Presently, LegalTech is developed to automate more and more workflows in legal practice, enhancing productivity and decreasing costs and risks of *certain* kinds of human errors. The good comes with the bad. Automated batch processing and production of electronic documents for litigation and regulatory disclosure to courts, regulators and opposing parties require heightened quality assurance and control. *Both* human- and system-generated errors could be propagated to massive databases of electronic documents in matters of seconds. Parties may enter agreements on safeguarding inadvertent disclosures, preserving confidentiality and providing for claw-back arrangements.

Increasingly, the output of artificially intelligent LegalTech resembles regulated activities that constitute legal practice. Chatbots can now address legal enquiries based on canned or preprogrammed responses (like an interactive FAQ) and generate bespoke recommendations and advice based on their machine learning-enabled databases. Furthermore, in making legal enquiries, if a user shared with a chatbot (operated by a technology vendor/non-law firm) information that should otherwise be protected by LPP, is LPP necessarily lost? If LPP protected this information and became purged from the chatbot's database, but the training algorithms remain, are the algorithms subject to LPP? These are highly factually dependent questions that get thornier with further hybridization of legal solutions.[7]

---

[4] See, e.g., Silvio Porcellana, "What the EU's Latest Data Protection Law Means for Chatbot Makers and Marketers", Venture Beat, 2018: https://venturebeat.com/2018/03/16/what-the-eus-latest-data-protection-law-means-for-chatbot-makers-and-marketers/ (last visited 20 February 2020).

[5] David G. Ries, "2018 Cybersecurity", American Bar Association, 2019: https://www.americanbar.org/groups/law_practice/publications/techreport/ABATECHREPORT2018/2018Cybersecurity/ (last visited 20 February 2020).

[6] The quote is from *2001: A Space Odyssey*, a film by Stanley Kubrick (1969).

[7] See, e.g., Gregory Bufithis, "Understanding the French Ban on Judicial Analytics", Gregory Bufithis, 2019: http://www.gregorybufithis.com/2019/06/09/understanding-the-french-ban-on-judicial-analytics/ (last visited 20 February 2020).

Likewise, if non-lawyers could sell will kits, then equally non-lawyers could sell "smart" or artificial intelligence (AI)-enabled will kits. The same logic could then be extended to a wide variety of document assembly and automation software, which can draft legal documents with less and less human input. It is unclear if this is a "slippery slope" and where the lines should be drawn to better define "legal practice" in the age of AI. While beyond the scope of this chapter, a deeper set of ethical, economic and legal problems arises where processes for making legally relevant decisions are delegated to, impaired or otherwise influenced by emerging technologies.[8]

Silver Lining, of Sorts

Improperly managed, LegalTech use could lead to the loss and impairment of fundamental rights, such as LPP and access to legal representation. Also, the effects may not be apparent until long after the event, as legal risks so often are. As highlighted above, there are legal and operational issues peculiar to the LegalTech market. On the sell side, there are market entry barriers and ongoing compliance and other operational costs driven by regulation. The different jurisdictional views on the regulation of activities connected with LegalTech has contributed to the fragmentation of the international LegalTech market. Germany and Malaysia, for example, are considering direct regulation and licensing of LegalTech vendors.[9] All these factors can be particularly detrimental to the growth of the LegalTech startup market.

On the buy side, these issues tend to deter adoption of new solutions as legal professionals and users of legal services have little tolerance for errors and favour familiar approaches. Innovation feeds on trial and error. Nevertheless, the legal profession's attitude towards innovation is beginning to transform globally, as lawyers slowly realize the value of technology use in staying competitive and managing costs.

Healthy growth in the adoption of LegalTech in legal services in the public, private and non-profit sectors would broaden access to justice. Simple, cheap and reliable LegalTech is critically required in many jurisdictions where legally aided services face increasing resource constraints.[10] The flipside or "dark side" to this is that access could be eroded severely in jurisdictions where technology adoption accelerates in small pockets or benefits only narrow segments of the legal services market, while it is stagnant in others. While LegalTech has its pitfalls and challenges, they can be managed well, and the fruits of innovation are plentiful.

---

[8] See Annabelle Ritchie and Siegfried Clarke, "The Ethics of Artificial Intelligence: Laws from Around the World", Lexology, 2019: https://www.lexology.com/library/detail.aspx?g=8a62e0af-8824-41a0-9602-9435b8a0f894 (last visited 20 February 2020).

[9] See Philipp Plog, "German Politicians Seek to Regulate 'Legal Tech' Companies", Artificial Lawyer, 2019: https://www.artificiallawyer.com/2019/06/03/german-politicians-seek-to-regulate-legal-tech-companies/ (last visited 20 February 2020).

[10] Magda Ibrahim, "Justice for All: How Technology is Promoting Public Access", Raconteur, 2018: https://www.raconteur.net/risk-management/technology-public-access-justice (last visited 20 February 2020).

Closing the Justice Gap – Technology is *Not* the First Step

Tresca Rodrigues
Dispute Resolution Designer and Mediator, Moralis Consulting

A cocktail of legal aid cuts, court closures, legal fees, reduced recoverable legal costs (and more) have led to many people on low income struggling to access civil justice in England and Wales. This scenario is the same across many countries.

Technological innovation presents an opportunity to address this problem and access justice efficiently and affordably. It is increasingly being adopted by courts globally; redefining justice as we know it.

England and Wales are seeing rapid court digitalization and a new "online court" involving the deployment of digital court forms, remote video conferencing, online case management and the like. With these developments occurring at pace it may appear that the central focus is only on injecting technology into the court process. This, however, would fail to recognize the importance of a fundamental part of a user's justice journey: *user support services.*

For those on low income, access to justice relies on both the support service network and the court process working effectively in tandem. Both are important cogs within the justice wheel for unrepresented litigants (hereinafter referred to as litigants-in-person, LiPs).

Solely injecting technology into a redrawn court landscape without doing the same for the support landscape risks not addressing the justice gap effectively. At worst, it may widen it, rendering digital court systems inaccessible to many.

This chapter explores how technology can be used to widen access within a support service strategy. It outlines why STEP 1 should be strategy and STEP 2 technology.

Accessing Justice Through a Supported Court Process

My research and experience working with charities and community projects has shown that LiPs fear embarking on and navigating a complex and confusing legal system – at a time when they face a life-changing crisis with little or no funding.

They need a practical understanding of legal process and rights as well as additional support dependent on circumstances such as a language barrier or disability.

A technology-enabled support network offering quality-assured services will reassure LiPs of support in understanding what to expect, make informed choices and feel empowered throughout. Without this, courts spend much time explaining processes to ensure procedural fairness.

Support Services – a Confusing Landscape

Support and alternative dispute resolution (ADR) services provide the LiP with assistance and opportunity for early resolution.

Support services are wide ranging, including legal information provision, pro-bono or unbundled legal advice, court attendance support, language services and legal aid. ADR services include mediation, arbitration, neutral evaluation and negotiation.

Dedicated support organizations provide a lifeline amidst a complex, underfunded sector comprising multiple providers with no clear single access point for the LiP. There are gaps in provision, areas of overlap and lack of enabling technology.

Step 1: Strategy Before Technology

People need clarity about what support is available and a simple way to access those services.

To achieve this, and address existing issues, requires strategically redrawing the support landscape *before* introducing technology.

This would create a comprehensive and coordinated network of services, allow targeted technology development where most needed and make technology available on a shared services basis for maximum cost–benefit.

Without putting strategy first, there could be danger of a scatter-gun approach where technology development may not be deployed to greatest effect, be duplicated across providers or unsustainable and fall into disuse. This cash-poor sector cannot afford the financial "hit".

More dangerously, without proper oversight and accountability, technology can put the public at risk of unintended consequences such as ethical misuse or data security (think Cambridge Analytica). Innovation potential is powerful but must be developed within a framework that safeguards the public – else we risk a public backlash on its use when trust is shattered.

Step 2: Technology to Support Lips

A guided pathway approach

The consolidated service network can be offered to the LiP as part of a technology-driven resolution pathway. There could be a single entry point and the support could be offered to the LiP before as well as during the justice process.

Technology can be a powerful enabler in this resolution pathway, providing legal information, integrating support services and ADR services. Additionally, there are opportunities for predictive artificial intelligence (AI), chatbot capability, data insight and more.

A guided pathway could take the LiP step by step through obtaining information on their legal issue, providing services to help them resolve their issue and identifying next-step options. The British Columbian Civil Resolution Tribunal and MyLawBC projects are examples of this kind of approach.

Additionally, a built-in triaging process could help identify what support a LiP needs. Telephone and face-to-face support offered in conjunction with this technology-based process will further assist and provide the all-important "human" element where needed.

Guided pathway steps: information provision

Research shows a LiP's first step is usually to search the internet to find out more about their problem and options. Many are overwhelmed by the vast amount of legal information available online, struggling to understand what is trustworthy information and relevant to their situation.

Information provision could be the first step in the LiP's pathway. This could be via a rule-based question set that presents resulting information obtained from trustworthy sources. Another option may be for an AI chatbot to accept a freestyle question and present the LiP with more tailored information about the law and options.

Information can be presented in a mixture of formats: text, video, picture, downloadable material, etc.

Prioritizing development where its most needed would maximize benefit. This requires identifying the most common and important problems people face? The public advice service, Citizens Advice, could provide underlying data for evidence-based decisions.

Guided pathway steps: legal advice

Depending on the type of dispute and personal circumstances, LiPs may need tailored advice.

The next pathway step could allow the LiP to access legal advice. This offering could include pro-bono, legal aid, law centre or paid-for limited scope (unbundled) legal advice. These services could be scheduled via the platform and delivered face to face or via secure video recording. Video services may help address the issue of "advice deserts" where people in certain geographic areas struggle to find help.

Another option, depending on dispute complexity, may be to use AI to provide the user with a range of outcomes within a given context. This could be driven by machine-learning AI or prescriptive analytics. Issues such as bias, data provenance, explainability, fairness, transparency and accuracy must be addressed. Regulators could issue a rule set governing ethical use of AI technology to protect human rights and personal data. Technology, likely to pose a public risk, could be vetted against this baseline before being approved for use.

Guided pathway steps: resolution

LiPs proceeding with a court application can use digital assistance and limited legal advice services to understand and complete the digital court application.

ADR, such as mediation, could also be built into the pathway for early resolution. It could directly link to either a face-to-face or an online dispute resolution platform. If full settlement could not be reached, parties would be able to proceed to court on the remaining issues. This aligns with the current court pre-action protocol encouraging the use of ADR.

Summary

This strategic approach could make the justice system more accessible for LiPs through a technology-enabled coordinated group of services that supports them through the justice process.

Overall governance of the service network could help to provide oversight and accountability to ensure efficient, cost-effective and quality-assured services that can scale to meet demand.

If technology support for the LiP journey is not properly designed, implemented and funded, the cost of digitizing court processes for them could be wasted.

Finally...

This is an ambitious vision that marries innovation and creativity with humanity to address a global problem.

Realizing the vision won't be about a single individual or a perfect plan, but a collective vision requiring us to collaborate, consensus-build and hold ourselves accountable.

There's room on the bus for everyone!

Combining AI and Digitization of Judgments for Access to Justice

Mikolaj Barczentewicz

Lecturer in Law and Research Director, University of Surrey School of Law

Litigation in lower-level courts and tribunals rarely attracts the attention of others than those directly interested in the given case. However, with computer analysis of such judgments it is possible to build algorithmic tools that can tell us a good deal about how the law works in practice. Such tools may even be able to predict how a court would decide a legal question, given a set of facts. Due to technological limitations, it may not be appropriate to offer such tools directly to consumers (e.g. litigants-in-person) in the near future. Nevertheless, a lawyer assisted by such a tool may even today be able to work more efficiently and thus offer legal advice to clients who now do not benefit from it due to cost.

Individual judgments of lower courts and tribunals do not normally have much influence on the development of the law. Also, in many areas of law there are so many such judgments that it would be very difficult to try to keep up with them. Academics don't teach about those cases, focusing instead on landmark judgments of appellate courts. For similar reasons, practitioners (judges, lawyers representing clients) mostly rely on appellate cases. And even though practitioners may know more lower-level judgments than academics, in many fields no one has a truly comprehensive perspective. We rely instead on more or less partial pictures. Because of the limited interest from lawyers, it is understandable that publishers of commercial databases of court judgments (e.g. Westlaw, Lexis) publish only small selections of lower court judgments.

The same lower court judgments that are of such limited interest today are crucial for developing artificial intelligence (AI) (machine learning) solutions that could assist in providing legal advice. With access to those judgments, it is possible to find patterns in how judges decide certain legal questions. Knowing those patterns, we can predict how a court would respond to given facts. Such prediction is not going to be perfect, but it can be very helpful to a lawyer. Especially when the prediction is accompanied by an explanation (legal reasoning) and by identification of similar past cases to the facts the lawyer is dealing with.

The law makes use of many multifactorial tests. Some are provided expressly by legislation, but many are at least partially developed by the courts. Part of what being an experienced lawyer means is that one is able to apply such multifactorial tests to the facts at hand, without necessarily having to spend days reading the relevant past cases applying the test. An experienced lawyer can either recall past cases with similar facts or use their professional intuition honed by reading many cases, even if the lawyer couldn't recall all of them. Of course, both methods available to an experienced lawyer are fallible. And those methods are not available to lawyers with less experience or to lawyers who would like to advise on an issue that is not within their strict specialism.

A machine-learning algorithm could build a model of how the courts have applied the law (on a particular issue) that works like an experienced lawyer's intuition and memory. The algorithmic methods have their limitations (more of which in a second), but there are ways in which they surpass human capability. An algorithm will always take into account all cases we feed it, not just a small subset that a human can remember and process. An algorithm will build a model using repeatable, deterministic statistical methods – human intuition is often fooled by biases and non-statistical thinking.

Consider the following example. One important multifactorial test in many jurisdictions is the one that determines who counts as an employee for the purposes of labour law and tax law. As Blue J Legal have demonstrated in respect of Canadian law, it is possible to build an algorithmic tool that would take the information about the facts of past cases and about how the courts answered the question of employment status in those cases and, in return, give us predictions about what a court would say in future (or hypothetical) cases, while also providing an explanation of the prediction and information in past cases that have similar facts.[1]

Using such a tool, a lawyer is less reliant on experience and can spend less time researching past cases. The lawyer should then be able to provide better advice and do so in less time. Of course, the lawyer should not trust any such algorithmic tool blindly, but the fact that the tool could provide an explanation and identify similar past cases may allow the lawyer to check the prediction. At the very least, the prediction provides a quick starting point for analysis, likely improving it and making it less time consuming.

Less-than-perfect reliability is just one of the current limitations of this technology. The other big limitation is the issue of legal change. It may be relatively straightforward to build a tool, like the one just described, that would be reasonably reliable relative to past court judgments. But what if the law changes, and especially if it changes merely by an unannounced and hard-to-perceive change of the courts' approach to certain legal questions? A tool developed on the pre-change judgment data may cease to be reliable in predicting the courts' approach post-change. There are methods to attempt to address this, but it is not a trivial problem.

Although we may not like to admit it, there is also the issue that the law in action follows patterns not only set by legal rules, but also determined by human biases. While developing an algorithmic tool predicting what a court would say to certain facts we may discover that among the factors that heavily and reliably predict the courts' judgment are not just extra-legal factors, but factors that we would be abhorred to know any court took into account (e.g. gender or race of the plaintiff, when they are legally irrelevant). It will be good for us to know this, and such "by-product" knowledge may on its own have important contributions to improving the law, by pointing out the ways in which the law (or at least the practice of law) must change. Nevertheless, before the law (or practice) changes, it may be a controversial issue whether to use predictive models which work well (in predicting what a court would say), but do so by taking into account facts that the court legally should not take into account.

The limitations of the technology I describe here are real and should be taken seriously, but the promise of the benefits it brings are real as well. I believe that, if developed and used responsibly, they can be a force for good – providing fairness and justice for society as a whole.

---

[1] https://www.bluejlegal.com/preview-tax-worker-classifier.

LegalTech Around the World

Executive Summary

Just as the legal services market is global and differs by jurisdiction, LegalTech also has a growing global footprint. This part looks at differing perspectives of its development in different jurisdictions – from the emerging new skills required, to the approach in Japan, through to what is happening in Malaysia. Each one of these contributions provides a small glimpse into the world of LegalTech as it begins to gain traction globally – highlighting both the potential and the many barriers which remain before it can truly have a transformational and positive impact on the delivery of legal services.

In their opening chapter Legal Implications of Artificial Intelligence in China, the authors Ron Cai, Xuezhou Chen and Sherry Zhang review the growth of artificial intelligence in China, investment going into the sector and how many of the concerns raised are comparable to those outside China.

In their chapter on tech adoption and skills demand, Dr Matthias Qian et al. seek to test the impact and degree of adoption of technology on the demand for lawyer and non-lawyer skills across jurisdictions. By comparing three leading jurisdictions, the UK, Singapore and the US, the paper sheds interesting insights on the degree of adoption and therefore real impact of LegalTech.

Clare Weaver looks at a country-specific example, examining the adoption of LegalTech in Japan. The counterpoint to a non-Western market provides an interesting overview of the barriers to adoption in Japan, but also highlights how many barriers in a globally conservative profession are shared across jurisdictions.

And finally, Jenna Beh Huey Ching provides a story of Malaysia's growing LawTech scene. Albeit a small nation in comparison to some of the other giant jurisdictions seeking to make a mark in their area, Malaysia has shown great enthusiasm in the support of the benefits of LawTech, a market worth watching closely.

Legal Implications of Artificial Intelligence in China

Ron Cai
Partner, Zhong Lun Law Firm

Xuezhou Chen
Associate, Zhong Lun Law Firm

and Sherry Zhang
Senior Associate, Zhong Lun Law Firm

Background

Artificial intelligence (AI) has been developing very quickly in China. According to a recent report from *iiMedia Research*, in 2018, the amount of financing in the AI sector in China reached RMB 131.1 billion (approximately US$20 billion), with a growth rate of 107% against year 2017.

Policies supporting AI in China started from intelligent manufacturing. Back on 8 May 2015, the State Council issued the *Notice on Issuing "Made in China (2025)"*, which paved the foundation for the development of AI in China. On 8 July 2017, China's State Council issued "*A Next Generation Artificial Intelligence Development Plan*" (AI Plan), which outlined China's strategy to build a domestic AI industry worth nearly US$150 billion in the next few years and to become a leading power for AI. This officially marked the development of the AI sector as a national priority. The motivations for pursuing the AI strategy include the potential of AI for industrial transformation, better social governance and maintaining social stability.

Despite the government's ambition, however, the development of laws and regulations governing AI is still at its early stage in China. In the AI Plan, the State Council proposed to "establish AI-related laws and regulations, ethical principles and policy system, and build up capability in AI safety assessment and control". However, no integrated law or regulation has been formed yet. AI technologies and products are regulated under the current general laws and regulations, particularly in respect of privacy and data, professional or regulatory permits, intellectual property, liabilities, bias and discrimination. This chapter discusses the legal implementations of AI from all these perspectives.

Legal Implementations

1. Privacy

AI technologies are developed based on massive data. However, data itself is intangible asset, which may involve personal privacy rights, in particular, personal information. AI developers need to obtain adequate high-quality data for AI development, while still staying in compliance with legal requirements on privacy.

Personal information under People's Republic of China (PRC) law generally refers to any information that independently or in combination with other information can be used to identify a person. Collecting and using personal information are required to follow the general principles of prior consent, relevance and legitimacy, etc. Specifically, before collecting personal information, collectors shall disclose their rules of data collection and use, purposes, means and scope of collection and use, and obtain the consent of the information source. The information collected shall be necessary for the products or services provided. Collection or use of personal information against laws, regulations and agreements with the information source shall be prohibited. For example, if a bank intends to install an AI device in the lobby to provide consulting services to its customers, the AI device would need to collect the customers' behaviours through its cameras, including facial characteristics and expressions, such collection may require the specific consent of its customers. However, we seldom observe that such prior consent is sought in practice.

Additionally, purchasing personal information from third-party vendors may also subject the purchaser to criminal liabilities if such information is acquired by the third party through illegitimate means, for example, theft or defending crawlers, etc.

2. Professional or regulatory permits

In China, some industries and professions are highly regulated and subject to special licences, such as the medical and finance industries. Individuals or legal entities doing business in such industries must obtain prior approvals or licences from authorities. Does an AI need a licence? This is a question with no clear answer for certain industries and professions under current PRC laws. PRC laws and policies will have to grapple with how to determine competency in an AI system.

For example, in the medical industry, an AI solution that can help detect eye disease and make diagnosis recommendations may be deemed to be a medical device under PRC law, and thus be subject to approvals. However, in practice, it would be difficult for medical AIs to obtain such approvals, given the authorities' lack of knowledge and experience in how to evaluate and regulate such medical AIs.

Another example is in the financial industry. If an AI developer develops a smart software that can advise users about purchasing or selling stocks, should the developer obtain a licence for the product? Under PRC law, a "stock pick software" without AI function would be considered to be providing security investment consulting services subject to a licence. However, Chinese financial regulatory authorities are not very clear on licence requirements on financial AIs.

3. Intellectual property

With respect to intellectual property (IP), one big issue is whether an AI could own the IPs of the works created by the AI. AIs today are clever enough to create works; XiaoIce, a smart chatbot developed by Microsoft, for example, has created numerous poems and pictures based on the user's input. Legally speaking, AIs are not qualified owners under PRC Copyright Law, as owners can only be individuals or companies. Therefore, an AI may not own IPs of such creations. Should the AI developers or the users who contribute to the final works own the IPs? These are questions to be discussed and answered in the future.

In a recent case between Tencent and the operator of the online platform "Wang Dai Zhi Jia", the court of Nanshan District in Shenzhen, Guangdong Province ruled that AI produced works are protected by the Copyright Law. In this case, writers from Tencent used Dreamwriter, an AI writing system developed by Tencent, to write a commentary article about the stock market based on massive data and personalized instruction from the writers. The court ruled that this article was displayed as a literary work, was created based on personalized choice and arrangement of the writers, and demonstrated creative analysis and judgement of stock market information. Therefore, this article should be protected as a literary work under the Copyright Law. Further, the court ruled that this article was created by the joint talent of Tencent team members, and its copyright should be owned by the Tencent company.

Another interesting topic is IPs of AI deliverables in joint development projects, where one party provides algorithms and modules, as the developer, and the other party provides data, as the customer, for the joint development. There would generally be two IP ownership arrangements for the final AI deliverables, i.e. sole ownership by the developer and licence to the customer for business use, or co-ownership between the developer and customer. Under the former arrangement, the developer has sole ownership and control of the IP. However, it may be difficult for the developer to negotiate the deal, and it would be subject to higher tax burdens than under the co-ownership arrangement. Under a co-development arrangement, however, it would be difficult for the developer to control IP and use of the deliverables by the customer.

4. Liabilities

One more legal issue would be, who would be liable for harm caused by an AI? Currently, there is no specific provisions in the law. The general rule is that if an AI is regarded as a product, manufacturers and resellers of the AI product would be subject to strict product liability, and the party suffering the losses may need to prove defect of the AI product under PRC Product Liability Law. If an AI is regarded as a service, the service provider would be subject to general torts liability, and the suffering party may need to prove fault, e.g. negligence, of the service provider under PRC Torts Law.

For example, if the AI solutions for eye disease detection and diagnosis made a mistake, and a patient lost vision after surgery by a doctor who relies on the advice of the AI solutions, the patient might choose to claim torts liability against the hospital and the doctor, or might claim product liability against the AI solutions developer. It is not clear under PRC law how to deal with such a situation.

5. Bias and discrimination

AI cannot always be fair and neutral. AI is created by humans, and may learn to incorporate human bias. A machine-learning algorithm can identify a data pattern and include it in writing predictions, rules and decisions. If such a pattern reflects current discrimination in society, then the machine-learning algorithm may magnify its adverse effect. For example, an AI search engine may recommend more high-salary positions for males than females.

Algorithm systems need to be improved to reduce discrimination. And laws and regulations are required to deal with the bias of AI technologies.

Conclusion

None of the issues described above are unique to China. AI is quite a new area, and we expect a lot of new issues and developments to come in the future.

Mapping LegalTech Adoption and Skill Demand[1]

Dr Matthias Qian
Lecturer, University of Oxford

Dr Adam Saunders
Research Fellow, University of Oxford

and Maximilian Ahrens
Machine Learning Researcher, University of Oxford

Introduction

With LegalTech innovation progressing at an ever-increasing pace, the jury is out regarding how fast the global legal services sector is implementing new technologies and what the impact is for lawyer and non-lawyer skills across jurisdictions. We shed new light on these questions by analysing LegalTech adoption and skill rates embedded in online job adverts posted in 2019 by legal services sector employers based in Singapore, the United Kingdom and the United States. Each country is in the running to become a globally leading LegalTech hub but with very different policy approaches to enabling LegalTech investment. These range from Singapore's coordinated *Smart Nation* initiative to the UK government's open R&D competition format under its *Industrial Strategy* and a market-driven yet anti-reformist stance in the US in which bar association opposition continues to prevent inward sector investment.

[1] This research was supported by the University of Oxford's *Unlocking the Potential of Artificial Intelligence for English Law* project, which is funded by a grant from UKRI-ESRC's *Next Generation Services Challenge* under HM government's *Industrial Strategy Challenge Fund*. The authors would like to thank both the funder and our project data partner, Burning Glass Technologies Inc., with further thanks due to Davor Miskulin and Dr Bledi Taska from Burning Glass for their ongoing support. The authors would also like to thank James Sayer for his excellent research assistance.

What we find from the results of a big data analysis of LegalTech operations and job roles across these countries is:

1. the market is in its infancy with fewer than 1% of legal services sector job adverts referring to LegalTech enabling technologies and skills; and

2. there is greater overall demand for LegalTech capabilities from UK law firms, yet higher demand in Singapore and the US for job roles that combine legal expertise with technical expertise, in particular coding.

The initial results suggest an emergent distinction in approach between a higher tendency towards non-lawyer technologist recruitment in the UK and a higher tendency towards the recruitment of hybrid lawyer-coder skill sets in Singapore and the US.

Approach

We analysed data from a corpus of more than 500 million online job adverts supplied by Burning Glass Technologies Inc., a globally leading labour market big data provider. Based on frequency counts of key term searches according to legal services industry and occupational classification codes, we calculated the percentage frequencies of job adverts in a given year that contained specified terms associated with LegalTech. This approach provides indicators for the comparative development of LegalTech capabilities across national legal services sectors.

LegalTech Markets Are in Their Infancy

Despite the hype surrounding the possibilities of LegalTech solutions, an analysis of legal services job advert data from each country shows that they are still in their infancy with respect to artificial intelligence (AI) and legal technology operations and job roles. As can be seen in Figure 1, calculations of percentage frequencies for key LegalTech terms embedded in 2019 legal services job adverts show very low adoption rates for the legal services sector as a whole in Singapore, the UK and the US.[2] In particular, fewer than 1% of job adverts in each case contained references to key thematic terms, including legal technology, AI, data science and automation.

This suggests that only a very small subset of legal practices in each country is actively engaged in LegalTech implementation strategies. The picture changes somewhat when focusing specifically on UK and US law firm job adverts. This disaggregation of the data for the US legal services sector shows that the percentage of US law firm job adverts containing the keywords "legal technology" is as high as 8% during the first eight months of 2019. The percentage of UK law firm job adverts that reference "AI" is 2% during the same period. Figure 1 therefore suggests an emerging disparity in LegalTech adoption not only between large and SME legal practices but also between those focused on courtroom representation and those focused on matters such as contracting and legal advisory services.[3,4]

---

[2] The 2019 Burning Glass data that was analysed extends to 31 July 2019 for the Singapore data, 5 August 2019 for the UK data and 12 August 2019 for the US data.

[3] Please note that data for the "legal services sector" is derived from Burning Glass data for the following industry codes: Singapore (2015 SSIC 691 – Legal Activities), United Kingdom (2007 SIC 69.10 – Legal Activities), United States (2017 NAICS 5411 – Legal Services). Data for "law firms" is derived from Burning Glass data for the following industry codes: United Kingdom (2007 SIC 69.10/2 – Legal Activities – Solicitors), United States (2017 NAICS 54111 – Legal Services – Offices of Lawyers).

[4] This last point is highlighted in the case of the UK in which LegalTech adoption is substantially lower in the overall UK legal services sector than amongst UK law firms. Further evidence is shown in that 2019 Burning Glass job adverts labelled as "2007 UK SIC 69.10/1 – Legal Activities – Barristers", in which the focus of that subsector primarily remains on courtroom advocacy, do not return any LegalTech term frequency counts for the entire corpus of data between 2012 and 2019.

Differential Demand for Machine Learning

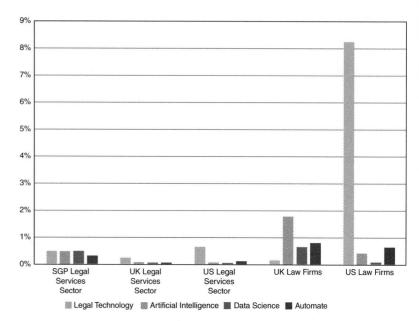

Figure 1: Percentage of legal services sector and law firm job adverts containing key LegalTech thematic terms, 2019

Source: Authors' calculations of 2019 Burning Glass data for: Singapore (2015 SSIC 691 – Legal Activities), United Kingdom (2007 SIC 69.10 – Legal Activities), United Kingdom (2007 SIC 69.10/2 – Legal Activities – Solicitors), United States (2017 NAICS 5411 – Legal Services); more detailed data for Singaporean law firms was unavailable so comparisons can only be made to the Singapore legal services sector as a whole.

With machine learning poised to become the driving force of LegalTech innovation, the demand profile for this, and the other underlying algorithmic-driven technologies that can power various forms of document analysis used in LegalTech applications, is a very telling indicator of how different countries are positioning with respect to LegalTech adoption. As Figure 2 highlights, 2019 UK law firm job adverts contain considerably more references to "machine learning", at 3%, than did either US law firm or Singaporean legal services sector job adverts. In addition, UK law firm job adverts contain comparatively more references to advanced machine-learning techniques for documentary analysis, including natural language processing (NLP) for textual analysis. This trend encompasses a small but comparatively higher number of job adverts that contain references to the most cutting-edge NLP methods of deep-learning neural networks, which enable pattern recognition embedded within a big data corpus of text.

Non-Lawyer Technologists versus Lawyer-Coders

This trend in machine learning is coupled by UK law firm demand for a growing number of solicitor job roles that place an emphasis on supporting skill sets such as algorithm development and coding in languages such as Python and R, as can also be seen in Figure 2. However, the data suggests that the broader trend in Singapore and the US is the recruitment of AI and coding skill sets amongst legal professionals themselves in contrast to UK law firms in which demand would alternatively need to be met through the recruitment of non-lawyer technologists. For instance, as can be seen in Figure 3, there is a robust demand for lawyers

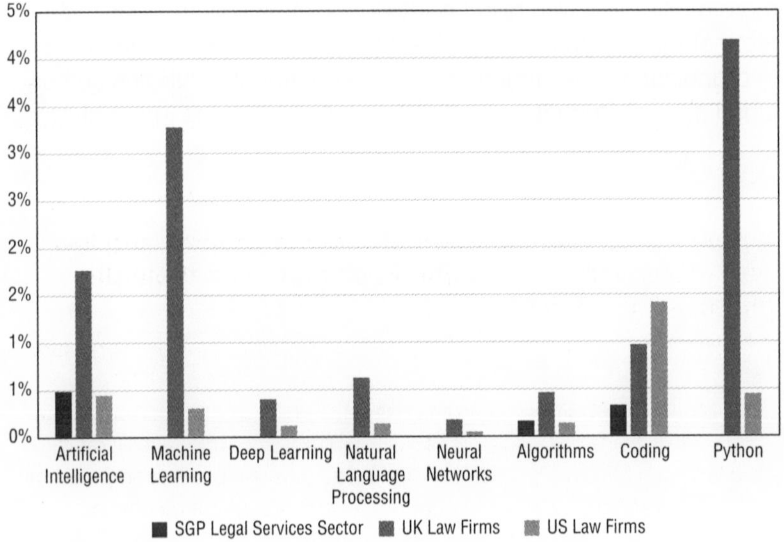

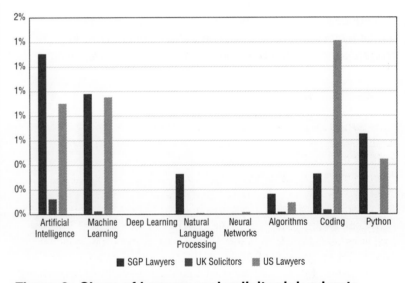

Figure 2: Percentage of legal services sector and law firm job adverts containing key terms for skills and capabilities that enable LegalTech, 2019

Source: Author's calculations of 2019 Burning Glass data for: Singapore (2015 SSIC 691 – Legal Activities), United Kingdom (2007 SIC 69.10/2 – Legal Activities – Solicitors), United States (2017 NAICS 54111 – Legal Services – Offices of Lawyers).

Figure 3: Share of lawyers and solicitor job adverts containing key terms for skills and capabilities that enable LegalTech, 2019

Source: Author's calculations of 2019 Burning Glass data for: Singapore (2015 SSIC 691 – Legal Activities), United Kingdom (2007 SIC 69.10/2 – Legal Activities – Solicitors), United States (2017 NAICS 54111 – Legal Services – Offices of Lawyers).

in Singapore and the US to know both AI and machine learning, which in 2019 stands at 1% of Singaporean and US legal services job adverts. Such trends stand in contrast to the demand dynamic in the UK where there are decidedly fewer job adverts for trained solicitors who also possess key LegalTech enabling skills. Beyond this headline finding, in Singaporean and US job adverts aimed specifically at legal professionals there is a comparatively higher emphasis on LegalTech enabling capabilities such as AI, machine learning, NLP and coding. This is in contrast to the UK where there is more demand for those capabilities in the round but without a move to recruit those skills from legal professionals themselves.

The Future Impact of LegalTech Adoption

If the question posed is whether LegalTech adoption is fundamentally changing the hiring patterns of law firms in Singapore, the United Kingdom and the United States, then the answer in 2019 has to be not yet. However, the initial findings above do highlight that certain legal practices are beginning to upskill their operations and their workforces with relevant technological capabilities. The next question which arises is how that trajectory will develop. As has happened to a large extent in the advanced manufacturing and financial services sectors, are some law firms on their way to becoming tech firms or LegalTech firms? The finding that some, even if a small minority, of law firms are seeking in-house advanced machine-learning capabilities which are expected to transform how the law will be practised in the years to come appear to suggest so. What is not yet known is whether lawyers in the machine-learning age will be required solely as domain specialists who will work in tandem with technology specialists in order to improve the delivery of legal services or whether the profession will expect lawyers to become more multiskilled with talent portfolios spanning both legal and technological areas of expertise. Finally, will there be differences in organizational arrangements and recruitment strategies across jurisdictions? On that point, the data tells us that the jury is still out.

A Case Study of Adoption of Legal Technology in a Non-Western Market

Clare Weaver

Consultant and Director, Putney Consulting Ltd

Introduction – A Legal Revolution

The global market for legal services is in a state of flux – clients are demanding "more for less", Western lawyers are proactively using new innovations to seek increasingly productive, efficient and cost-effective ways of providing legal services, whilst Japan with its reputation as a highly technologically advanced economy has yet to make any significant technological changes in its legal services industry.

A case study of innovativeness in Japan, an advanced non-Western market, in contrast to the US and UK legal markets, was undertaken to consider the following questions:

1. What factors influence the rate of adoption of new innovations?

2. What recommendations can be made to increase such adoption?

3. What can the wider legal industry learn from this case study on Japan?

The Western Legal Services Market Today

The work of Western academics and commentators along with the Law Society of England and Wales, which undertook its own review of the legal services market in the UK, "The Future of Legal Services" (The Law Society, 2016) (Figure 1), promoted three key themes for the future of legal services in the UK and US coming out of research on the UK and US legal services market, which can be summarized as follows.

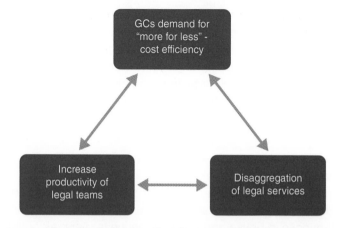

Figure 1: **Key themes for the future of legal services**

A Case Study of a Non-Western Market

New legal innovations are gradually diffusing the legal markets in Western Europe, North America and Asia Pacific; however, key adopters of these innovations are predominantly in European or Anglo-Saxon markets, familiar with the provision of Western-style legal services. The point in case here, Japan, with a civil law-based legal system and very traditional, hierarchical and conservative legal services market, has not yet embraced legal innovation or new technologies in the legal services market as a whole and has a strong scepticism about adopting innovations in this market, the reasons for which formed the basis for this research.

Recent commentary on innovation in Japan poses an interesting dichotomy – Japan is universally known as one of the most technically advanced nations, leading the global charge on technological development in the 1980s and 1990s, yet is seen as lagging behind the West on the development and adoption of innovative technologies by members of Japanese society in general.

The Japanese legal services market reflects this paradox more starkly – Japanese companies are highly active in the development of artificial intelligence (AI) (including production of AI and technology being applied for legal services outside of Japan) but anecdotally it appears the legal teams in those companies have not yet adopted many technological advances in providing their legal services.

Research on the Japanese legal market was undertaken from late 2017 to early 2018 of the Tokyo legal services market, first by way of an online questionnaire sent to legal department heads in over 20 of Japan's largest companies, followed by one-to-one interviews with Japanese in-house and private practice lawyers, alongside key expatriate leaders.

Findings from the Research

The research found that whilst there was interest in new legal technologies, and innovation exists amongst legal department heads in Japan, little innovative change has been adopted to date and strong scepticism remains about benefits, costs, applicability and usability of adopting such innovation; hence, there has been little uptake of any of the available technologies or alternative legal services in Japan so far:

"The reason for slow speed of change in Japan is the lack of change thinking."

Several patterns emerged from the data collected:

1. **A general lack of *awareness* or *knowledge* about the offerings of legal technology:** including opportunities it can bring and how other countries are increasing the use of legal innovation. Nearly all respondents noted some sense of lack of general knowledge on the matter:

    "We don't hear very much at all in Japan about this innovation. I think it is about new things, they don't want to take risk, they don't

want to make mistakes, that's the mentality. They want to rely on humans.

"[the Japanese] don't see how innovation might work and if they don't see it they don't know how to use it nor what benefit they might get."

2. **The sense of paradox or conflict in the Japanese market:** a majority of respondents acknowledged that Japan creates innovative products and the Japanese like novelty. However, whilst AI and digital transformation are management "hot topics" at the moment, there is little action beyond information gathering, indicating a longer-term view on changes than may be expected in the West:

    "I think the main problem here is people don't feel there is a need for change – why do we need to change?

    "We have incredible profits now, next year will be a good year for the [trading companies], so they don't worry about [change] at all. If one day they have real problems, they might try to change then."

3. **A critical view from the legal market that what might be good for Western lawyers or clients is not necessarily *best* for *Japan*:** there is a general sense that current tools or applications made in the US or UK were "not appropriate" or "not accurate" enough for use in Japan or, more strongly, that the fact the technology comes from the US or the UK, it is not trusted for use in Japan, unlike some new tech products being developed by Japanese AI companies:

    "Japanese don't trust foreign technology, if they didn't create it, they don't know how to adopt it."

4. **The *follow-the-leader strategy* of Japan's biggest corporates and law firms:** many respondents confirmed no one firm would likely stick its neck out to develop a new technology or pioneer the implementation of existing products, giving a sense that all firms are playing a "wait-and-see" game, but do not want to be left behind when the others do move:

    "If 1 or 2 leading companies start to use this [technology] then all the market will follow."

5. A surprising "outlier" response was in relation to the subject of **leadership of innovation** in Japan:

"Japanese leadership is all about Japanese culture – leaders are made that way by others, they are not natural leaders, but when they become leader they are too old to do anything … the people that grew up with innovation want change but if the group don't see innovation, they don't choose leaders for innovation. That's why it takes so long to change in Japanese organizations."

This comment added an additional dimension to the adoption decision process: that the wider corporate climate of innovativeness may have a direct effect on the decision to adopt or reject new innovations in an existing market.

Outcomes and Recommendations

The research raised three paradoxical outcomes that influence how adoption of innovations may differ in diverse markets.

This case study of a paradoxical, non-Western market provides food for thought in relation to the factors that influence how technology is regarded in a local market and provides recommendations for increasing the rate of adoption of legal innovation in any legal market, regardless of location or technological development.

Whilst the US and UK legal markets and regulators have become increasingly liberalized and open to innovative providers of legal services, the Japanese Bar Associations, supported by traditional Japanese law firms, have not yet accepted alternative legal service providers or liberalization of the Japanese legal market, stifling the growth of innovation and change.

However, there are some similarities with Western markets, as the Law Society report "Artificial Intelligence and the Legal Profession" (Law Society, 2018) found – lawyers in both markets do not yet trust the data and insight that the systems provide, nor do they have the skills or training necessary to see the benefits of or use the technology products to their best advantage.

Therefore, the recommendations for adoption of legal technology that could be applied equally to Western and non-Western markets can be summarized as set out in Figure 2.

Figure 2: Recommendations for the Japanese legal services market

Why Now Is the Time for LegalTech to Boom

Lawtech Malaysia

The way our society perceives and accords to laws has come a long way since laws were first codified back in 2000 BCE under the rule of Mesopotamian kings. In today's digital age, legal professionals are able to look up centuries-old cases within seconds, facilitate commercial deals with parties from multiple geographical locations concurrently, review and analyse bulky documents within minutes, or even hire robot lawyers to undertake grunt work; all thanks to technological advancements. Legal technology – technology platforms or software that aid the provision of legal services – started budding in the early 1970s when Lexis' UBIQ was invented to allow lawyers to search case law online rather than laboriously pore through books.[1] By the 1980s, the more adventurous law firms started adopting the use of personal computers for word processing, calendar/diary management and the storage of digitally created documents. According to *Forbes*, investment in LegalTech grew by a staggering 713% in 2018.[2] Technological innovations have allowed the legal industry endless possibilities in terms of efficiency and efficacy, and there is no better time for LegalTech to boom than now.

Time, in essence, is the critical ingredient for many innovations and technologically historical moments. Do we recognize it as striking it at the right time or do we have the right building blocks that pave towards the innovation success and technological wave in this era?

Amongst the Asian countries, Malaysia may be considered as a late bloomer in the LegalTech space, which leads us to trace the origins of how it all began. The Malaysian legal system was built on the backbone of the English legal system due to Malaysia's rich history and the way the country was built after gaining independence. Until today, we still refer to and apply case laws and precedents from the United Kingdom, which leads us to the next question: can we springboard ourselves to achieve the growth of the robust LegalTech ecosystem in the UK that remains one of the powerhouses globally? The LegalTech race became far more exciting when Barclays Bank UK launched a LegalTech incubator, Eagle Lab, in London.[3]

Returning to the Asian landscape, in Malaysia, as a new area which lacks precedents and guidelines to navigate, the early stages of LegalTech have been sluggish. LegalTech startups from abroad were shopping for a base country from which to launch to tackle the Asia market and indeed some have actually landed in Malaysia. Like many beginnings, it had its teething problems and this resulted in many LegalTech startups opting to go elsewhere, outside of Malaysia.

The words legal and tech combine two areas that on the surface look remarkably different. Legal stands on the premise of legacy systems, knowledge and existing precedents, while tech builds innovations as if it is racing against time. Therefore, due to the stark nature of the two worlds of legal and tech, it is essential to build a LegalTech ecosystem that focuses on working with stakeholders in both the legal and tech worlds closely to address the problems in the legal industry. We must also appreciate and strengthen international collaboration across borders to enhance the growth of LegalTech regionally.

The birth of the Asia-Pacific Legal Innovation and Technology Association[4] and ASEAN LegalTech[5] shows the timely transition

---

[1] https://prismlegal.com/back_to_the_future-a-history-of-legal-technology/.

[2] https://www.forbes.com/sites/valentinpivovarov/2019/01/15/legaltech-investment2018/#4a2d45c7c2ba.

[3] https://www.thomsonreuters.com/en/press-releases/2019/february/ai-powered-legal-technology-startup-selected-to-join-thomson-reuters-labs-incubator-programme.html.

[4] https://www.techlawfest.com/alita/.

[5] https://www.artificiallawyer.com/2019/07/25/se-asia-launches-alt-the-regions-first-legal-tech-organisation/.

for stakeholders in the region to invest in time and resources to fortify collaboration to increase awareness, working with regulatory bodies, startups and academics. On the other hand, those members who are part of these initiatives are also reminded to put their best effort and strategy into building the LegalTech ecosystem where the results of innovation, existence of bustling startups, commitment of investments and adoption of technology will surface in this race regionally.

There is also a wave of LegalTech-focused events and initiatives that carries specific objectives such as hackathons, Legal Hacker[6] chapters and LegalTech conferences. The global effort organized by Global Legal Hackathon,[7] which spreads across cities globally, led by community builders in growing LegalTech, marks the rising awareness and efforts from individuals, organizations, regulatory bodies and countries. Hackathons became an interesting tool, depending on the design of the competition and event, to kickstart the collaboration between legal and tech communities to work together during a confined time to address specific problem statements by building a minimum viable product (MVP). There are many ways to categorize what is considered to be an MVP, such as business plan pitch, a rough design of what a solution looks like or a solution that has code written that then allows a demonstration of the MVP during the hackathon. The metrics of a successful hackathon can be manifold, including the number of participants, the number of MVPs created, the number of investments, the number of partnerships fostered or changes of policy of regulators and/or governing bodies that are assisted by the awareness raised by the hackathon.

This was how the budding Malaysian LegalTech ecosystem, which stems from the first LegalTech hackathon (LawTech Malaysia), began, organized as a grassroots movement in 2018.[8]

The idea was to create a platform that gathered individuals from legal, tech and other fields to put their best efforts into experiencing, learning, networking and building during say a 48-hour period. Mentors and judges with different expertise and backgrounds are invited to enhance and guide the teams during the hackathons. The premise is to show what is possible, albeit in such a limited time, to those who attend (which may be in different capacities – whether they are participants, mentors, judges, organizing teams or volunteers).

How do we get the next generation ready for LegalTech? There is a rise in legal technology, legal design, innovation workshops and similar events globally, which suggests that there is great demand for us to shape and groom talents to be ready for this wave and for the LegalTech industry to grow. Notably, the College of Law based in Australia (a pure digital learning portal) has launched a Centre of Legal Innovation – a think-tank to focus on legal innovation and transformation.[9] In the UK, both undergraduate and postgraduate courses focused on LegalTech and innovation are offered at the University of Law, amongst others.[10] This shows that there is a rise in the drive to shape these future talents, for those who are yet to enter the workforce and those who might currently be in the legal industry but working in a more traditional manner.

The combination of building blocks sparks the excitement to build the LegalTech ecosystem right now, wherever you are and no matter what capacity and backgrounds you have. Both at the local and international level, collaboration drives, and whole communities are emerging in support of the growth of the LegalTech market. From creating new job opportunities, revenue streams, and making the legal system efficient and accessible to revitalizing the profession, LegalTech is set to trailblaze – across the globe.

---

[6] https://legalhackers.org/.

[7] https://globallegalhackathon.com/.

[8] https://www.thestar.com.my/metro/metro-news/2018/10/02/legal-and-tech-experts-to-compete-in-hackathon.

---

[9] https://www.collaw.edu.au/about/centre-for-legal-innovation.

[10] https://www.artificiallawyer.com/legal-tech-courses/.

The Future of LegalTech

8

EMPOWERING THE LEGAL FUNCTION

Harnessing a disruptive agenda

- Unprecedented pace of change in regulation, data demands and service expectations
- A highly disruptive industry landscape that brings winners and losers
- Upsides available through grasping the digital journey. Highest risk is inaction

Leverage this disruption to business advantage

Empowering the legal function

Enterprise Integration
The power of a joined up agenda

Hyper-Digitization
The power of an end to end digital model

Digital Roadmap

Data-Driven Intelligence
The power of insight into reliable data

Now-Generation Working
The power of virtual and flexible working

- Radical ground-up rethink typically betters incremental change onto a weak legacy model
- Rethink brings new opportunities for driving value
- Digitization and data-connectivity drive streamlining and de-duplication – both are key to flexible and enduring service models

Shape the 'Legal Digital Agenda'

Building a secure and value-adding roadmap

- Many technology opportunities, big $s invested
- Mixed outcomes: overcommitting to an unproven solution is all too common
- Pioneering *should* now be over (and generally is)
- Experience and knowledge of paths already trodden is key

Develop the digital roadmap

Emerging technologies are transforming financial services globally. No function is immune and **– that includes the Legal function.**

Source: O2 Legal Technology

Executive Summary

"The only constant in life is change." For many, the legal profession and industry had often seemed the exception to this quote of Heraclitus, the pre-Socratic Greek philosopher. The culture, norms and ways of working are steeped in tradition and precedent, with many criticizing its clinging on to the past.

Edgar Bodenheimer, in his 1948 paper on "The inherent conservatism of the legal profession", noted that "judges and lawyers, as such in their capacity as professional men, have rarely been the primary architects of basic legal change". It is for good reason that decisions of the court are rarely "revolutionary", for the judiciary understand the need not only to consider forwards, but also to be fixed in the past – an attempt to build on what earlier generations have done, or to determine what is reasonable and necessary within the context of the state of society around it and government. For if the legal framework on which so much of life depends changes unexpectedly, we might lose the very fabric of society and commerce which the law brings to us. The law often is that inertia which means we are not that ship seeking to turn direction too hastily, tipping over – as it finds its direction to its final destination. It is a great brake, checking the free and unbridled play of the dynamic forces around us.

The preceding parts of this book have shown that we are at a crossroad. The rate of change, innovation and disruption in everyday life has certainly picked up in pace with technology enablers, meaning we continue as people to push the boundaries of what we thought was possible – harder and stronger. We have explored the importance and explosion of data that fuels much of the changes for businesses and people, which both creates opportunities to reimagine the practice of law, as well as requires a need to put controls in place around its use to protect many of our basic freedoms and rights, such as the right to privacy. There is a tension that often arises as we seek to use technology to undertake legal activity, with many of the rules and regulations across industries (as well as professional standards expected of the legal profession) written without expecting the rapid rise and possible utility of tools such as artificial intelligence (AI). We have also discussed the emergence of cryptocurrencies and distributed ledger technologies such as blockchain, which threaten to be true game-changers for business and the way in which we carry on our daily lives – although for the most part, perhaps remain solutions looking for the right problems. Of course, the legal framework surrounding these technologies will need to develop to support this journey, including its application to smart contracts. These are of particular importance to the law, as automatable and enforceable agreements.

Access to justice is of paramount importance if we are to ensure our future societies are fair and just – and if legal technology does have the impact we have discussed in this book, it is critical that this area is not neglected, rather a focus to ensure the law is utilized to protect those most in need is necessary. The submissions in this part certainly explain the opportunities in this area, as well as the dangers at hand. Finally, the preceding part took a broader global view of LegalTech around the world, exploring differences in approach or focusing on particular cultural or jurisdictional challenges to its use and development.

It is only right that this final part now seeks to firmly look at what the future may hold. We have discussed above the inherent slow pace of change in the law. But the rate of change is exponential in the areas the law seeks to support, across the spectrum from human rights, travel, leisure, finance and trade. It is, therefore, inevitable that both the practice and business of law, and especially the latter, will quickly iterate and evolve for a faster and better world for all.

We begin with a consideration of what this future state looks like – is it the death of lawyers, or in fact simply the need for more? There is a consideration of the amount of disruption that we can handle and what is needed to make use of technology enablers in a new landscape for commercial and legal relations. With the clear impact of AI in our everyday lives, we then look at the use of natural language generation and processing to explore how far into legal knowledge and reasoning AI might wander and the implications of letting AI put words in our mouths. We then consider the path we are taking to the future – and whether we are being swayed by glittering technologies, rather than the building blocks we need to best reach the art of the possible. Finally, we ask what it means to making legal better. Thankfully, we conclude that this means making it start and end with people.

LegalTech's Legacy?

Mitchell E. Kowalski

Gowling WLG Visiting Professor in Legal Innovation, University of Calgary Law School

The foregoing chapters have illuminated technology's disruption of the legal services industry. And make no mistake, over the past 20 years, legal services has transformed from a profession into an industry with a number of different players, not all of which are lawyers and not all of which are human. And while several factors have driven this transformation, such as more aggressive client-buying behaviour and generational change, the key enabler has been technology. Without an enabling set of technological tools, legal services industry transformation would not and could not happen.

As it turns out, technology's cool kids, who for the first decade or so of this century were creating technology for the masses, have now turned their sights toward legal services. They've begun "hacking the law", exploring new ways of delivering legal services – ways that are better, faster and cheaper. Unconstrained by legacy, image or prestige, the cool kids are excited by the challenge of using technology to break into a centuries-old profession, turning it upside down for the benefit of clients – even lawyers.

At present there seems to be no end to their passion for change – a passion that also comes with a purpose. Many countries have an ever-widening access-to-justice gap and lawyers continue to have disproportionately high rates of addiction, depression and suicide; legal technology is one way to fix these problems, making its creation more purposeful than generating money and doing cool things – in the eyes of some entrepreneurs, this is "a mission from God".

LegalTech enthusiasts gather monthly in an ever-growing number of cities around the world. Every meeting fertilizes new ideas on how to "fix" legal services. And "in need of repair" is very much how the inhabitants of the LegalTech world see legal services. They view law as nothing but code and decision trees (if this, then that), and they pay little heed to tradition. They fearlessly tread where most lawyers dare not, asking questions most lawyers refuse to even contemplate. There's no tinkering, maybes or hesitation at "legal hackathons"; these events are for believers who want full-bore transformation. The energy is high, the discussions excited and fully engaged. No one questions the premise that technology will improve legal services delivery. No one says, "Hang on a moment, law is really complicated – maybe we shouldn't go there." No one asks for permission from the legal establishment or its regulators. Taking their cue from the likes of Uber and Airbnb, the prevailing philosophy is that asking for forgiveness is preferable to seeking permission.

And whether I'm sitting in a brick-and-beam loft space watching computer science engineers drink beer from plastic cups while mingling with young lawyers in jeans, or I'm absorbing the ideas put forth at a loud and brash pitch competition that has more in common with *American Idol* than *Dragon's Den*, I'm hard pressed to see how traditional legal services can withstand this onslaught of new ideas and new tools.

Backlash

But not everyone sees the benefits of a brave new LegalTech world because with change comes fear; a fear of obsolescence, a fear of competition and a fear of exposure. All of which manifested themselves in Europe during the last half of 2019.

In Germany, a Hamburg court prohibited DIY contract platforms from offering their services directly to consumers, on the basis that it was very important for lawyers to be involved in the contracting process; contracts should not be drafted by regular people aided by technology.

Prior to that a Berlin court determined that an app built to assist regular people with obtaining lower rents from their landlords was perfectly valid LegalTech. However, that decision is currently under appeal as the Berlin Bar Association feels the app is encroaching on the practice of law.

Also in 2019, the government of France passed legislation which made it a criminal offence to publish any statistical information about court decisions. Maximum punishment? Five years in prison. This law effectively shields judges from scrutiny by data analytics firms that have been harvesting court data in many other jurisdictions in an effort to determine the chances of success in front of certain judges.

Clearly, technological encroachment into legal services touches a very raw nerve and some lawyers (and judges!) are not about to go quietly into the night.

Time for a Reality Check

Notwithstanding the current level of cool kid enthusiasm, at some point the legal technology market will become saturated. After all, legal services is a very niche market that cannot sustain the large number of companies selling the same type of technology solution; at the time of writing there are more than 1,500 LegalTech companies globally, so we may have already reached the upper limits of the LegalTech bubble. And with upper limits comes the silly season, where every new legal technology boasts that it's "fuelled by AI" or that it's "on the blockchain", and every law firm adds "innovation", "AI" and "blockchain" to their marketing materials. The silly season has also spawned cynicism within the legal community itself led by the rallying cry of "bring back boring"; a call for less hype, and a more disciplined, practical and realistic approach to technology in legal services.

Sadly, the prevailing wisdom among law firms and in-house legal departments has become that technology = innovation. Never mind that adding technology to a process for the sake of adding technology is neither innovative nor useful – and may in fact make things worse. Consider the current hype that blockchain is a solution to everything from international borders to paying for petrol. In connection with the latter, the world already has a convenient, reliable and secure payment system for purchasing petrol; it's called credit cards. While a new blockchain system could be used as a new payment system for petrol purchases (and make the system really "cool"), that system would require massive investments by suppliers, retailers and consumers for little, if any, appreciable benefit in reliability, security or convenience. As such, adding a new technology to an already useful, convenient and efficient process for little, if any, gain is a terrible idea. Put a different way, the benefits gained through implementing technology must not only be appreciable and measurable, they must be greater than the costs (money, training time for user and consumer, etc.) of adopting the legal technology.

What seems to have been lost during the silly season is that legal technology must have a clear purpose. It must solve a problem, and it must create value for the customer or the firm – or both! If it doesn't, there's little point in proceeding with it. Therefore, before embarking on any LegalTech journey, the following questions must always be asked:

1. What problem do we have?

2. How does the new technology solve that problem?

3. Do the benefits of the new technology outweigh its costs?

Asking these questions at the start of every LegalTech journey would not only save a great deal of money, time and effort, it would also form a better framework for the creation and implementation of workable and successful legal technology. Bring back boring, indeed.

The Path Forward

Richard Susskind facetiously wrote about the end of lawyers in 2008, and yet at the close of 2019, the legal profession continues to grow throughout the world. It therefore seems that whatever the LegalTech cool kids have come up with to date, they haven't succeeded in eliminating lawyers from legal services. But what they have done is to force us to look at legal services through a different lens. A lens that focuses on output, rather than input; a lens that forces providers to assemble the best combination of people, processes and technology so as to achieve that output, regardless of the weighting within the mix.

Over the coming decades, the talent mix within legal services providers will continue to adjust as the cool kids relentlessly experiment with legal technology, reducing the need for large masses of lawyers. How can it not? Technology gets better, not worse, giving legal services workers, who did not go to law school, the ability to do more work, with greater accuracy and in less time, from anywhere on the planet. This will allow legal services providers to look at scale in a completely different way; scale no longer means hiring more (expensive) lawyers, since a legal solution no longer involves something that can only be delivered by a lawyer. Scale will be achieved through technology, workflow, and process, with lawyers being hired only when absolutely necessary. Just as economists once spoke of a jobless recovery from the financial crisis of 2008, lawyer-less growth is not only imaginable, it's now possible. A handful of savvy law firms are already grasping this reality.

Lawyer-less growth means that job creation in the legal services sector will favour those who did not invest in a law school education but bring other valuable skills to the table. It will also favour those who can skill-up through workflow and technology to provide a certain layer of legal services. As a result, legal services providers will start to more aggressively trim their high-priced legal talent and replace it, wherever possible, with smart, engaged employees having less intensive legal training but fully supported by workflow and technology. All of this will require a dramatic rethinking of compensation, career paths, career advancement key performance indicators and hiring practices at incumbent legal services entities.

All of which suggests that the ultimate legacy of legal technology will not be AI-powered lawyer robots on the blockchain, but rather the transformation of legal services from a lawyer-dominated industry into a service fuelled by a human–technology combo that is merely augmented by lawyers.

Back to the Future: How LegalTech Is Changing the Law Firm

Benjamin Silverton
Head of Legal Product, LitiGate

As a legal technologist and a (lapsed) lawyer, the first thing practising lawyers say upon finding out about my job is "when are you replacing me?", generally accompanied by a nervous chuckle. Lawyers should relax. They aren't being replaced any time soon. However, the provision of legal services will dramatically change over the next decade.

Technological Revolution: More Law, More Lawyers

The legal profession has always been shaped by accessibility to information. Prior to the printing revolution, lawyers were generally noblemen or clergy who had been granted access to the original manuscripts. These lawyers were largely amateur and part-time; the practice of law was part of their general standing in society, rather than a particular profession. Printing widened the scope and reach of legal information by allowing these manuscripts to be accurately copied and distributed far and wide. This development allowed rapid advances in legal scholarship and opened the legal market to anyone who was educated to a requisite standard. This flourishing of the legal ecosystem led to increased specialization; being a lawyer became a full-time profession.

For around 500 years, while the law evolved greatly, the legal profession remained largely the same with individual practitioners advising clients on all aspects of the law. However, by the beginning of the last century, the Industrial Revolution had led to a shifting structure for the legal profession. In order to provide services of sufficient quality and speed for the large industrial companies of the day, leading lawyers grouped together into firms of increasing size. As Ronald Coase famously noted, joining together reduced both the transactional and information costs of providing legal services. However, these new law "firms" were frowned upon as negatively impacting the quality of lawyering. In 1933, US lawyer and philosopher Adolf Berle bemoaned the fact that law firms were "legal factories contribut[ing] little of thought, less of philosophy and nothing at all about responsibility or idealism".[1] It should be noted that, despite the description of these firms as "factories", they would be considered small by today's standards. Even in the late 1950s, only thirty-eight law firms in the United States had more than fifty lawyers.[2] Across the pond, in the UK, prior to 1967, partnerships could not exceed twenty members.

The Information Age of the latter part of the twentieth century led to an explosion of information that lawyers were required to process. Particularly when servicing large companies, one or two lawyers could no longer be expected to process enough information to provide the highest quality service. Indeed, the current economic model of a modern law firm is predicated on partners establishing a relationship with clients, expending time in establishing detailed knowledge of the client and having an extensive knowledge of the required legal processes. However, the voluminous amounts of information required to be processed and created in order to actually provide legal services are too much for partners to complete alone. Indeed, it is this surplus of human capital which allows the partners to hire associates and convert the human capital investment into profit.

This commoditization of the law has, largely, been good for lawyers, with the largest firms now having thousands of lawyers around the world. Partner incomes have risen, as have associate

---

[1] Laura Kalman, "Professing Law: Elite Law School Professors in the Twentieth Century", *Looking Back at Law's Century*, edited by Austin Sarat et al., Cornell University Press, Ithaca; London, 2002, pp. 337–385.

[2] Marc Galanter and Thomas M. Palay, "Why the Big Get Bigger: The Promotion-to-Partner Tournament and the Growth of Large Law Firms", 1990, 76 *Va. L. Rev.* 747.

salaries. The rise of the *MegaFirm* has yet to be tempered despite well-documented increases in job dissatisfaction among lawyers.[3]

The New Wave: More Law, Fewer Lawyers

Knowledge used to be power; but now information is cheap. A litigator can search through millions of judgments in a second; corporate lawyers have precedents of thousands of complex agreements at their fingertips. An internet connection and a subscription have replaced the law library. LegalTech is allowing lawyers to break the chains of the structures that were previously required of a modern law firm: many lawyers working on low-value, time-consuming and repetitive tasks.

LegalTech is changing the game, conducting simple tasks, thus freeing lawyers to focus on actually giving legal advice. The Boston Consulting Group suggests that LegalTech solutions could perform as much as 50% of tasks carried out by junior lawyers today. Even today, lawyers now regularly use artificial intelligence to assist with due diligence, e-Discovery and even legal research. There are platforms to assist with practice management and billing. Short-sighted lawyers will see this as a glorious method of reducing headcount while ensuring partner profits remain high. However, this trend has the power to change the provision of legal services itself, where quality of advice reigns supreme over quantity of resources.

The Rise of the Boutiques

One trend that has already started to take hold is the rise of the boutique. By outsourcing many business functions of the law firm and using LegalTech, smaller but laser-focused firms can produce high-quality work for lower cost than many larger firms. The power of one or two brains can again compete with the might of thousands of others. As LegalTech grows, boutiques will be able to increase their efficiency at a rate faster than larger, less agile, firms, and therefore will be able to offer a more attractive offering to clients and lawyers alike. Clients will appreciate lower costs for high-quality work conducted by more senior lawyers, whereas lawyers will be free to develop more attractive working cultures, increasing lawyer happiness.

Law Firms as Legal Ecosystems

This is not to sound the death knell for *MegaLaw*, but it needs to respond to this changing landscape. The answer is to focus on what they offer to clients: not just legal advice but outstanding holistic legal services. Just as those trailblazing lawyers that joined together as firms over a century ago, it is those at large law firms who are best placed to traverse the complex informational and operational costs of managing legal risk for large companies in the twenty-first century.

As functions that have been traditionally undertaken by lawyers are carried out by technology, law firms must be able to harness those technologies effectively to increase the quality of their own offering. LegalTech allows the law firm to provide traditional solutions such as analysis, draftsmanship and good advice as a truly modern service.

By using technology to structure data, by conducting a review of the entirety of the case and measuring the relative success of different arguments, or classifying certain types of higher risk documents in a diligence exercise, law firms can advise clients to make smarter decisions and continue to retain their status as an indispensable advisor to business. Lawyers themselves will be able to focus on lawyering and working on complex bespoke legal advice, in turn providing a better incentive to stay at larger firms.

Law firms have not dropped the proverbial ball with LegalTech. By developing links with the LegalTech community and establishing incubators to assist the LegalTech community in developing

---

[3] Jerome M. Organ, "What Do We Know About the Satisfaction/ Dissatisfaction of Lawyers? A Meta-Analysis of Research on Lawyer Satisfaction and Well-Being", 2011, 8 *U. St. Thomas L.J.* 225.

solutions that they encounter most frequently, law firms have ensconced themselves as a leader in the space.

This synergy between law firm and LegalTech is vital for both communities. Talk about technology replacing lawyers is both incorrect and unhelpful; man and machine are a symbiotic relationship. Our futures are entwined. Lawyers should understand that they themselves should be in the driving seat of this technological innovation. The dog must always wag the tail.

While the method of delivering legal services may change, the place of the lawyer and the law firm at the heart of its delivery will remain as it has for centuries. This brave new world is actually starting to look quite familiar.

How Much Disruption Can We Handle?

Magnus Lindberg
Chief Enabler Officer, SKYE Contracts

Looking at the future of all this interesting technology, the world, and the landscape we all work in, will change. The question is, will we work in a similar way – simply with parts of the process automated? Will we work less and faster? Or will it just be totally different to today and beyond our comprehension. In this chapter we will see if there is a limit to how much disruption we can handle as human beings and what the future holds.

As a baseline we can establish that the technologies described in this book will, eventually, lead to change. How much the change will affect us is dependent on how it is used if used at all. As a reader of this book, there cannot be any doubt that all this technology is a part of the promise for an automated legal process. But what is needed to make use of the inventions in a new landscape for commercial and legal relations?

The Current Situation

In relationships, verbal and written communication is the foundation. In commercial ones, we use word processing, we use the internet, we use email, we talk to each other and we use a multitude of software and systems. However, there is not one solution for managing all parts of these relationships. MS Word was released in 1983 and is the one thing all LegalTech tools currently tend to need to relate to in one way or another. It does not cover everything, and it does not give us an automated legal process. But it does support the understanding of the agreement. That is clear. Over the years, different software offerings have promised a lot for how legal documents can be managed. Some of the solutions have definitely improved some parts of the process. None of them solve the whole process. But do we need one

thing to do that? Perhaps it is more important to look at what the knowledge worker needs to have to get the right flow in the legal process. And fundamentally what all human beings need to thrive.

The Cognitive Advantage

This is important because all usage of technology starts with people agreeing on something. And usually that something is not too far from what we already have experienced. But they are initiated to solve problems, because we want to know and understand. These are cognitive needs, as defined by Maslow.[1] Let us link these with the future of LegalTech.

1. Know

Knowing is more and more important, with exponentially growing data volumes. Finding data and information is core to take legal work forward. With machine learning and artificial intelligence we dramatically increase the availability to this data. Current and new legal technology needs to bring clearness to the increasingly vast ocean of data. Otherwise, it will be impossible for people to know and they will resort to an inefficient and impractical way of working.

Within the legal sphere, I have not yet seen that truly simple solution to find data, even if some solutions have the capability to learn fast and understand. Until legal text is simple and straightforward (never, or…?), the semantic piece of understanding is crucial.

Before a high level of adoption of a technology by the legal community can be achieved, the profession needs to know and feel that it can trust the new technology. For example, digital signatures solve a problem, but is not yet widely adopted in line with its potential. Why is that? It could be that the lawyers do not

---

[1] A.H. Maslow, "A Theory of Human Motivation", originally published in *Psychological Review*, 1943, 50, 370–396.

understand the technology. However, another scenario is apparent when implementing digital signatures, which is that the users seek knowledge – knowledge about the technology and comfort that it is safe and something that can be trusted.

2. Understand

Having an understanding of the technology is important. But for most legal knowledge workers the most crucial thing is actually not to know how to code, but to understand the basics of information technology. Here we are talking about the true basics in producing (writing), sharing and finding information. Understanding the functionality that exists today in the systems from the 1980s and 1990s, I believe, will bring automation on faster. Yes, new technology will still be developed and deployed, but the uptake can go faster when people have already taken a step in their process of understanding how to keep things truly simple.

With technology we can also get a better understanding of the case, the matter, the business. The ongoing trend in the field of legal design is addressing the feeling of not understanding legal. Redesigning a document is well intended and needs to be done. The ease of understanding a document can only help matters! It is the future-proofing of the document to make it ready for automation on a full scale that is often missing. And the fact that the intention for much of the technology described in this book is to erase the need for documents.

3. Solve problems

Humans will always communicate with each other in order to solve problems. What technology we use does not matter, but as you have seen, the tools can make it much easier. As long as knowledge and understanding of the tools and the process of using it in a user-friendly way are there.

If the tools and infrastructure we use also solve some of our problems in an automated process, then the future has something to promise.

The Future Is Always Bright – How Do We Get There?

What comes next? Will we have a new equivalent to MS Word that we all will baseline our agreements upon? I am not suggesting an improved word processor here. With the uptake of newer technologies, such as distributed ledger technology and software connectors, we can skip many tedious steps in negotiations. But in the near future, it is less likely that technology will fully overtake and change our way of deciding the rules: agreeing in person and then writing them down.

Once in a while, new tech comes along. But it is when that tech is arranged in a system, a system that just makes things flow, that we see the commercial benefit from innovation. This usually does not happen immediately when the tech is released, but when a collective group of innovators leads us to a totally new way of satisfying our cognitive needs. Then I believe we are getting closer to that more automated legal flow. And I think we can handle the disruption when the described needs are fulfilled.

We can transform a whole industry if the disruption, in process and technology, is positive and gives us the speed and simplicity we all want. More problems will be solved when we know and understand and have the technology, the process and the way of working with the tools we have at hand and the ones that will come. Perhaps you as an interested party have that next idea that will be deployed on the infrastructure at hand and disrupt the way we work in a way we cannot understand today. At least, let us all be prepared for a totally different invention to pop up and disrupt legal work as we know it today.

The Role of RegTech in Delivering Better Regulatory Compliance

Patricia Peck
Head of Digital and Cyber Law, PG Law

Technological development has brought several impacts on society: distances have been shortened, time has been relativized and behaviours have changed. Solutions that were once sufficient or at least satisfactory to ensure social development today are archaic and often misplaced with digital reality.

In this context, the law and the ways to ensure the enforcement of the regulations towards civil society and institutions are being reinvented to keep up with the new demands of the digitized and digitizable world. Regulation plays a number of fundamental roles in guaranteeing the safety of society, equality, fairness and accountability. The challenge that regulators and policymakers face is how to support and stimulate a free market at the same time as securing responsible outcomes. In the advent of RegTech the core question is, how can technology innovation be used to ensure that technology is itself deployed responsibly?

It is very hard to balance individual rights and common good (collective rights of society) especially in a global approach, although it has always been natural for law and its regulation to change to reflect the changing dynamics and values of sociocultural change. However, the challenge in the technology field is how to keep pace with change which is almost immediate and global. Is domestic regulation sufficient to deal with the global impacts? And can innovation happen equally and harmoniously around the world?

These and other issues – and the lack of solutions in the *traditional law* model – have led people around the world to question the current regulatory framework and propose solutions that focus not only on conflict resolution tools, i.e. the traditional ex post regulatory responses, but also on investing in preventing such problems in the first place.

One approach has been to look to technology itself for ways in which to address the risks. The capability of technology in these fields – commonly referred to as RegTech – has come a long way, enabling companies and regulators to have better visibility of activity.

According to the "Cost of Compliance 2019: 10 Years of Regulatory Change" study by Thomson Reuters,[1] 63% of companies surveyed[2] expect compliance budgets to continue to grow. Similarly, 71% of companies expect regulatory information to grow next year with regulators and exchanges.

This data demonstrates that the so-called "pacing problem"[3] has become a hindrance to technological and economic development, so that the solution is not to think about contemporary conflict resolution but to prevent these conflicts.

And what's more, since there's no point in thinking about conflict prevention in the digital and globalized world locally and domestically; solutions must be global, which means compliance must be global and not just local anymore. It also changes the way we think about governance in the world. Although this is still somewhat difficult to achieve – as it requires harmonization of standards at a global level – the technologies available are able to make this far more achievable. At a minimum they allow globally active companies to have a better degree of vigilance as to their compliance with differing regulatory regimes – a task which is done manually that is both lengthy and also prone to error.

---

[1] Stacey English and Susannah Hammond, "Cost of Compliance 2019: 10 Years of Regulatory Change", Thomson Reuters, 2019.

[2] About 900 senior compliance practitioners worldwide were consulted, representing global systemically important financial institutions, banks, insurers, broker-dealers and asset managers.

[3] According to Adam Thierer "the pacing problem" can be summarized as the situation "when technological innovation outpaces the ability of laws and regulations to keep up".

One area in which there has been significant change in recent years is data protection.

Following the advent of the General Data Protection Regulation (GDPR) in May 2018 in the European Union, there was a great scramble, not just in Europe, but also in many other parts of the globe, to revisit data protection legislation. Companies operating in and with the EU reviewed their compliance.

Although initially derided by some, the ripple effect of the GDPR has spread far. A number of other countries have revised their data protection laws to mirror some or all of the GDPR, such as Argentina, Uruguay and Brazil. This has also impacted the way we do business around the world. Aside from having to revisit compliance arrangements, global companies have faced fines in many countries[4] for failing to comply with data protection regulations – albeit this remains an ex post impact on the businesses at this stage.

Interestingly, the European Union did not focus only on hard law when dealing with the GDPR. The GDPR was accompanied by a heavy emphasis on education and behaviour change – both corporate and consumer.

The challenge facing regulators is how to guarantee that the same institutions that safeguard the personal data will not misuse the information?

Clear rules to comply and transparency are crucial to achieve digital governance and in turn the transparency enables accountability which ultimately creates the conditions for trust between corporate firms and regulators, and in turn civil society.

In the field of technology regulation, soft law is as important as hard law, with an emphasis on multidisciplinary mechanisms that help create culture and enforce compliance in organizations.

In the words of Hagemann, Skees and Thierer "soft law is in the process of becoming the primary modus operandi of modern technology policy and the governance of fast-moving, emerging technologies in particular".[5] It may also be the case that in fast-moving sectors such as artificial intelligence (AI), governments are reluctant to commit regulations to the statute book for fear of either stifling innovation or being desperately out of date by the time they come into effect. Standard setting, certification, codes of conduct – developed in partnership – are seen as much more achievable routes.

Alongside this is the market-side response – the growth of RegTech. In the case of the GDPR there has been a proliferation of tools designed to help companies manage their compliance risks – categorized under the following considering the last IAPP Privacy Tech Vendor Report 2019: (1) privacy program management; (2) assessment managers; (3) consent managers; (4) data mapping tools; (5) incident response; (6) privacy information managers; (7) website scanning; (8) enterprise privacy management; (9) activity monitoring; (10) data discovery; (11) de-identification/pseudo-anonymity; and (12) enterprise communications.[6]

Therefore, there are RegTechs focused on delivering a specific demand for the regulation (Anonos, BigID, InfoSun, ProofPoint, Radar) and there are others that promise to help the institution to address all the needs to become data protection compliant (full

---

[4] Companies like Google, Facebook and British Airways were fined in different European countries for breaking GDPR rules throughout 2018 and 2019; this has set a new standard for working with data-based digital businesses around the world as technology giants and other companies are setting an example by adopting irregular behaviour.

[5] Ryan Hagermann, Jennifer Huddleston and Adam D. Thierer, "Soft Law for Hard Problems: The Governance of Emerging Technologies in an Uncertain Future", *Colorado Technology Law Journal*, February 2018, p. 40.
[6] https://iapp.org/resources/article/2019-privacy-tech-vendor-report/ and contributions to the research of this part of the article by Larissa Lotufo, research assistant at UNESP University.

solution such as AV Point, Content Space, Integris, One Trust, Poslovna and Wizuda).

For example, BigID can deliver automated data inventory, personal data classification, data subject rights fulfilment, breach assessment response and consent governance. Ave Point works for activity monitoring, assessment management, consent management, data discovery, data management, de-identification/pseudo-anonymity, privacy information manager, incident response and website scanning.

On the other hand, there is a huge new market for de-identification/pseudo-anonymity solutions and companies such as Anonos, Arcad and DE-ID Data Corp have specialized just in doing this.

A Brazilian RegTech that has grown quickly in the last year because of data protection regulation is Privally, which does consent management and website scanning. The same phenomenon was observed in financial regulation worldwide. The changes experienced in the financial regulatory world are the result of two central factors: the 2008 financial crisis and the emergence of new digital technologies.[7]

It was in this context of the need for innovation and agile, creative and practical financial recovery that the so-called RegTechs emerged, laying the foundations for a new tool in the regulatory toolbox and inaugurating a new way of thinking about compliance. The impact of the aftermath of the 2008 financial crisis is critical in the growth of this sector. The regulatory responses worldwide posed a significant challenge to the financial institutions. From repapering in derivatives, through to ring fencing in the wholesale markets, the breadth of regulatory changes was vast, the impact high and the time frames limited. The problem for financial

institutions was how to keep up with new regulatory needs quickly, efficiently and satisfactorily.[8]

But what exactly is RegTech?

Conceptually, RegTech or regulatory technology is understood to be a group of companies that offer technology solutions to meet all regulatory demands required in the financial world to make compliance easier and more agile.[9,10]

RegTech's central features can be listed in three pillars as seen in Figure 1.

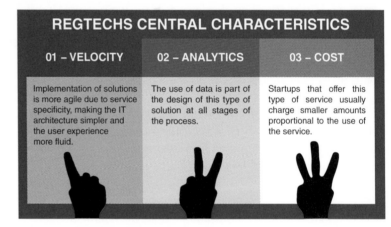

Figure 1: RegTech's main features

Source: Finnovation, 2016; Design: Presentationgo.

[7] According to Yvonne Lootsma: "The backlash of the 2008 financial crisis and new technology are the main drivers that have shaped the new paradigm in the financial industry. […] In addition to regulating financial and technological matters, regulators have also actively introduced policies in the domain of customer due diligence", Loostma, 2017, p. 16.

[8] Veerle Colaert explores the subject: "In the aftermath of the financial crisis, the financial sector was hit by a tidal wave of new legislation. The question of how financial institutions can remain compliant with this ever expanding financial legal framework has however been largely neglected", Colaert, 2017, p. 2.

[9] Raphael Melho, "Regtechs e o Futuro da Regulação", Idwall, 2019.

[10] UNSGSA Fintech Working Group; CCAF, "Early Lessons on Regulatory Innovations to Enable Inclusive FinTech: Innovation Offices, Regulatory Sandboxes, and RegTech", Office of the UNSGSA and CCAF: New York, NY and Cambridge, UK, 2019.

This concern to make compliance more effective has created a new market for innovation. According to Trulioo reports, investments in RegTechs were about $300 million in 2012 and up to $1 billion in 2017, and in the first quarter of 2018 half a billion dollars had already been invested in these types of niche companies around the world[11] (Figure 2).

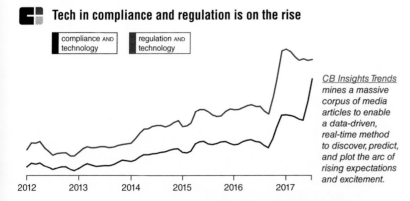

Tech in compliance and regulation is on the rise

compliance AND technology

regulation AND technology

CB Insights Trends mines a massive corpus of media articles to enable a data-driven, real-time method to discover, predict, and plot the arc of rising expectations and excitement.

2012   2013   2014   2015   2016   2017

Figure 2: Tech and compliance regulation growth

Source: CB Insights, 2017.

---

[11] General information provided by Trullioo: "From investments in fraud protection to identify verification, funding across the space has been on an upward trajectory over the past five years. In 2012, just over $300 million was invested in RegTech companies. Five years later, that had more than tripled with just over $1 billion in 2017. Within the first quarter of 2018, half a billion dollars have already been invested, indicating that this could be another banner year for RegTech investment. The recent spate of mergers and acquisitions in the identity space, as well as recent investments by American Express Ventures and others underscore the rise of value and valuation in this arena. RegTech is also a growing international business. Of the 600 companies in the space, the bulk of these – 75 percent – are found in just five countries: the U.S., U.K., Switzerland, Australia and Ireland. But the prospects are spreading out as the funding spreads out. Looking at the five-year period between 2012 and 2017, RegTech investments have become more global in nature. In 2012, a bulky 81 percent of investments happened in North America alone. By 2017, European and Asian companies had, respectively, picked up 41 percent of the global RegTech investment circuit", Trulioo, 2018.

All this investment does not happen without a reason – the sums are simple – the cost effectiveness of investing in compliance mechanisms is much more attractive than the cost effectiveness of investing in legal response solutions or facing regulatory reprimands for failure.

There will remain a challenge for governments – how to keep pace with technology, develop regulatory responses which balance innovation with core needs to protect society, whilst also utilizing the maximum new emerging approaches such as RegTech. There is good evidence that in sectors such as financial services this has proven to be successful.[12,13]

Game changing new technologies such as the Internet of Things, AI and facial recognition will demand new legal solutions to allow the application of its useful capabilities and mitigate risks and eventual collateral damages. RegTech can play a vital role in offering solutions to some of these compliance challenges.

References and Further Reading

CB Insights. CB Insights trends. 2017. Available at: https://s3.amazonaws.com/cbi-research-portal-uploads/2017/10/26204600/Regtech_trends.png (accessed on 28/08/2019).

Finnovation, "Regtech: Uma Nova Onda de Startups", 2016. Available at: http://finnovation.com.br/regtech-uma-nova-onda-de-startups/ (accessed on 28/08/2019).

---

[12] N. Gurung and L. Perlman, "Use of Regtech by Central Banks and its Impact in Financial Inclusion: Evidence from India, Mexico, Nigeria, Nepal and the Philippines", KU Leuven, 2017.

[13] Ibid.

Herrera, Diego and Vadillo, Sonia, "Regulatory Sandboxes in Latin America and the Caribbean for the Fintech Ecosystem and the Financial System", Inter-American Development Bank, 2018.

Loostman, Yvonne, "Blockchain as the Newest Regtech Application – the Opportunity to Reduce the Burden of KYC for Financial Institutions", Banking & Financial Services Policy Report, v. 36, n. 8, August 2017.

Murphy, Dan and Mueller, Jackson, "Regtechs: Opportunities for More Efficient and Effective Regulatory Supervision and Compliance", Milken Institute, 2018.

Packin, Nizan Geslevich, "Regtech, Compliance and Technology Judgment Rule", *Chicago-Kent Law Review*, 2017.

Tan, Alan, "IoT Innovation Outspaces Regulation for Now", FutureIoT, 2019. Available at: https://futureiot.tech/iot-innovation-outpaces-regulation-for-now/ (accessed on 28/08/2019).

Thierer, Adam, "The Pacing Problem and the Future of Technology Regulation: Why Policymakers Must Adapt to a World That's Constantly Innovating", The Bridge, 2018. Available at: https://www.mercatus.org/bridge/commentary/pacing-problem-and-future-technology-regulation (accessed on 28/08/2019).

Trulioo, "The Rising of RegTech Tide", Trulioo, 2019. Available at: https://www.trulioo.com/blog/rising-regtech-tide/ (accessed on 28/08/2019).

Creating Supervised Independence for FinTech Companies via Regulatory Sandboxes

Sebnem Elif Kocaoglu Ulbrich
Consultant and Author, Contextual Solutions

The rise of financial technology caught the regulators off their guard. Banking regulations that are designed for traditional institutions and business models haven't responded well to the needs of the FinTech companies, not giving them enough space to innovate and explore in particular. Getting used to receiving superior customer experience, consumers are expecting to "swipe right" from the comfort of their home to find the perfect financial services provider. Clearly, ignoring the potential of FinTech and failing to support a new approach to financial services through an innovative approach and enabling technology is not an option. On the other hand, letting the new generation of financial institutions explore the market without sufficient supervision exposes consumers to a number of unacceptable risks. FinTech is threatening the meticulously built consumer and investor protection mechanisms, mainly because FinTech startups do not fall under and are not subject to the same licensing, reporting and disclosure obligations as traditional financial service providers – nor can their activities and services be viewed through the same lens as those applied to traditional providers. Over-regulating FinTech activities as a whole might slow down or even hinder their development. The question is clear – how can we fit customer experience, market development and consumer protection all together?

Trying to categorize FinTech within the existing regulatory structures has been a challenging task for the regulators. FinTech startup business models do not easily fit within the current regulatory frameworks, forcing the regulators to create ad hoc precedents. The market quickly understood that directly integrating new institutions and practices into the old system or these ad hoc workarounds would not suffice, and the adoption of new and innovative approaches to regulating innovation was required. Among the many approaches to control the use of technology in banking, the creation of controlled testing environments for new business models ("**regulatory sandboxes**"), creating a safe space within the FinTech ecosystem – are the most promising. This mechanism aims to construct a "supervised independence" structure, creating an area for trial and error, whilst ensuring regulatory compliance and creating a buffer against potential legal consequences.

Arising as a project from the FCA Innovation Hub, this has been a British initiative that identifies policies and processes which need to change to support innovation,[1] with the initial goal defined[2] as "reducing the time and the cost of getting innovative ideas to market; enabling greater access to finance for innovators; enabling more products to be tested; allowing the FCA to work with innovators". This move indicated that regulators were evolving into more mentor-like roles.

Using its first-mover advantage to encourage innovation and foster competition, the FCA paved the way for a practice that has now become popular and spread to more than twelve countries in a short time period. In addition to providing a safe space to foster technological developments, regulatory sandboxes disrupt the way regulatory agencies function and shift regulators' static position to a dynamic one, allowing regulators to actively seek out innovation and form a strong connection and direct bond with the inventors.

Highly dependent on the local legal structure, regulatory sandboxes usually consist of *application, admission, customization* (of applicable rules and conditions), *compliance* (identification of licensing and exclusion criteria) *testing* and *review* processes.

[1] https://www.fca.org.uk/news/speeches/innovation-regulatory-opportunity.

[2] https://www.fca.org.uk/publication/research/regulatory-sandbox.pdf.

The regulatory sandboxes help the regulators to have an eye on the market practices and educate themselves about the uses of technology. Regulators are not the only ones that benefit through these programs though; sandboxes also educate the FinTech companies in respect of applicable laws and regulations. As a matter of fact, one of the directors of Bud, the FinTech company that participated in the very first FCA sandbox cohort, stated[3] that, although the sandbox didn't change their operations, after the cohort they were able to grasp the regulations and the compliance barriers applicable to their area much better. Regulatory coaching is amongst the most positive aspects of this exchange between the parties, allowing FinTechs to evolve their offerings to better consider financial stability, consumer protection and the regulators' concerns more broadly.

Having a controlled test environment sounds like a magical solution to all our FinTech inflicted regulatory problems, but it's not plain sailing. Like all tools, regulatory sandbox units best serve their intended purposes if managed systematically and methodically. The use and the rules of the programs should ideally be set from the outset, in a clear way, including functional conflict resolution and appeal mechanisms. Unfortunately, due to the lack of standardization, this can't be guaranteed in all practising regions. On another note, it is also debatable whether all regulators will be able to correctly and fairly assess the innovative aspects of business models when selecting and filtering the right candidates for a cohort. After all, regulators are experts in consumer protection rather than technology and innovation and, therefore, might have not be best placed to make the judgment required. To improve their assessments, regulators need to feel the pulse of the market and the consumers they are seeking to protect and look after.

Regulatory sandbox practices are often criticized[4] for turning a blind eye to consumer protection mechanisms and often

being used as a PR tool or "*stamp of approval*" for FinTechs. If true, claimed practices of de-prioritizing consumer protection would be apparent negligence of regulators' office duties and thus unacceptable. Providing it is done with fairness and with considerations of competition laws and regulations in mind, a stamp of approval should not be viewed in this manner – it should actually be counted among the responsibilities of the regulators. In a market filled with many companies that offer (somewhat similar) financial services, which are neither regulated nor provide (sufficient) creditor protection mechanisms, a pre-filtering of the market, giving guidance to the consumers and understanding of new business models and companies before they enter the market should be counted as a success and priority for regulators.

It should be kept in mind that the information gathered by one regulator through its local sandbox practices will not be enough by itself to understand FinTech and upcoming trends. Regulators need to actively participate in research, exchange data, and seek collaborations with other regulators to understand international developments and, therefore, contribute to the standardization of global practices.

All in all, there seems to be enough positive evidence to conclude that regulatory sandboxes should be more inclusive than selective. Instead of cherry-picking companies that sound innovative, use fancy buzzwords for their pitch decks or master the art of lobbying, more FinTech companies (regardless of their licensing requirements) should be allowed to be a part of these programs. They should all be listed under a simple register, which would provide transparency and accessibility for consumers and the creditors. Among the registered, those that fulfil the criteria should receive exemptions and an ability test their business models, but all registered FinTechs should nevertheless have the chance to enter discussions with the regulators. Although this approach might be criticized due to the extra burden it will bring to the regulators' plate; it would prevent the FinTech companies from manipulating the sandbox experience and pretending that they are favoured against others. Also, by taking a broader part

---

[3] https://www.bbva.com/en/participated-regulatory-sandbox/.

[4] http://ftalphaville.ft.com/2018/12/05/1543986004000/A–fintech-sandbox–might-sound-like-a-harmless-idea–It-s-not/.

of the FinTech community under the wings of the regulator, it will prevent poor judgment on what could evolve into to positive new business models and products and what could not – the regulators might not be the best authority to decide what's innovative and what will remain significant or successful in the long run. In the long term it would be more productive to keep the FinTech companies at arm's length, instead of handpicking some applicants and leaving the rest to stew in their juice. After all, it's not the technologies, infrastructures and the practices we know that are threatening the market, but more the ones that we can't predict and therefore control. In this sense, providing FinTech companies *supervised independence* and letting them explore and innovate under the roof of the regulator might prevent future supervisory failures.

Patterns of Speech: A Future of AI-Authored Legal Reasoning and Arguments?

Dr Tara Chittenden
Foresight Manager, The Law Society

Mastering human language requires common sense and an understanding of context and creativity, currently limited in artificial intelligence (AI) systems. In recent years, there has been great progress in the domains of natural language generation (NLG) and natural language processing, thanks to advances in deep learning. This chapter looks at the use of NLG in LegalTech to explore how far into legal knowledge and reasoning AI might wander and the implications of letting AI put words in our mouths.

Smartphones have been reading the words we type, predicting what our next word will be and making suggestions for years now, and yet Carty suggests this is really only an exercise in statistics, "slightly better than a random walk through the dictionary".[1] In other words, machines are writing based on mathematical values, the probability of a particular word or letter occurring next. The system does not understand the context of its conversations, it is merely converting human language to computer commands and computer output into human language. Recurrent neural networks are a type of machine-learning algorithm which can create a model from source data and then use it to predict new content. Neural network algorithms have been applied to a variety of writing challenges, including US political speeches. The guest curator at the 2019 Cheltenham Science Festival was an algorithm which generated topics for talks such as "Aliens What What?", "Flying Cars for the Mental" and "Everest Spoon Science", after being fed 10 years' worth of Science Festival event titles and descriptions. Attempts to train AI on natural language have resulted in plausible-sounding narrative and text, yet underlying these quirky outputs is the reality that AI can replicate human phrasing and rhythm but does not understand the concepts behind the words – which is why after being trained on 1,000 cupcake recipes, AI thinks we might enjoy a cake of "blueberry with a twig and wire dusting".[2]

AI is Already Involved in Content Creation and Editing

It is not unusual today to encounter political news stories, sports write-ups or financial trading reports that are automated. One reason for this improvement is structure. Stories tend to follow a formula and programmers can create a framework that allows AI to mimic this approach, including jargon familiar to readers of particular topics. *Narrative Science* is the leader in automated narrative generation for enterprise. Its Quill™ platform analyses data from disparate sources, understands what is important to the end user and automatically generates written narratives to convey meaning for the intended reader. Good legal briefs also follow a predictable structure. They recite the rule of law, summarize the salient facts and argue that those facts dictate a particular conclusion. However, human language is inherently "fuzzy", and persuasion requires not only logic, but such qualities as empathy and analogy. Legal systems work to incorporate nuanced reasoning that takes into account the special circumstances of individual cases, alongside the larger goals and purposes of society.

An AI That Debates

Over the past six years, IBM has endowed an AI system with three capabilities: (1) data-driven speech writing and delivery;

---

[1] R. Carty, "The Thing Speaks for Itself – Why Computer-Written Legal Briefs Are Closer Than You Think", Artificial Lawyer, 11 April 2019. Available at: https://www.artificiallawyer.com/2019/04/11/computer-written-legal-briefs-are-closer-than-you-think/ (accessed 25 July 2019).

[2] Tiny Giant, 2019. See www.tinygiant.io/ and www.cupcaikes.com/.

(2) listening comprehension that can identify key claims hidden within long continuous spoken language; and (3) modelling human dilemmas. The resulting Project Debater is the first demonstration of a computer that can digest mass bodies of information, and given a short description of a controversial topic, write a well-structured speech, delivering it with clarity and purpose.[3] The goal is to help people build persuasive arguments and make well-informed decisions.[4] Legal reasoning and argument offer the ideal testing ground for these capabilities. Legal questions have competing yet reasonable answers and these too evolve. The underlying expectation in the legal domain is that, through the adversarial process, ideally the "truth" will prevail. Jurisprudence stems from a human culture of discussion and the value of arguments that is often inherently subjective.

Harish Natarjan, Grand Finalist in the 2016 World Universities Debating Championships, found that the differences between debating IBM's machine and debating a human competitor were not enormous: "after the first minute of getting used to the shock of it not being a human being, or the surprise of what that actually meant, it became much like debating against a human being".[5] Given the same short time, the computer was able to summon evidence and examples from a vast database, while the human participant had to rely on his own knowledge and rhetorical skills. The machine excelled at finding relevant evidence, but Natarjan was impressed by the system's ability also to explain why the evidence mattered in the context of the debate.[5] This suggests that technology is starting to eat away at issues of context in its use of human language; however, Project Debater struggled responding to the subtler claims of the debate and lacked the skills to play with the mood of the room. Through this example we can begin to divide legal reasoning into evidence and persuasion; the machine excels on the former and persuasion through logic, yet lacks the rhetoric or cadence that humans use to coax each other.

Implications for Lawyers

Situations in the legal domain are challenging in the respect that laws are invariably conveyed through natural language, and in ways that make specific use of lexical and syntactic peculiarities, thus modelling the complex reasoning and knowledge abilities of the lawyer as machine learning requires solving issues of natural language processing.

This challenge throws light on what is "special" about the language of law that might make it the domain of human lawyers rather than machines. Are lawyers trained to frame and argue cases in particular ways and, if so, can algorithms recognize these patterns? If machine learning can generate credible approximations of legal reasoning or argument, does it matter that it does not understand what it has produced? For Richard and Daniel Susskind, it does not. The Susskinds have written about the mistaken notion that computers must emulate human thinking processes in order to do what humans do.[6] The "AI fallacy" assumes that there is only one way to approach complex intellectual tasks. In this argument, all that matters is the end product; as long as the system produces a credible brief it does not matter if the system has "understood" what it is writing. Furthermore, thinking like a lawyer becomes irrelevant.

[3] A. Krishna, "AI Learns the Art of Debate", IBM blog, 18 June 2018. Available at: https://www.ibm.com/blogs/research/2018/06/ai-debate/ (accessed 20 July 2019).

[4] IBM, 2019, Project Debater: https://www.research.ibm.com/artificial-intelligence/project-debater/.

[5] G. Joyce, "Interview: Harish Natarajan on Beating IBM Project Debater and Restoring Everyone's Faith in Humanity…for Now", 2018. Available at: https://www.brandwatch.com/blog/interview-harish-natarajan-on-beating-ibm-project-debater/ (accessed 20 July 2019).

[6] R. Susskind and D. Susskind, *The Future of Professions*, Oxford: Oxford University Press, 2015.

Buchanan and Headrick discussed the possibilities of modelling legal reasoning, particularly for advice-giving, legal analysis and argument construction, where a model might show how a decision's justification, not just its facts and outcome, influences how it can be used to make arguments about other cases.[7] It also permits portions of multiple decisions to be combined to form new arguments. Nearly 50 years on and combined with the advances of systems such as Project Debater, we might be finding a way to give AI the tools to explain itself out of its black box.

The systems developed in the course of IBM's (and others') research into AI and cognitive simulation indicate a potential for machine performance of rhetoric processes similar to those at times used by human lawyers. Once an AI is capable of persuasive arguments, it can be applied as a tool to aid human decision-making, though questions of ethics and bias remain alongside the dangers of persuading individuals towards a detrimental path. Lawyers might use Project Debater's technology to identify and develop legal arguments that best advance their clients' interests. The AI system could, without emotion, listen to the conversation, take all of the evidence and arguments into account and challenge the reasoning of humans where necessary (perhaps pre-empting the role of an AI judge). The machine would contribute to the discussion and act as another voice at the table.

Ross Goodwin's experiment, driving an AI system across America for it to narrate its own cross-country road trip, Kerouac-style, led him to question what "an AI author might teach us about a world already so totally sculpted and impacted by the kind of data it's gathering that a human writer can't?";[8] or, as the Susskinds infer, if we do not train and restrict machines to process the world in exactly the same way as us. Machine-learning techniques help to reveal patterns and relationships in large volumes of legal documents. When these patterns are based around legal concept and legal language rather than transactional information, there arises potential for machine learning to highlight unseen associations leading to new legal arguments and improvements in the application of law.

[7] G. Buchanan and T. Headrick, "Some Speculation About Artificial Intelligence and Legal Reasoning", *Stanford Law Review*, 1970, 23, 1, 40–62.

[8] B. Merchant, "When an AI Goes Full Jack Kerouac: A Computer has Written a "Novel" Narrating its Own Cross-Country Road Trip", The Atlantic, 1 October 2018. Available at: https://www.theatlantic.com/technology/archive/2018/10/automated-on-the-road/571345/ (accessed 21 July 2019).

From Innovation Frenzy to Productivity Steadiness

Grégoire Miot
Head of New Markets and Chief Evangelist, Wolters Kluwer
(Legal & Regulatory – Legal Software France)

The Nokia 3210, one of the most popular cell phones in history and the best-selling device of the twentieth century, had as its most cutting-edge feature an integrated antenna. Only seven years elapsed before we discovered Apple's masterpiece and the first smartphone ever: the iPhone. So much distinguishes both devices, and decades seem to separate them. Yet, innovation cycles seem to come round ever more rapidly and blow our minds with fantastic inventions.

Indeed, the past decade saw lots of excitement and passion about new legal technology and how it could help the progressive evolution of the practice of law. "Disruptive technologies" and "groundbreaking solutions" have flustered legal practitioners, as much as they dusted off old habits. Yet, adoption is anywhere near a consensus and, while a lot of awareness has been raised, new solutions keep sprouting up at a much higher pace than the adoption rate.

With so much on the market than one could possibly understand, solutions are still continuing to reach maturity – and with so much creativity, this has ultimately generated more apprehensiveness. In fact, Wolters Kluwer's most recent survey (2019 Future Ready Lawyer Report) emphasized, amongst various findings, that there is a global lack of understanding of the most promising "transformational technologies" (including artificial intelligence (AI), blockchain and predictive analytics), although it should be noted that respondents also acknowledged a significant likely impact of such technologies over the next three years.

The innovation frenzy around legal technology greatly contributed to this miscommunication and lack of understanding – with wild promises from so-called disruptive technologies, as we often forget that there is no smart software, only smart data. This has also led legal professionals into a tech-based choice regardless of their needs and potential technological overlap in their organizations. With so much misunderstanding of the purpose and possibilities of legal technology, could we still believe the right choices are being made to foster efficiency rather than fancy choices promoting glittering technologies?

Where Are We Heading with Technology?

"Transformational technologies" based on – often abusively called – AI, keep widening the gap between the real level of digital maturity of legal professionals and their supposed level of technological need. At the same time, this tendency also significantly contributes to feeding the fantasy of robots replacing the legal profession, as we reach the point of "inflated expectations" described by the Gartner "hype cycle".

Yet, as promises of automated legal work seem to have exhausted many of the most fervent legal technology defendants, a new innovation cycle has dawned, focusing on productivity and efficiency. Cutting down low-value work is not about assisting a lazy legal generation but helping them focus on strategic and high-value work in highly challenging times for the legal profession.

This efficiency-based approach is eventually taking over to help the legal market transition from "foundational technologies" (basic technologies that organizations rely on to conduct business) to optimized ways of dealing with recurring legal tasks and exploiting the (legal) metadata they have in their possession. Basically, transitioning from flat spreadsheets to smart automating engines.

Changing Product Philosophy

A common confusion between information accessibility and data exploitability lets us think that multiple software solutions are better than no software at all, without considering the risks of dealing with multiple and legacy systems. It has created generations of software built from scratch to meet isolated needs, locked-up data in static environments rather than developing the required understanding of the subtle challenges and requirements of day-to-day legal work.

Software philosophy has to change to provide business and client-oriented solutions, understanding the new role legal departments are taking, as well as the new way legal firms are providing their services to their corporate clients. This means software providers need to stop imposing rigid solutions which should recognize the complexity, but also the great diversity clients. Legal technology is still for many legal professionals an unaffordable desire which rarely manages to understand their organizational needs.

Obviously, such changes are shaking the legal software market with a growing need to provide more contextual data from various sources: linking precedent to litigation data or legal references to contract projects, while at the same time retrieving, assimilating and suggesting strategies and experiences based on previous matters. Connectivity between different types of software is allowing us to radically transform the way legal work is being done, without having to deal with software silos which do not capture the global environment of a legal project and therefore could complicate the work of legal professionals.

New Solutions for New Professionals

Praising only legal technology as the main changing factor for the legal profession would be a mistake. Legal technology has been walking side by side with the profession, as new legal roles emerged in the last few years: from legal operations to legal data scientists, including legal innovation officers and project managers, in both corporate legal departments and legal services firms.

However, technology always had a crucial role in the ongoing evolution of the relationship between legal services providers – law firms and alternative legal services providers, if we were to distinguish them – and their clients. Technology seriously increased expectations

in terms of responsiveness as much as predictability and preciseness in the services provided. Corporate legal departments are progressively internalizing low-value work, achieved more easily and quickly with structured data and tech-trained workforces.

The best example of this can be found in due diligence activities requiring agile teams for fast-paced operations and daunting amounts of information – which has to be processed, structured and organized to extract only relevant data. Such typically time-sensitive operations also bear a risk of human error, which companies and law firms strive to minimize at all cost.

What Will the Future Look Like?

Efficiency and productivity are the bedrock of the next generation of software. The new generation goes beyond analysing merely legal information but will also take on board business dimensions and communicates globally, to anticipate and avoid legal chaos. Legal technologies will progressively rationalize their scope and mutualize their goals, while the legal profession will be less concerned with technology adoption but instead driven by a different mindset of its transformed environment: focusing on strategic business-driven legal analysis.

The frenzy around the diversity of solutions is indeed a temporary phase, and so-called AI technologies, as we know them today, will really demonstrate their true value with semantic analysis engines capable of understanding the legal language within its more subtle meanings. With less and less volumes of data required to build up their legal intelligence, these tools have a bright future in providing more meaning to scattered sources of information in wide IT environments.

The next legal technology burst will doubtlessly take us on the path of integrated solutions, gathering legal data from a wide spectrum and allowing us to have tools which can do so much more with less: precisely what is being asked of the legal profession today.

Legal professionals: it is time to unfurl the sails and not let technology currents guide you too far out to sea!

The Humans Strike Back: The Fall of the Robots in LegalTech's Future

Richard Mabey
CEO, Juro

Last year I found myself giving a demonstration of our product to a prospect on a Thursday afternoon. Our sales team was tied up and I thought it would be fun. They'd requested the demo online, and I had some basic information about their role (assistant general counsel) and company (mid-market corporate). I ran through the high-level messages we usually use to frame these meetings, and then before jumping into the product, asked if they had any questions so far.

"Yeah, thanks, Richard – can you tell me, does this do blockchain?"

Confused. I'm not sure blockchain is something you "do", but regardless: "Blockchain …," I said, "well we don't incorporate any blockchain technology as such, but can I ask what it is you're looking to achieve with it?"

"Not sure – I just need to know if it has blockchain. OK, it doesn't. Does it do AI?"

Now I start to regret taking this demo. By Thursday afternoon, founders have fairly serious accumulated fatigue, which isn't helping. The week's coffee ran out hours ago. "Well yes, there are machine learning models in the product – but can I ask, why? What are you looking to solve?"

"Just need to know if has AI – thanks."

Needless to say, this particular lead didn't go anywhere. Heading out into the market to procure LegalTech with a mandate to "get some AI" and "do blockchain" is a pretty terrible way to buy, but we can hardly blame people for succumbing to the hype and asking the wrong questions. The narrative in this industry is changing, but the overhyped idea that big data, blockchain, machine learning and the rest of the buzzwords are enough, on their own, to solve all our problems is as sticky as it is misguided.

Human Beings First

To really solve problems, the legal industry must learn from the successful pioneers in other industries. Apple didn't get to a trillion-dollar valuation by making empty promises built on hype. It did it by building a phone with which you can literally run your entire life, and which people can also use intuitively out of the box with no instructions. The actual technology (and the marketing) behind the iPhone's success is staggering too, but the reason it worked quite so transformatively was the focus on human-centred design.

Haptics and gestural design are well-established disciplines now, but they were far from the mainstream even in recent memory. The reason they worked so successfully in the iPhone was that for Apple they were just a means to an end – a monomaniacal focus on how human beings like to use stuff was what really mattered, and the tech was just there to facilitate it. The secret to their peerless solution was forgetting about bells and whistles, and instead starting and ending with human beings.

In finance, companies like Monzo emulated this approach. They looked at how modern consumers live their lives and built a bank that lets you run your finances intuitively on your phone. Again, the software engineering behind that platform is incredible – the algorithms for selfie video ID verification are mind-boggling – but Monzo has no interest in shouting about what's under the hood. They just want people to be happy.

This raises the several-hundred-billion-dollar question that the legal industry must answer: are the consumers of legal services happy? Can we all – lawyers, vendors, educators – look around at the average human being interacting with the law and say that they are happy?

Overwhelmingly, the answer is no.

We might argue, by way of mitigation, that of course they aren't – legal issues arise at stressful times in people's lives. Making a claim, signing a contract, buying a house, writing a will – these are serious moments, unlikely to have people dancing on chairs. But doesn't that make our obligation to put people first even greater? Why wouldn't we do everything we can to make that difficult time a little easier? Can we look at any of these fundamental legal processes and say that we as an industry have enabled people to carry them out in a way that's intuitive, accessible and doesn't require instructions?

Lawyers Are Still People

There are champions in this space who've grasped the idea that human beings are the key to legal technology. Joshua Browder's DoNotPay made contesting fines something anyone can do, rather than an impenetrable bureaucratic nightmare. Farewill takes the paperwork burden out of the end of life. But these are the exception, not the rule – and it's important to remember that the main consumers of legal services are other lawyers. This is where the rubber meets the road in terms of commercial impact.

Lawyers are people too. Really. What's more, lawyers (and I say this as an ex-lawyer) are not renowned for their willingness to change processes and adopt new technology quickly. We're trained to be professionally risk averse. This means the burden for anyone who wants to change, improve and disrupt the legal industry with technology is much higher in terms of making products human-centric.

The evidence for this is everywhere: both in private practice and in-house, legal teams are surrounded by the metaphorical

wreckage from failed tech deployments. Often this failure isn't because the solution in question didn't work, or that the implementation team did something wrong. It's not because it didn't "have AI" or "do blockchain". Time and again, it's because the solution in question forgot about the key to LegalTech: human beings. Without human-centred design at the core, asking successful professionals like lawyers to adopt and adapt to a new technology or process is a losing game.

The Fall of the Robots

Thankfully, the way to solve this, defeat the hype robots and elevate the human beings, is surprisingly simple (but not easy). Talk to people. Ask them what they want. Watch how they use stuff. Go and sit with your customers and see for yourself the problems they run into and the workarounds they create for themselves. And don't limit it to lawyers – at Juro we work with sales teams who create large volumes of contracts, and their pain points and user journeys can vary wildly from their colleagues over in legal. HR and procurement teams are different again. If a legal process isn't limited to lawyers, then don't limit your input in trying to solve it to lawyers either.

Without re-establishing human beings as the core focus of the legal industry – pre- or post-blockchain, big data, or whatever else people are marketing today – we're likely all participating in a huge collective waste of time. I see software engineers and product managers accomplishing incredible technical feats, bringing us so close to changing a sector that seemed destined to be stuck with the billable hour forever. But if we want to make that final step, take transformative LegalTech from the margins and actually make people's lives better, then the latest tech buzzword is the last thing we need to worry about.

Making legal better means making it start and end with human beings. Only by forgetting about hype, robots, jargon and whatever else gets in the way of that laser focus on people, do we have any hope of achieving it.

List of Contributors

Enrique Agudo Fernández
Magistrate
www.twitter.com/Enrique53348449

See chapter:
Cryptoassests and Market Abuse

Maximilian Ahrens
Machine Learning Researcher, University of Oxford
www.linkedin.com/in/maximilianahrens/

See chapter:
Mapping LegalTech Adoption and Skill Demand

Mikolaj Barczentewicz
Lecturer in Law and Research Director, University of Surrey School of Law
www.linkedin.com/in/mikolajbarczentewicz/

See chapter:
Combining AI and Digitization of Judgments for Access to Justice

Pierre Berger
Partner, DLA Piper UK LLP
www.linkedin.com/in/pierre-berger-3780071/

See chapter:
Cryptosecurities: Traditional Financial Instruments on a Distributed Ledger

Raymond Blijd
CEO, Legalcomplex.com
www.linkedin.com/in/raymondblijd/
www.twitter.com/legalpioneer

See abstract:
Cyber Security Companies vs LegalTech

Struan Britland
Head of Legal Operations Solutions, Simmons Wavelength
www.linkedin.com/in/struanbritland/

See chapter:
Educating for Disruption, Innovation and Legal Technology

D. Ann Brooks
President, Ann Brooks Law P.C.
www.linkedin.com/in/ann-brooks-law

See chapter:
LegalTech in our Daily Lives

Liam Brown
Chairman and CEO, Elevate
www.linkedin.com/in/liamjmbrown/

See chapter:
We Are Voyagers

Christian Bunke
COO, Aalbun
www.linkedin.com/in/christianbunke/
www.twitter.com/aalbunIP

See abstract:
Technology the Breakdown of our Legal Services Value Chain

Ana Burbano
Legal Support, GLS
www.linkedin.com/in/aburbano/

See abstract:
Smart Contracts, Challenges for Lawyers

Mike Butler
Tutor, The University of Law
www.linkedin.com/in/mike-butler-60626421/

See chapter:
Technology and In-House Counsel

Laura Bygrave
Innovation and Ventures Lead, Deloitte Legal
www.linkedin.com/in/laurabygraveuk/

See abstract:
Overcoming Barriers When Reality Bites to Scale Up Change Beyond the Hype

Ron Cai
Partner, Zhong Lun Law Firm
See chapter:
Legal Implications of Artificial Intelligence in China

Cemile Cakir
Teaching Fellow, The University of Law
www.linkedin.com/in/cemile-cakir
See chapter:
Fairness, Accountability and Transparency – Trust in AI and Machine Learning

Israel Cedillo Lazcano
Lecturer in Law/Researcher, Universidad de las Américas Puebla
www.linkedin.com/in/israel-cedillo-lazcano-07966913/
www.twitter.com/IsraelCL
See chapter:
The Electronic Creation Right (ECR)

Xuezhou Chen
Associate, Zhong Lun Law Firm
See chapter:
Legal Implications of Artificial Intelligence in China

Dr Tara Chittenden
Foresight Manager, The Law Society
www.linkedin.com/in/tara-chittenden/
See chapter:
Patterns of Speech: A Future of AI-Authored Legal Reasoning and Arguments?

Qiyin Chuah
Founder and Director, QC Immigration
www.linkedin.com/in/qiyinc/
www.twitter.com/QCimmigration
See chapter:
Humanize with LawTech Lawyering

Martin Davidson
Chief Legal Intelligence Officer, ThoughtRiver Limited
www.linkedin.com/in/martin-davidson-ThoughtRiver
www.twitter.com/ThoughtRiverCI
See chapter:
Smart(er) Contracts – Digitizing Contracts for a New Age

Dr Sam De Silva
Partner, CMS Cameron McKenna Nabarro Olswang LLP
www.linkedin.com/in/sam-de-silva-6b15102/
See chapter:
Cloud Computing Contracts

Emanuela Denaro
Legal Engineer, ThoughtRiver Limited
www.linkedin.com/in/emanuela-denaro-122947ba/
See chapter:
Smart(er) Contracts – Digitizing Contracts for a New Age

Dana Denis-Smith
CEO, Obelisk Support
www.linkedin.com/in/ddenissmith/
www.twitter.com/Ddenissmith
See chapter:
Legal Talent Platform Economy – The Beginning of the End?

Nilixa Devlukia
CEO, Payments Solved
www.linkedin.com/in/nilixa-devlukia-49162a35/
See abstract:
FinTech, PayTech, LegalTech – The Perfect Storm for Open Banking

Pascal Di Prima
CEO, Lexemo LLC
www.linkedin.com/in/pascaldiprima/
www.twitter.com/pdip74
See abstract:
The Possibility of the Virtual General Meeting – Legislative Avant-Garde and Skepticism in Practice

Dr Anna Elmirzayeva
PD National Lead in Legal Technology and Innovation, The University of Law
www.linkedin.com/in/dr-anna-elmirzayeva-b9592288/
See chapter:
Cryptoasset Regulation: Clarification and Guidance

Dr Andreas Fillmann
Partner, Squire Patton Boggs
www.linkedin.com/in/andreasfillmann
www.twitter.com/andreasfillmann

See abstract:
LegalTech versus GDPR and AML

John Finnemore
Partner, CMS Cameron McKenna Nabarro Olswang LLP
www.linkedin.com/in/johnfinnemore/

See chapter:
Legal Technology: Increasing or Impeding Access to Justice?

Eleftherios Jerry Floros
CEO, MoneyDrome X
www.linkedin.com/in/jerryfloros
www.twitter.com/jerryfloros

See chapter:
The Legal Implications of Digital Security Offerings

Alessandro Galtieri
Deputy General Counsel, Colt Technology Services
https://www.linkedin.com/in/alessandrogaltieri/

See chapter:
An Introduction to Mapping and Classifying LegalTech

Simon George
Associate Professor, The University of Law
www.linkedin.com/in/simongeorgelaw

See chapter:
An Introduction to the Internet of Things

Charlotte Gerrish
Founding Lawyer, Gerrish Legal
www.linkedin.com/in/charlottegerrishlegal
www.twitter.com/gerrish_legal

See chapter:
Can the Law Keep Up with the Growth of AI?

Stevan Gostojić
Associate Professor, University of Novi Sad, Faculty of Technical Sciences

www.linkedin.com/in/gostojic
www.twitter.com/gostojic

See chapter:
From Legal Documents to Legal Data

Lachlan Harrison-Smith
Head of Lexible, ThoughtRiver Limited
www.linkedin.com/lachlanhs

See chapter:
Smart(er) Contracts – Digitizing Contracts for a New Age

James Hazard
Founder, CommonAccord
www.linkedin.com/in/jameshazard/
www.twitter.com/commonaccord

See chapter:
Legal Prose to Code: Restructuring Contract Templates for Blockchain Automation

Paula Hodges QC
Partner, Head of Global Arbitration Practice, Herbert Smith Freehills LLP
www.linkedin.com/in/paula-hodges-qc-64416b9

See chapter:
Dispute Resolution 2.0: The Era of BIG Data, AI and Analytics

Sally Holdway
CEO, Teal Legal
www.linkedin.com/in/sallyholdway/
www.twitter.com/legaledge

See abstract:
Disruption from the Inside Out: Is Better LegalTech Developed by Lawyers – Or Does this Disruption

Thomas Hyrkiel
Head of Publishing, IFRS Foundation
www.linkedin.com/in/thomas-hyrkiel

See chapter:
I Make the Rules – Why Should I Care About LegalTech?

Bukola Iji
Partner, SPA Ajibade & Co
www.linkedin.com/in/bukolaiji
www.twitter.com/bukolaiji

See abstract:
How Will LegalTech Catch Up with the Fast-Developing FinTech Revolution in Nigeria?

Dr Asim Jusic
Attorney at Law, Law Office Jusic
www.linkedin.com/in/jusic/

See chapter:
Dealing with Tensions Between the Blockchain and the GDPR

Mehran Kamkarhaghighi
NLP Data Scientist, Ontario Tech University
www.linkedin.com/in/mehrankamkar/

See chapter:
Acquisitive Information Extraction Framework for Legal Domain

Rebecca Kelly
Partner, gunnercooke LLP
www.linkedin.com/in/rebecca-kelly-46444817/
www.twitter.com/Lawbyrebecca

See chapter:
Tech vs Law: Consent

Sebastian Ko
CEO, A.I. Vermont
www.linkedin.com/in/sebko/
www.twitter.com/ko_sebastian

See chapter:
The Dark Side of Technology in Law: Avoiding the Pitfalls

Sebnem Elif Kocaoglu Ulbrich
Consultant and Author, Contextual Solutions
www.linkedin.com/in/sebnemelifkocaoglu/
www.twitter.com/sebnemelifk

See chapter:
Creating Supervised Independence for FinTech Companies via Regulatory Sandboxes

Achim Kohli
CEO and Co-Founder, legal-i
www.linkedin.com/in/achim-kohli-a3460012b/

See abstract:
80% Efficiency-Gain for Insurances: Automated Legal Document Study in the Field of Personal Damage

Bhagvan Kommadi
CEO and Founder, Quantica Computacao
www.linkedin.com/in/bhagvan-kommadi-b463a6
www.twitter.com/bhaggu

See abstract:
Legal AI Platform for Future: Singularity is Near

Mitchell E. Kowalski
Gowling WLG Visiting Professor in Legal Innovation, University of Calgary Law School
www.linkedin.com/in/mitchkowalski/

See chapter:
LegalTech's Legacy?

Brie Lam
Founder and Regulatory Compliance Consultant, Brie Lam Regulatory Advisory Services
www.linkedin.com/in/brie1986/

See chapter:
The Role of LegalTech in Financial Services: A Case Study

Pinaki Laskar
CEO and Founder, Fisheyebox
www.linkedin.com/in/pinakilaskar
www.twitter.com/fisheyebox

See abstract:
Cyber Transcendence – Cyber Spirituality and Immortality

Lawtech Malaysia
www.linkedin.com/company/lawtechmy

See chapter:
Why Now Is the Time for LegalTech to Boom

The Law Society of England and Wales
www.linkedin.com/company/the-law-society-of-england-and-wales/

See chapter:
The Crucial Role of LegalTech in Access to Justice

Kate Lebedeva
Junior Research Fellow, University College London and PhD candidate, University of Southampton
www.linkedin.com/in/katelebedeva/

See chapter:
Can Intelligence Be Appropriated: Ownership Over AI

Laurence Lieberman
Partner, Disputes and Investigations, Taylor Wessing LLP
www.linkedin.com/in/laurence-lieberman-09406244
www.twitter.com/LMLieberman

See chapter:
Digitizing Disputes

Magnus Lindberg
Chief Enabler Officer, SKYE Contracts
www.linkedin.com/in/the-magnus-effect

See chapter:
How Much Disruption Can We Handle?

Charles Lombino
Attorney and Counselor, Lombino Law Studio
www.linkedin.com/in/charleslombino

See chapter:
New Privacy Laws Require Changed Operations on Commercial Websites

Richard Mabey
CEO, Juro
www.linkedin.com/in/rmabey/
www.twitter.com/RMabey

See chapter:
The Humans Strike Back: The Fall of the Robots in LegalTech's Future

Masoud Makrehchi
Associate Professor, Ontario Tech University
www.linkedin.com/in/makrehchi/

See chapter:
Acquisitive Information Extraction Framework for Legal Domain

Paul Massey
CEO, Tabled.io
www.linkedin.com/in/paulmassey/
www.twitter.com/paulmassey

See chapter:
In-House Counsel Can Drive Industry Change through Legal Technology

Elly May
Legal Engineer, Simmons Wavelength
www.linkedin.com/in/elly-may
www.twitter.com/iamellymay

See chapter:
Educating for Disruption, Innovation and Legal Technology

Natasha McCarthy
Head of Policy, Data, The Royal Society
www.linkedin.com/in/natasha-mccarthy-4a7a5522/

See chapter:
Technology and the Law – Data and the Law

William McSweeney
Technology and Law Policy Advisor, The Law Society
www.linkedin.com/in/william-mcsweeney/

See abstract:
Automating Dispute Resolution to Facilitate International Trade

Grégoire Miot
Head of New Markets and Chief Evangelist, Wolters Kluwer (Legal & Regulatory – Legal Software France)
www.linkedin.com/in/gregmiot/
www.twitter.com/gregmiot

See chapter:
From Innovation Frenzy to Productivity Steadiness

Željka Motika
Lawyer, Motika Law Office
www.linkedin.com/in/zeljka-motika-00921b39/
www.twitter.com/Zeljka38983339

See chapter:
Smart Contract and Traditional Contract

Charlie Morgan
Digital Law Lead (UK), Senior Associate (International Arbitration), Herbert Smith Freehills LLP
www.linkedin.com/in/charliemorganhsf
www.twitter.com/C_MorganHSF

See chapter:
Dispute Resolution 2.0: The Era of BIG Data, AI and Analytics

Lily Morrison
Legal Consultant, Gerrish Legal
www.linkedin.com/in/lily-morrison123/

See chapter:
Can the Law Keep Up with the Growth of AI?

Shaun Murray
Managing Director and CEO, Margin Reform
www.linkedin.com/in/shaunmmurray/
www.twitter.com/shaunmmurray72

Oliver Rostron
Co-Founder, Amare James Ltd
www.linkedin.com/in/oliverrostron
www.twitter.com/OliRostron

See abstract:
The 'Uberization' of Law: Lawyers Hired and Fired Through Apps

María Ruiz de Velasco
Of Counsel, ECIJA
www.linkedin.com/in/mar%C3%ADa-ruiz-de-velasco-a41537142/

See abstract:
Is a New Legal Paradigm Needed to Cope with Technology?

Ekaterina Safonova
Founder, CEO/Board Advisor/Founder, CTO, CS Consulting and Advisory/ Cybertonica/FemFinTech
www.linkedin.com/in/ekaterina-safonova-03959830/
www.twitter.com/KaterinaSafo

See chapter:
Smart Home or Spy Home?

Nita Sanger
CEO, Idea Innovate Consulting
www.linkedin.com/in/nita-sanger-a656199/
www.twitter.com/Nita Sanger@Idea_Innovate

See chapter:
Distributed Ledger Technology and the Legal Profession

Dr Adam Saunders
Research Fellow, University of Oxford

See chapter:
Mapping LegalTech Adoption and Skill Demand

David Schmitz
CEO, Techmedev Lux
www.linkedin.com/in/davschmitz/
www.twitter.com/TechMeDave

See abstract:
Distributed Ledger Technology and Smart-Contracts: Which Incorporation into the Usual Law?

Benjamin Silverton
Head of Legal Product, LitiGate
www.linkedin.com/in/benjamin-silverton

See chapter:
Back to the Future: How LegalTech is Changing the Law Firm

Peter Smith
CEO, FinTechReguLab and Seneca Investment Managers
www.linkedin.com/in/PeterSmith
www.twitter.com/SmithyChat

See abstract:
Collaboration Conundrum

Clive Spenser
Marketing Director, LPA\VisiRule
www.linkedin.com/in/clivespenser/
www.twitter.com/CliveSpenser

See chapter:
Legal Expert Systems

Christian Spindler
CEO, DATA AHEAD ANALYTICS GmbH
www.linkedin.com/in/dr-christian-spindler/
www.twitter.com/datagmbh

See chapter:
The Legal Framework of Commercial Pay-Per-Use Financing

Anshul Srivastav
Chief Information Officer and Chief Digital Officer, Confidential
www.linkedin.com/in/anshul-srivastav-b57b514/
www.twitter.com/anshulsrivastav

See abstract:
Algo Lawyer

Ben Stoneham
Founder and CEO, Autologyx
www.linkedin.com/in/benstoneham
www.twitter.com/autologyx

See chapter:
Why All LegalTech Roads "Point" to a Platform Strategy

Laura Stoskute
Independent Researcher
www.linkedin.com/in/laura-sto%C5%A1kut%C4%97-71a817113

See chapter:
How Artificial Intelligence Is Transforming the Legal Profession

Brian Tang

Founder, ACMI and LITE Lab@HKU

www.linkedin.com/in/brianwtang

www.twitter.com/CapMarketsProf

See chapter:

The Chiron Imperative – A Framework of Six Human-in-the-Loop Paradigms to Create Wise and Just AI-Human Centaurs

Luigi Telesca

CEO, Trakti

www.linkedin.com/in/luigitelesca/

See chapter:

Legal Prose to Code: Restructuring Contract Templates for Blockchain Automation

Graham Thomson

Chief Information Security Officer (and interim Head of Data and Analytics), Irwin Mitchell LLP

www.linkedin.com/in/grahamjthomson

www.twitter.com/grahamjthomson

See chapter:

Cybersecurity: Myths and the Hero's Journey

Andréa Toucinho

Director of Studies, Prospective and Training, Partelya Consulting

www.linkedin.com/in/andréa-toucinho-95102597

www.twitter.com/AToucinho

See abstract:

Artificial Intelligence: For an European Legal Framework

Afsaneh Towhidi

Graduate Research Assistant, Ontario Tech University

www.linkedin.com/in/afsaneh-towhidi-625660a4/

See chapter:

Acquisitive Information Extraction Framework for Legal Domain

Marc Van de Looverbosch

Lawyer, DLA Piper UK LLP

www.linkedin.com/in/marc-van-de-looverbosch

See chapter:

Cryptosecurities: Traditional Financial Instruments on a Distributed Ledger

Laura van Wyngaarden

COO, Diligen

www.linkedin.com/in/lauravanwyngaarden/

www.twitter.com/@lauravanwyn

See chapter:

Lawyers' Ethical Responsibility to Leverage AI in the Practice of Law

Daan Vansimpsen

CIO, Ethel

www.linkedin.com/in/daanvansimpsen/

www.twitter.com/zetdaan

See chapter:

Mapping and Classifying LegalTechs

Clare Weaver

Consultant and Director, Putney Consulting Ltd

www.linkedin.com/in/clare-m-weaver-mba-bb8121101/

www.twitter.com/PutneyConsult

See chapter:

A Case Study of Adoption of Legal Technology in a Non-Western Market

Oliver Werneyer

CEO and Cofounder, IMburse AG

www.linkedin.com/in/oliverwerneyer/

www.twitter.com/OliverWerneyer

See abstract:

Evolving the Billing Culture and Match Services

Ivy Wong

Product Manager, HighQ, a Thomson Reuters Company

www.linkedin.com/in/ivywong26/

www.twitter.com/operationivy_

See chapter:

The Evolution of the Legal Marketplace

Lubna Yusuf

Founder, La Legal

www.linkedin.com/in/lubnayusuf/

www.twitter.com/Lubna_LaLegal

See abstract:

Law – With or Without Bots

Sherry Zhang

Senior Associate, Zhong Lun Law Firm

See chapter:

Legal Implications of Artificial Intelligence in China

Index

W

W3C 67
Waymo 38
Westlaw, Lexis 202
Wizuda 234
World Economic Forum 44

X

Xero 21
XML 67

Y

YouTube 39